Butte: An Unfinished Story

Butte: An Unfinished Story

Wedgwood, Darwin, Ryerson, Hawkesworth—
Related Men of Genius

Montel Hawkesworth Menting

To order additional copies of this book, contact:
Xlibris Corporation
1-888-795-4274
www.Xlibris.com
Orders@Xlibris.com
33577

CONTENTS

Introduction 9

1. An Illustrious Background 13
2. Progeny and Inventions-1912-1920 21
3. Just a Little Bit 24
4. New Places 28
5. Daunting Demonstration 32
6. Second Eastern Trip 36
7. Lucid Explanations 41
8. Trip Number Three 48
9. Progress: Slow and Steady 57
10. Grinding Machines and Prices 66
11. Potpourri 76
12. A Plant 85
13. Butte, A Welcomed Sight 95
14. Pre-Depression Days 99
15. A Mysterious Purchase 106
16. The Great Depression 109
17. Maurice Aims For Gold 116
18. A Duo In Canada 121
19. High and Low Levels 128
20. Pivotal Events 133
21. 1939 138
22. A Family Challenge 147
23. Safety First 161
24. Butte on Strike 176
25. A Bright New Beginning 179
26. Butte and Beyond 185
27. Reflections 197

Epilogue: Arthur and Gar Hawkesworth's Descendants 201
Glossary 209
Endnotes 211
Bibliography 217
Additional Web Sites 219
Private Family Collections 221

Dedicated to all my friends wherever they may be.

Introduction

Southwest Montana Territory slumbered. The town to become Butte quivered. Arthur Lee Hawkesworth entered the world in Bay City, Michigan. The year was 1869.

Deep from within the magnificent Rocky Mountains a saga of wealth, mystery, deceit, bravery, and greed was about to surface. A state, a city and individuals would be exploited in the process. A country would be enhanced in exchange.

Energetic entrepreneurs began to arrive in Butte. Most notable were the men soon to be designated *Copper Kings*: Marcus Daly, William Clark and Fritz A. Heinze followed later by Dan Ryan and Cornelius Kelley. The stage was set. The power plays were about to explode. After the glory days of the Comstock Lode in Nevada, this became the ideal site for expansion.

Marcus Daly prospected for gold in 1876 and found instead a fifty-inch copper vein. With initial financial investments from Hearst, Haggin, and Tevis, Daly began the battle for dominance of what soon would be deemed *The Richest Hill on Earth*.

William Rockefeller and Henry Rogers, of Standard Oil fame, infused more money along with influential New York financiers and bankers. Daly, a control addict, supervised the purchase, by any means available, of mines, railways, timber, acreage, banks, newspapers, power companies, brick factories, and foundries.

These conglomerates, aside from department stores, elegant hotels, race tracks, and horses, including the famous Tameny, all came under his control. Together they became known as *The Amalgamated Copper Company*. Rogers was the first president followed shortly by Daly.

William Clark at the same time wanted control of the Butte Hill. He had amassed his fortune through banking, mining, freight, smelter operations and reduction plants. A twenty-year economic battle commences between the two titans.[1]

During these encounters a royal war in the political arena erupted as well. Clark wanted Helena to become the Capitol of the new state. Daly declared for Anaconda. Pamphlets, scathing, satiric and prejudiced, proliferated. "Legislative bodies must be removed from contact with the common people" one Clark devotee wrote. As a political ploy Clark changed from a ten-hour day to an eight-hour day in his mines, something Daly refused to follow. Clark's supporters won this round. Helena became the state's Capitol in 1894 by 27,028 votes to 25,118.[2]

Montana politics became more corrupt. It was promulgated that Clark paid $431,000 to forty-seven senators for votes in order to procure for himself a U.S. Senate seat.[3] Clark served six months in 1899-1900 before he was forced to resign rather than to face fraudulent election charges. Unbelievable as it seems, the legislature appointed him to fill this vacancy but he did not qualify. Elected once again in 1901 he served until 1907. After a dinner in New York City to honor the Montana Senator at the end of his term, Mark Twain wrote, "Senator Clark was as rotten a human being as could be found anywhere under the flag."[4]

Daly's forces, who were supported by Butte labor unions, controlled the judges. Many bitter legal embroilments ensued over mining rights.

Political power domination by the Copper Kings became a given. For example, Montana's Supreme Court stated stock transfers from one company to another were illegal without the consent of minority stockholders. In January of 1899 the legislature passed House Bill No.132 which provided for stock transfers without minority consent. The Governor vetoed this but was overruled. Control of the senate was securely in the hands of the Copper Kings.[5]

Two indispensable commodities at the turn of the century were vital to the growth of America, oil and copper. One-fourth of the world's copper was being produced from the Copper Kings' mines while Rockefeller controlled the oil. Like a swirling hurricane that could not be satiated while its force expanded with ease, these tycoons knew the magnetic power of money and their appetite was ravenous.

The first Copper King, Daly, died in 1900 from complications of a disease considered incurable at the time, diabetes, but the Amalgamated Copper Company's management continued the battle with Heinz, Copper King number three. This resulted in a paralysis of the state's entire economy in 1903. Heinze finally capitulated and sold out his interests for $12 million in 1906.[6] Amalgamated now represented a capitalization of $1,555,000,000.[7]

By 1905 Amalgamated took the name *Anaconda Copper Mining Company*, later called just ACM or *Anaconda* and finally, *the Company*. After purchasing Clark's principal assets, the newly named company had the largest payroll in the world, in proportion to the population, $1,500,000 a month with 12,000 workers employed.[8]

John Ryan, the fourth Copper King, appeared at the turn of the century, a handsome, cunning business man. With money from an inheritance, he invested in the Daly Bank and Trust Company. Daly's widow, Margaret, provided additional financial backing. Ryan, in turn, purchased the First National Bank of Great Falls and its city utilities. Daly's heirs selected him for President of the newly named mine company.

Electric Power was needed in the mining industry and copper was needed to generate this power. Ryan was able to consolidate eleven small hydroelectric plants and four steam plants. He created and became the President of the Montana Power Company. Price control factors came into play. More wealth was available for ACM's kingdom with this new electrical source. It would replace steam power which cost $125 horsepower/year with the new hydroelectric source which was only $35 horsepower/year.[9]

The two giant corporations, Anaconda Copper and Montana Power, never totally merged but Ryan as President of both was able to utilize the same lobby, legal and PR staffs. His political power was intimidating, over powering and not to be challenged without dire consequences. The Anaconda Copper Mining Company was virtually a dictatorship ruling Montana.

Wealth for Ryan, as well as the three Copper Kings before him, was an end in itself not a means to increase the quality of his worker's lives or their surroundings. Ryan had little concern about their dangerous working conditions except when cost factors could be diminished by making mine improvements. He, unlike Daly, had never mined. Wages, though above the minimum, were not commensurate with the danger involved in mining.[10]

Ryan became associated with Cornelius "Con" Kelley, as brilliant a lawyer as he was a businessman, during 1905. Kelley ascends to second in command and, subsequently, Copper King number five. Together they used stringent tactics with the Butte unions. Strikes, riots and murders erupted as a result. Federal troops were called in by the two magnates to end the union uprisings. Omar Bradley, later a famed General of WWII, led a decisive charge September 13, 1918 while Butte was under Martial Law. The unions were momentarily quieted.[11]

With labor under control, Ryan and Kelley's expansions spread like a crown forest fire. To the south a lead-copper smelter at Toole, Utah, to the east a lead refinery in East Chicago, to Mexico a copper mine in Cananea which is sixty miles south of Arizona, and to South America the Potrerillos copper mine in Chile were acquired. ACM became a multi-national Corporation. It was listed among the top twenty Wall Street firms all during the 1920s. Ryan and Kelley would in today's world be called "Corporate Raiders of Wall Street." In the next 50 years 36,900,000,000 pounds of copper would be produced by this newly formed corporation which was on track to becoming the world's fourth largest enterprise.[12] Butte mines would produce copper; Americans would have radios, automobiles, telephones and wide spread electricity.

Numerous companies, individuals and small businesses became affected by ACM's decisions. *The Gilded Age of Capitalism* was at its apex. Greed was at its heart.

On the brighter side stories of courage, of racial and religious integration emerged. Butte people became known for their warmth and hospitality, for their delicious ethnic foods and for their superb theatrical productions. The later featured popular stars of the American stage in ornate Opera Houses.

Into this territory Arthur Hawkesworth arrived with his inventive powers. Mining and construction methods would be revolutionized by him. But mysteriously, mention of Arthur and his part in these inventions is expunged from the known records. Eighty years later a new generation discovered a densely packed, old wooden Hercules powder box which figuratively exploded. Missing records about Arthur tumbled into view. Bound patents, fascinating pictures, fragile letters, penetrating diaries, well-written newspaper articles, revealing magazine stories, encyclopedia articles and a brown leather autograph book were among the exposed treasures. Stock certificates with their mint green borders from the twenties and thirties even fluttered out from the bottom layer.

First source information about Ryan, Kelley, The Daly Bank and Trust Company, The Anaconda Copper Mining Company, The Hawkesworth Drill Company, political figures, lawyers and mine personnel lay scattered as fodder. To digest the contents would be a fascinating adventure. How did one family encounter a super conglomerate like the ACM and survive? Were similar American history stories to follow?

Arthur Lee Hawkesworth-16 years old-1885.

Chapter One

An Illustrious Background

With a profound loving gaze at the scattered contents from the aged box, Tecla whispered for no apparent reason, "These are some items Maurice could never bear to throw away so I just kept them."

This unexpected distraction was a grateful relief for her daughter, Montel. The uprooting of her mother from her home of thirty-nine years had taken an emotional toil on her usual resilient parent. Quick to capitalize on the situation, Montel remarked, "I really don't know much about my Grandfather. You, Dad and Grandma never talked about him much. Who really was he and what actually happened to his inventions?"

"It's a poignant story," Tecla reflected. Then on an impulse she blurted out, "Here, take all of this." A sense of relief passed through her entire body and the subject was momentarily dropped.

Montel loved challenges, mysteries and above all genealogy. This treasure box oozed with potential wealth and needed organization. Months later she began to unravel the documents.

Her grandfather, Arthur Lee Hawkesworth, was born on August 25, 1869 with genes from illustrious ancestors. His father, James Hawkesworth, was a scholarly person who was educated at a Canadian college. Early in life he emigrated from Ontario and became superintendent of a sawmill where he planned and erected shafting, maintained and built mechanical equipment. James "was broad-minded, liberal in his religious views, and a prominent member of the Universalist Church. Politically, a Republican, fraternally he belonged to the Masons."[1]

"With regard to Arthur's ancestry on his father's side," his mother once wrote in elegant script to her future daughter in law, "he was a fifth generation descendant from Josiah Wedgwood, the famous English potter. The lineage being traced through Elizabeth Wedgwood who married Adam Hawkesworth. They emigrated to Nova Scotia."[2]

Arthur was a cousin of Charles Darwin four generations removed. When Charles' father disapproved of his sailing on the famous Beagle ship, he uttered one line, "Find me one man of common sense who believes you should undertake this expedition and I will give my permission."[3] The man Charles found was his uncle, Josiah Wedgwood. Darwin's book, *Origin of the Species*, written as a result of this journey still evokes controversy and discussion to this day.

Julia Clark Hawkesworth, Arthur's mother, was born in Hamden, New York. She descended from the Canadian Ryerson family.

Arthur's great-uncle, Dr. Egerton Ryerson, is remembered in the name of the Ryerson Poly Technical Institute located in present day Toronto. Here his life-sized statue greets visitors and students.

After Ryerson's death in December 1882, thousands of mourners lined Yonge St. for his funeral procession. He was honored as one of Ontario's founding fathers of education while also being a Methodist minister. Appointed Chief Superintendent of Education in 1844, he opposed High Church monopolies and pushed for free schools. As a result, legislation passed between 1846 and 1850 provided the basis of Ontario's public school system, using ideas he had borrowed from other countries in his travels. For example, he got the idea for schools supported by a property-tax system from Massachusetts, textbooks from the Irish National Republic and the teacher-training system from Germany.[4]

Arthur's second cousin, Dr. George Ryerson, became the founder of the Red Cross Society in Canada. During one of the most decisive battles ever fought on Canadian soil, the North West Rebellion, the young Toronto doctor cut two strips of red cloth and hastily sewed them onto a piece of white cotton. On a hill above the Saskatchewan River at Batoche, he raised the first Red cross flag to fly over Canada. Dr. George became the champion and founder of the Red Cross Society of Canada. Another achievement was his being named Honorary Colonel-in Chief of the Canadian Army Medical Corps.[5]

In the U.S. Census of July 5, 1870, the Hawkesworth family of Bay City, Michigan is listed as: James, 35, Millwright: Julia, 27, Keeping House, Lulu, five, Keeping House; Frank three and Arthur, 11/12 (eleven months!) Their real estate value was $2500.[6]

When Arthur was three years old, his father died prematurely of a spinal disease. Life changed dramatically for the young family. Julia was forced to support the fledgling family by taking up her former teaching profession. Creative education was a top priority for her. As a child she could quote Shakespeare, Aristotle, Carlyle, Plato and Tolstoy. "I was brought up on them," she laughed much later in life. "I could recite whole plays." For the present she delved into the more structured world of teaching for a livelihood.

Arthur was instilled at an early age with the principal tenants of his parent's Universalist faith: make others happy, be honest, develop good habits, work hard, persevere with cheerfulness. Above all he was told, love God and you will have a happy life and the special favor of Our Father in Heaven.

From this environment Arthur's wondrous adventure through life began. At an early age he became fascinated with mechanics and machines, in inventing and discovering. This was part of the young lad's genetic makeup.

After he obtained his first knowledge of books in the public schools of his native city, his teenage years were spent at a technical school in Flint, Michigan. One vacation he boarded a train and then ferry boat for a trip to Walsingham and Tillsonburg, Ontario. Here he visited the Ryerson family and witnessed the large tobacco farms for which the town was famous. A well-preserved autograph book contained comments from his many friends and teachers while at school and during this trip. He finished the equivalent of a high school education at 15 years of age.

At the age of sixteen without funds for college, he entered the Standard Machine shop in Bay City and served as a machinist apprentice for three years. When an unexpected offer came, he accepted work as a tool maker in a watch factory in Chicago. Then the lure of the West drew him to Helena, Montana in 1888.

Arthur became politically active, first as a member of the city council. Cascade County elected him as a state delegate to the convention. He helped nominate Joseph Toole who became the first Governor of the new state in 1889. Tales of Helena's ascendency to fame as the Capitol amazed the young man. He learned of a classic satiric work that had appeared in the *Anaconda Standard* regarding Helena's Social Supremacy: He wrote to his mother and laboriously summarized the gist of the campaign article.

Helena was aristocratic and Anaconda along with Butte provided the work force which made wealth possible for the few. Common laborers should not control the politics of the state. The capitol should be located in more dignified surroundings.

In Helena men who wore silk hats, number 7 sized shoes, were seen with kid gloves and at night wore silk night shirts and patches on their consciences.

In Anaconda and Butte men wore cotton night shirts, number 9 sized shoes, overalls and patches on the knees of their trousers.

Drink was a necessity in any Montana meeting. Manhattan cocktails and champagne by the quarts were consumed by the gentry in Helena while the miners and smelter workers imbibed in beer and whiskey. Dinner buckets were in daily use.

In Helena the fair sex had wet nurses and maids. Babies were born with silver spoons in their mouths. The average family had ½ child compared to 5 3/4 children per household in Anaconda.

Children rode Shetland ponies and had dinner at 6 o'clock in Helena while in Butte and Anaconda the mothers nursed their own babies, did their own washing and ate according to work shifts. The children of these manual laborers made mud pies.

Ladies with poodle dogs strolled the clean avenues of Helena while the cities to the south had only mutts or no dogs at all. Ladies who ripped other ladies up the back were aplenty in Helena. They also had many" skeletons" in their closets.

A 1,910 margin from the 52,146 votes cast gave Clark's Helena supporters the victory.[7]

However, mechanics were his heartbeat. For the next eighteen years he worked four Montana boomtowns in the roles of machinist, master mechanic and foreman of mechanics. Thirteen years in Elkhorn, four in Helena, one in Great Falls and six months in Marysville enlightened him as to the needs of miners.

While in Helena, Mamie Winifred Lynch entered his life and sparkled his day. This beautiful, vibrant woman had come with her eight siblings and parents from Minnesota in 1891 to Helena though she was born in Dunsmore, Pennsylvania, March 21, 1876. The lure of the railroads brought the Irish family West.

Wedding bells rang for Arthur and Mamie July 24, 1895. This Catholic marriage performed by Rev. Clarebeek in Helena was unusual. Many American communities did not tolerate the marriage between two different nationalities. Often, in the case of the Irish, marriage was acceptable only with a person from within the same county. Western pioneers accepted the liaison of an English man with an Irish woman in good spirit. The newlyweds settled in Elkhorn where the population numbered around 2500.

The Elkhorn Mine during these boom days was on course to produce $14 million in silver, 8500 oz. of gold and four million lbs. of lead. The monthly net income from the mine totaled approximately $30,000 in its "heyday," a great deal of money more than 125 years ago.[8]

Up until 2003 this settlement was among the five better ghost towns of the West. At this time the remaining homes were moved to Big Sky, Montana or disassembled because of potential danger for tourists. A picture of their quaint log cabin home is depicted on the cover of *Pictorial Ghost Towns of the West*.

Deep sorrow enveloped Arthur and Mamie when their three-year-old daughter, Margaret, died Christmas Eve from diphtheria. Death was common among families before the development of vaccines and other cures for contagious diseases. Environmental regulations were sorely lacking to provide some respite for miners and their families from the polluted atmosphere caused by the mines. Again the young couple grimly faced the death of their one-year-old girl, Hazel, who was sickly from birth. Both these children were buried in Great Falls. A. son, Lee, was born in July 1897 followed by Arthur (Arkie), in June of the following year. Both claimed Elkhorn as the place of birth.

Mamie Lynch Hawkesworth's childhood home in Helena, MT.

Arthur and Mamie's Elkhorn, MT home-rear view.

Arthur and Mamie's Elkhorn home-front view on the right.

Upon occasion Mamie's father, Michael Lynch, a section foreman for the Northern Pacific in Elkhorn, worked out of state. While engaged with a steel gang in Oregon, an essential division responsible for bridge building which included any structure that had a span of twenty feet or more, Michael fell from an embankment sustaining severe injuries. He died soon after from effects of this fall in 1902.

His death initially was attributed to suicide and a small disclaimer three days later in the Helena paper was not noticed until seventy-five years later when additional research discovered the errata. The morphine discovered by his body was issued by a doctor and Michael had not overdosed.[9] Suicide was a stigma which burdened family members many times in the first half of this century. His burial in the Catholic cemetery and a funeral Mass at the Cathedral would never have been condoned at this period of church history if suicide had occurred.

At the turn of the century, 20,000 railroad employees were killed or injured each year. Human life was sadly and foolishly squandered. A rule of law rendered the railroads exempt from damages in the case of injuries to employees.[10] Life in the West was like a roller coaster with its high moments and low depressions.

Just as suddenly as death, a joyous moment arrived when Arthur's dream of a piano became a reality. This illustrious 1898 instrument, a 56" walnut Bush and Gerts upright, began its history in Chicago and stopped first in

Elkhorn. Its melodious tunes matched the joys and sorrows of the family. When Arthur's mother came for a visit, she brought a copy of John Phillip Sousa's, "The Stars and Stripes Forever." Her train stopped in San Jose en route from San Diego where she had just visited her brother and his wife. At Ferguson's Music Julia purchased this first edition piece, copyrighted by the Agricultural Department in 1897.(This government department issued music copyrights at the time.)

The next evening Arthur bought home asparagus, an unusual treat in Montana. Mamie rushed to get a beautiful vase as she thought they were rare flowers! But the first party around this beloved, sturdy piano was a grand success.

Arthur, an affable person, made friends easily and was well liked even though diminutive in stature with a size seven shoe and a 16½ shirt. To his delight the New Year of 1899 began with his first patent approved, a *Metallic Packing for Piston Rods*.

Four years later, still active in politics, Arthur was elected Alderman of the sixth ward on April 13, 1903. While employed by the largest in the state, The Caird and Hawkesworth Foundry (Arthur's older brother was the junior partner,) he was recommended for the position of State Boiler Inspector by Caird. "He is a thoroughly competent, careful, skillful engineer and machinist and eminently qualified in every respect to hold the position of Boiler Inspector."[11]

But fate and the Anaconda Company would have him continue as a machinist. Dan Ryan, along with Con Kelley always knew who, what, where and when their next conquest was to be. They began watching Arthur closely when he joined the migration into Butte in 1907. For a brief time he was a machinist at the Speculator Mine owned by the North Butte Company.

Miners gravitated to Butte from over the world like Olympians who flocked to a site to reap gold, silver and copper. Lesser awards of zinc, manganese, uranium and aluminum were also rewards. So well known was Butte nationally that non-English speaking immigrants needed only to produce a picture of the Butte Hill and Ellis Island officials knew where to directed them. Butte had the fourth largest immigration office in the country. In teams of two, these men delved into the boiling bowels of the earth and extracted ore worth billions of dollars. This fantastic wealth was being mined in Butte but many ecstatic stock holders had their mansions in Helena where there were more millionaires per capita than anywhere else in the nation at the turn of the century. Boston and New York investors reaped an abundant share from Butte for their coffers as well.

In these cities there was no air pollution from smelters. By contrast many miners in Butte survived in *Dublin Gulch* shacks, *Cabbage Patch* lodgings or hastily built boarding houses in the midst of life threatening fumes and filthy, thick smoke. Exploitation of resources and people was a mute issue. Wealth flowed to a favorite few.

Family, politics, music and above all dedication to his field of endeavor, mechanics, occupied Arthur's life during the first decade of the twentieth century in the heart of Butte. The birth of his third son, Maurice, pronounced "more is" not "more ease", born nine years after his older brothers on August 21,1907, was a great moment of joy at 1010 Nevada Street as it was also the first Commercial Holiday ever to be had in Butte.

Chapter Two

Progeny and Inventions-1912-1920

After his first promotion in Butte, Arthur could afford to move and escape away from the sulphurous-enveloped hill to an area called the flats on Harrison Avenue. Two daughters had died from lung afflictions. Innumerable hard rock miners had met the same fate. Air pollution was a harbinger of a like outcome for Maurice, now four, as well as their expectant child. Arthur's grasp of the need for better air in the mines and in their living environments set his creative mind whirling. He came up with an idea for a more effective mine ventilator.

When Mamie was five months into her pregnancy, she and Maurice enjoyed a train trip to Helena to visit her mother, "Grandma Bridget." They remained a few extra days in the fresh air while his grandmother and aunt enjoyed a short vacation to Missoula. Master Maurice received his first postcard. "Be sure and take good care of Grandma's chickens till we get back. I think we'll have a kiss left for you when we do. Unkie Ed and Auntie Rose."

Larry was born a "sickly baby" in Butte Aug.26, 1912. While his mother was busy with their newborn and his father busy with experiments, Maurice found fascinating friends at the fire station three doors away. On his fifth birthday he was made honorary Fire Chief. "My Aunt Rose bought me an appropriate coat. Now I got to help with the horses. But the minute the bell rang, I had to hit for the designated chair and not move a muscle. Oh, how I loved riding on the exotic wagon when the prize horses were taken out for their daily exercise," he fondly remembered.

But this active black curly-haired boy was given to explore the expanding neighborhood and admitted that he was a bit spoiled while his father was off inventing things.He reflected, "After my fifth birthday my friend, Shorty, and I climbed into the back of a Chinese farmer's vegetable cart which abruptly jerked into motion like a cannon ball. The driver headed back to the "Nine-Mile", an area away from town, oblivious of his cargo. We two frightened boys failed to make our presence known and fell fast asleep lulled by the steady clop of the horse only to wake up in a dark strange barn. Hurriedly, we crawled into the safety of a nearby hayloft and wondered what to do beside return to sleep."

In the meantime the alarm sounded back home. Everyone including the Sheriff was sure the Gypsies who had been through town that day had taken the carefree boys. Next morning hunger drove the two lads into the farmhouse. No one was happy at the silent breakfast. The farmer had an added trip to make to bring the errant boys back to their homes.

"I got the hair brush and was tied to the clothes line with copper wire for a punishment," Maurice shuttered. Later in the day Shorty entered the scene. After assessing the situation, he hurriedly scampered home, seized an oversized old ax and successfully cut the shinny wire. We gleeful boys headed to an abandoned ore car and started to use it for a slide. Trouble is we couldn't get out. A mine watchman heard our plaintiff cries and brought us home by the scruff of our necks. To my chagrin I was dressed as a girl for the rest of the day. Well, now that cured me but not before a picture was taken."[1]

New opportunities greeted his brilliant father. He became the master mechanic for the East Butte Mining Co. Next he hired on with the Butte & Bacorn, each change a promotion. In 1914 he accepted employment with the formidable Anaconda Copper Mining. Here Arthur advanced in position with each change of venue from the Anaconda to the Tropic and on to foreman of the Leonard machine shop.

This unique, indefatigable man was also a strong union leader who continued his avid interest in politics. He played a prominent part in the machinist union statewide. Butte unions and their influence on the Labor Movement in America are well documented.

Montana's political history was unique. Once before the turn of the century Marcus Daly let all the miners out at three p.m. and sent them to the polls. When hired to work, all miners had to indicate their political persuasion. Daly hired Democrats. Democrats won.

Another scheme widely used was for each party to outdo the other by trying to be the first in a precinct to vote for those who had expired since the last election! Ambitious miners even bet on which one could engender the most votes that way.

In 1916 Arthur ran for the legislature on the Democratic ticket, but the ACM controlled all elections and he lost the race. The ACM officials either saw his potential as a machinist or more importantly they didn't want him in Helena influencing labor issues.

A contemporary, Jeanette Rankin, of whom Arthur spoke highly, was elected to the US Senate from Montana, 1917-1919, three years before women were guaranteed the Constitutional right to vote. Her platform, *Preparedness that will Work for Peace*, resulted in her being the first woman senator. She earned the distinction of voting nay for entrance of the US into World War I. Another of her honors included that of being the only woman to vote for the Constitutional right for the fair sex to vote. She ardently believed in negotiations over war and in furthering women's rights. She was not a threat to mining interests.[2]

Two other Montana contemporaries, Gary Grant and Bernard Russell, began making their presence known as actor and artist respectively. Montana was a rich state.

Ryan successfully kept the bright forty-seven-year-old inventor in the company's employ with an offer of a prestigious position and an increase in wages as the *Master Mechanic* of the elite Butte Mines Machine Shop located in the center of the Butte hill where 150 men were employed. This post he "filled with credit to himself and he received gratification from his employers."[3]

After accepting this advancement, the mechanic moved his family to the newly established Daly neighborhood on Argyle Street. Until their lovely home three houses away at 2124 Argyle was finished they had no indoor plumbing. For a sum of $3,000, the new home and all related expenses were paid by Arthur at year's end 1916.

His mechanical genius flourished. To his delight Arthur procured patents in 1918 including one for his Ventilator, June 26, and one for an Oil Pump, July 10. Both were most efficient. But most importantly, Arthur obtained several drill patents. For 15 years he had labored and experimented in all kinds of terrain to solve a problem that had taxed the ingenuity of the entire mining and construction world. He invented the first detachable drill bit that worked.

Scrutinizing the scene closely, Anaconda Copper Mining Company officials secretly prepared for the possibility of a coup. *The Wild West Show* of *Mining* was at its height of power. A new player was being brought onto center stage.

Chapter Three

Just a Little Bit

"Every now and then comes word of an invention so startlingly simple, yet so important as to promise to revolutionize an entire industry, that the world sits up amazed and each individual wonders why he hadn't thought of it. Of course, the man who did think of it is usually the one who has given his lifetime of work to the industry his invention affects and has burned midnight oil to perfect the ingenious thing which is his big contribution to posterity",the *Anaconda Standard* reported May 14, 1922. It went further and stated, "This bit may prove as revolutionary as the locomotive in transportation or the wireless in long distance,"

News of the detachable drill bit on the Butte Hill by mine officials and miners rippled like an uncontrolled river. The entire world would be revolutionized if it were the truth, a detachable drill bit that worked! This challenge had vexed the brightest engineers and inventive genius of the mining, oil and construction industries.

While scarcely initiated to mining, Arthur perceived the great hazard and the enormous economic wastefulness of the prevailing method of handling and sharpening drill steel. Strong beliefs carried him through the fifteen years he had devoted to this invention. "Mechanically, there are only a few problems that training and practical genius cannot solve. Meticulous care, countless tests and experiments are a necessary component to success," he once uttered to some friends. Tenaciously, he had clung to his set goal as had his forefathers, Wedgwood with his pottery, Darwin with his evolutionary insights and Ryerson with his Canadian educational system.

A major operation in hard rock mining was the task of drilling holes in virgin rock, preparatory to loading with powder and shooting. The miner must inevitably look to the drill for every inch of progress. Whether it be a shaft, drift, tunnel, stope or raise, the whirling point of steel must lead the way to the hidden treasures of mother earth. The miner's primary and almost exclusive effort was that of drilling.

One of ACM's greatest costs was to provide drills. Air driven machines had superseded hand drilling. "Go down into any of the mines of Butte, and if you are sensitive to impressions, you will bear away with you an unforgettable picture of this tireless 'machine gun of industry', delivering its 1,800 to 2,000 blows per minute against the age-old battlements of mother nature."[1]

To keep these drills sharp was a constant problem. Nippers who were accountable for the distribution of steel underground and its proper return to above ground searched continually for dulled bits which were still attached to a steel shank. These were taken to an underground station, hoisted to the surface, transported by truck to the shops, resharpened and returned underground. "In the mines of Butte alone, 10,000 pieces of steel went through this tedious and costly process every day."

A reporter requested an interview and posed Arthur this question, "Just how did you envision this bit?"

With excitement in his voice and animation in his demeanor, the inventor exclaimed, "One night as I lay abed, turning the problem over in my mind for the thousandth time, I had an inspiration. I rose, dressed hastily and with the few simple tools I had at hand quickly fashioned a wooden model of a one piece, detachable bit without threads, springs or pins, with nothing to lose and without delicate or flimsy parts to be marred or destroyed in the hard and exacting task for which it was designed. The thing was so simple, so plain, so absolutely foolproof, that I was amazed that such an obvious solution of the matter had never before occurred to me."[2]

A life altering moment arrived for Arthur when his patents were secure both in the United States, Canada and those in other countries pending. It was time to focus on the future. He wanted to form his own company.

Past discussions at political conventions in Helena had brought him into association with vibrant and ambitious personalities. As a member of the Central Committee for the 71st precinct of Silver Bow County, Arthur met one such person, Roy S. Alley, who was born in Wilbur, Nebraska, March 20, 1876. The men had kept in sporadic contact after Alley finished his term in the Twelfth Legislative Assembly. Dan Ryan, the present Copper King, had secured this election for Alley in order to have someone represent the ACM's interests in Helena. Roy had previously concluded a year as deputy Silver Bow County Attorney in 1899. Both Roy and Arthur were strong Democrats, men alert to their surroundings and knowledgeable about current affairs. As a lawyer, Roy had good advice to share. He became Arthur's first partner.

After agreeing the new company would be called, *The Hawkesworth Drill Company*, the two determined men elicited financing from the Daly Bank and Trust Company. With the help of E. J. Bowman, President, they secured capitalization for

$100,000 on April 13,1920. Articles of incorporation were filed with the county clerk with Directors listed as Arthur L. Hawkesworth, Mary W. Hawkesworth and Roy S. Alley. The later became first President of the company while Arthur would be General Manager.

Dan Ryan, Con Kelley, the future Copper King, W. Daly and C. Berrian, head ACM mining officials, knew what they wanted and needed, the rights to this bit. Time was their ally. These men and their company had extensive experience planning and plotting exploitation. "The Hawkesworth patents and their rights were presently secure but this brilliant genius couldn't make it on his own," they reasoned. "Who were his friends, whom would he chose for partners?"

They brought together a few top ACM officials for a high level meeting. Arthur, they knew, liked these men who were in pivotal company positions.

"Give support to Arthur," instructed Ryan. "We need to get this bit working for the good of all. We heard Hawkesworth plans to form a Board of Directors. Accept if he asks you."

Ed Bowman, President of the Daly Bank, could see the possibility of potential future profits from this bit. He was honored to become the treasurer and joined the board despite his heavy schedule. His son, Ted, wanted to study machinery and perhaps an opportunity would become available through this contact for him. ACM was pleased with this choice as they could easily gain access to the financial records, if the need arose. They owned the Daly Bank!

State Senator Harry Gallwey became the vice-president of the fledgling company. He was a protege of Marcus Daly who had placed implicit confidence in him. Harry was born in Virginia City, Nevada, August 16,1866. Through hard work he became manager of the Western Union Telegraph in Reno. In 1884 he came to Butte and began a long career as Manager of the Butte, Anaconda, Pacific RR (BA&P). He married Mary Fagin Kennedy in 1913. She was a native of Salt Lake City and a graduate of St. Mary (of the Wasatch). Coincidentally, two of Arthur's future granddaughters would graduate from this school.

His friendship with Arthur extended back a few years. This man was a special person, one who could listen to both sides of the factions found in Butte, management and labor. He was faithful, kind, and helped lay good foundations for the new *Treasure State* when he served during twelve sessions of the State Legislature, two of those in the senate.[3] Harry was an asset to any board. Arthur was delighted with his acceptance.

Two long time family friends added their support: J.D. Murphy, who was a capable secretary and notary while always loyal to Anaconda and secondly, John J. Riley who was a good person, but a man who had no actual mining experience. The six member board was complete.

Time arrived to begin manufacturing this marvelous bit, but first Arthur had to design the machines needed for mass production. The next six months found the inventor working out the details. Plans were laid for him to travel East to oversee the manufacturing processes. Montana with all its potential mineral wealth did not produce much iron ore. Steel and iron fabrications were manufactured in Eastern shops.

ACM watched and waited. They would endeavor to contract the best deal for themselves for the use of this drill when the proper time presented itself. They also began to formulate plans for a research department which would attempt to produce a bit of their own.

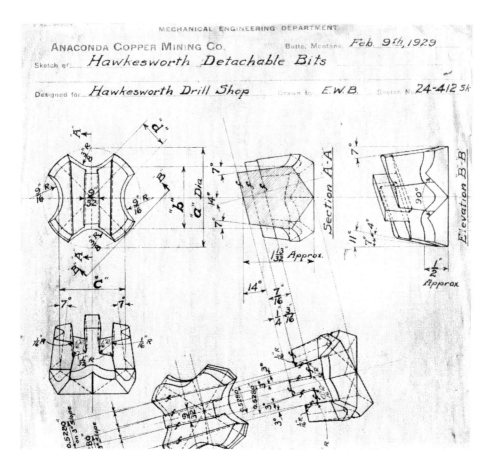

Blue Prints of Hawkesworth Drill.

Chapter Four

New Places

At home both Arthur and Mamie guided their energetic boy Maurice. His father watched carefully over his education. A precise homemade diary developed by the young lad recorded his Greeley school days from January 1 to June 10, 1920. Every square box and entry date was perfectly and identically drawn. Each sentence was complete. Life for a twelve-year-old boy from an economic secure family in Butte exuded from these entries.

Weekends were free! Daily chores of getting the coal and wood before school in the morning, lessons and practice on the prized family piano, trips to church filled his weekday routine. His school interests included the study of early America History, information about animals native to his continent, and the importance of manufacturing in the New England States. In addition he enjoyed Manual Training where he designed and made book ends.

Marbles, swims at the high school and uptown YMCA pools, baseball using his bright as copper catcher's glove, football, hikes to the hills provided his athletic activities.Boy Scouts, weekly shows, and card playing diversified his youthful days.

Special moments from the routine included going to see an airplane, seeing bluebirds in April, selling junk to the junk man and saving enough money to buy a fifteen-dollar bicycle in time for his summer vacation.

Excitement was captured as he told of getting his kite with its rag devised tail up and flying. He helped his mother make candy especially fudge. Occasionally, he did dishes and even went uptown on errands for his mother or his older brothers. In April their cellar flooded and he hauled out all the water.

One show he saw was, "Best Boy Dressed As a Girl." Memories recalled at this moment of his past were not shared with his peers but were written in his diary. Life flowed gently these years. The only rapid he encountered seemed to be a sprained wrist from swing acrobats. So ends his diary the last week of June.[1]

A sad period interrupted his carefree life. For the first time in the young lad's memory, his adored father was not going to be home at the end of a day. He had gone East for machinery.

Two weeks later Maurice's mood changed to that of elation when he received his very first letter from his father postmarked, Green Island, New York. "I will never throw away a letter from my father," he adamantly informed his mother. A promise he kept.

"I am so glad you passed in school. I hope you will always pass and be a doctor some day like your cousin, Maurice Miller. He is a Doctor in the largest hospital in Providence, Rhode Island. He is twenty-six years old. You just keep on passing and I will send you to one of the best colleges in the United States. I am sending one dollar with this letter for passing and when Lawrence passes, he will get one too, and when you pass again I will give you two dollars and again three and again four and so on. Be a good boy and I will be back some of these days. How are Mother, Lawrence and Elva? I suppose you are having a great time with your bike. Tell Lawrence I will write to him tomorrow. With lots of love to all. Papa"[2]

Two months later while in Troy, New York working on a machine, Arthur received an unexpected letter. The first to personally congratulate him in writing was the powerful Con Kelley, the Copper King. This corporate giant had great foresight into the legal and financial portions of business. If this bit were successful, what a boon it would be for the ACM!

A. L. Hawkesworth
c/o The Troy Times

New York, August 10, 1920

My dear Mr. Hawkesworth:

I am in receipt of your letter of July 31, in which you detail the result of tests made with your new drill bit.

I am very much pleased that the results were so satisfactory to you, and that you are so sanguine as to the successful outcome of the Bit.

Very truly yours, C.F. Kelley (Personally signed)

Costs had been creeping upward for the ACM. Freight, steel shipments from the East and wages were far above pre World War I figures when the ACM's tax rate was only 8.7 percent while the farmer paid 32.14 percent. This was not information published in the ACM controlled daily papers. After the war Federal and State taxes did rise for the ACM.

Scrutinizing care was given to lowering the cost per ton of ore mined. Savings of even a few cents per ton are significant when it is realized that a cost decrease of five cents per ton of ore mined to one Butte mining company alone meant an annual savings of $225,000. Many ramifications could be envisioned from the implementation of this drill bit.

Upon his return to Butte, Arthur continued to test and to refine the bit manufacturing processes. He began at the same time to negotiate with the ACM. Ground work was in progress on all fronts. The next challenge would be to get the bits into all the mines on the Butte Hill and convince the world mining leaders of its worth.

Abruptly, the first delay occurred in 1921 during a long mining strike. Miners were out of work. People began starving in the city. Arthur, Roy and Harry helped with food distributions to the needy as overseen by the Butte Elk's Lodge #240. All three were members and Harry had been Butte's first Exalted Ruler and at one time was the State President for a term.

After the interminable strike was over and mining commenced, Arthur received an honor. Two long columns praising his accomplishments appeared in *Montana its Story and Biography: A History of Aboriginal and Territorial Montana and Three Decades of Statehood*. Forecasting into the future, the article stated in part:

"Possessing great mechanical skill and inventive talent of a high order, Arthur L. Hawkesworth, master mechanic of the Butte Mines Machine Shop, is thoroughly acquainted with every branch of the machinist's trade, and in the various places in which he has been employed has won an enviable reputation for efficiency and dexterity in the use of the machinist's tools.His inventions will eventually revolutionize the rock drilling industry of the World, and will undoubtedly be to him a source of great revenue."[3]

Mamie encouraged her well-liked husband to purchase a prized, gold embossed Elk's Tooth along with a gold watch and chain to honor the occasion. Both these items were symbolic of financial success in Butte.

An agreement was drawn up by four HDC members as the owners, officers and directors of the company January 12, 1922. It was their mutual desire that control of the company stock "be perpetuated in and among themselves . . . and that pending the completion of plans for the beginning of manufacture of said drills and bits, and plans for reorganization and recapitalization complete . . . the stock interests of the parties hereto shall not be changed by sale or pledge."[4]

The Board drew up a contract for Arthur's sale of his patents to the company as the next order of business. "The parties of the second part agree to pay to the said party of the first part(Arthur Lee Hawkesworth) the sum of Two Million Dollars($2,000,000.00) together with a license fee of four cents ($.04) on each of the devices made under the Hawkesworth patents and on each and every article upon which any of the devices covered by the above letters and patents may be used payable as follows: Fifty thousand dollars shall be paid not later than thirty days after the formation of the afore-said corporation, the balance to be paid in five equal annual installments; the first of the five payments to be made one year from the formation of the corporation and the other four to be made on the first day of June of each following year."[5]

One evening Maurice inquired of his father, "Why do you sell things to yourself?" He could not grasp the concept.

After a brief explanation he believed along with his father that the proposed contract would come to fruition. As a result of this Arthur would have the means to send his two younger sons to college, an opportunity denied him because of family financial problems. Arthur and Mamie had great hopes for their new company. The horizon beckoned.

Chapter Five

Daunting Demonstration

As implementation of the bit continued to be slow, Gallwey suggested to Hawkesworth, "Suppose you give a demonstration to the representatives of all the companies in and around Butte."

Acting on this suggestion, Arthur arranged for a test to be held beneath the engine room of the St. Lawrence Mine on May 18,1922. The drill was mounted against the face of the solid granite rock that formed the foundation on which the huge hoisting engine rested at the surface thirty feet above.

A reception committee consisting of Senator Gallwey, C. L. Berrien, General Superintendent of Mines for the ACM, and Wm. Daly welcomed shift bosses, foremen, master mechanics, mine superintendents, managers, practical and technical mining men representing all the operating companies in Butte to the momentous demonstration. Professor Oscar Dingman from the math department of the School of Mines was among the fifty spectators.

"We appear to have the brains of the mining world present," said Senator Gallwey. "Let her go, Mr. Hawkesworth."

Two tests were made before the distinguished gathering. A new, old style drill and a new Hawkesworth drill were first tried out in succession for a two-minute interval each. The old style drill showed a somewhat corrugated hole, nine and one-half inches deep. The Hawkesworth drill showed a hole as clean as though driven by a diamond drill twenty and one-half inches deep. In the second test a used reground Hawkesworth drill was pitted against a new old style drill. The old style drill drove nine one-half inches. The Hawkesworth drill beat its former record driving a hole twenty-two inches deep.

An excited reporter from the *Anaconda Standard* began to interview everyone within sight. To have more than fifty dignitaries from so many mining interests was indeed a coup.

"That looks awful good to me," said Angus McLeod, superintendent of the Butte and Superior Mining Company. "If it had nothing to commend it but the safety of the men it would be enough. We lost six men in raising and lowering tools on one occasion. No question but that the company can make the points cheaper than buying them."

McLeod knew the operations of drills from alpha to omega and there was real affection in his fondling of the magic bit of steel as he examined it.

He was thoughtful for a moment, "Why, a man can carry a whole can of steel in his pocket!" he exclaimed. "Nine of these little bits will give the same results as thirty pieces of steel four feet long. The Hawkesworth drill point will save labor, save money, and save hazards."

"Mr. McLeod has covered the subject," said E. H. Parker of the Elm Orlu, a W.A. Clark, Jr. Property. "It was a fine exhibition."

"It is an unqualified success," said W.B. Daly, assistant general manager of mines of the ACM company. It will save a large outlay of money to every mining company by its use."

"Thank goodness that the mine companies are cooperating with the drill machine manufacturers," said James G. Graham, manager of the Sullivan Machine Company. "For years we have been drilling with doorknobs and urged-compelled, in fact-to-make machines heavier and heavier. With this device we can reduce the weight of our machines from 200 pounds to 115 pounds-a one-man drill. The Hawkesworth drill means universal steel throughout the mines. I tested that drill ten days in the Badger mine. We had good results. The mine managers do not realize what this drill means to them in the price of rock drills, steel, and their entire investment. It means savings in investment, in labor, in time, in risk and in loss of tools. In another year the mining world will be amazed at the results achieved through the use of this drill."

"It looks like an immense savings," said R.F. Banks, manager of the Sullivan Machine Company of Spokane. "It looks very good to me, indeed."

"It means a savings in raising and lowering the steel down the shafts. These bits can be given out just as carbide is given out now. There is the advantage of a better cutting edge, a more uniform hole. The new bit has many advantages."

"It is a practical drill," said Samuel Worcester, mechanical foreman of the Davis-Daly, "that is, unless something now unforeseen should develop. I haven't any idea what that might be. As I see it, the new drill means a handsome saving on drills, time, labor and investment."

"This is the first opportunity I have had to observe this new drill," said D.J. McGrath, foreman of the Davis-Daly. "Judging by the test I have just witnessed, I would say that it is a great success."

"I think it a perfect success so far as drilling is concerned" replied Elmer Williams, foreman of the North Butte. "I would not imagine that there is any chance for loss of the points through carelessness. The miners would sign up for them just as they do for other tools."

"It looks good to me," said A.G. Ray, foreman of the Pittsmont. "If the men will only give it half a chance, it will win. Better track can be kept of these points than of other things. Half of the spikes that go into a mine are wasted; also half the powder. All of the steel is wasted.

Sooner or later the steel is all used up, isn't it? This device will deliver the goods."

"The new drill appeals to me from the standpoint of 'safety first' and cost," said W. H. Carrick of the U.S. Bureau of Mines who was thoroughly convinced of its efficiency.

"I have no doubt it will be a great success," said E. V. Davelen, general superintendent of the North Butte.

"It looks like a good all-around proposition," said C.E. Dobbel of the engineering department of the North Butte. "From the standpoint of safety, it has great value."[1]

Then Arthur shared a letter dated April 4,1922 from The Waihi Gold Mine Co. Limited, Waihi, New Zealand. It read in part:

We wish to try out the Hawkesworth detachable bits and will be obliged if you will quote for a set of bits for each of the following machines: No. 248 Leyner-Ingersoll drill using 1 1/4 hollow round steel. CCW.II. Ingersoll stope hammer using 1 inch hollow hexagon steel. If you consider that we would be able to shape the steel to hold the bit, following instructions given by you, it would not be necessary to send any shanks with the bits; failing this please quote, for, say, three lengths of steel for each bit."

What do I think of our experiment today?" Arthur confidently responded to another reporter, "Why it was satisfactory as all tests have been. The experimental stage has passed. The bit has proven its worth. One feature which I wish to call attention to is the saving on the drilling machines. We make more footage with the same amount of stroke and power than with the present steel. Consequently, the new bit will give a longer life to the machine or in other words a machine with the new bit will make more footage than the same machine could do with the present steel."[2]

It certainly had been a red letter day for Arthur. He never felt better.Orders for the new device began pouring in from Michigan, Nevada, Utah, Arizona, British Columbia, Africa, Australia and New Zealand. Railway contractors of the United States had their attention aroused and wished to try the new drill.Demands far exceeded the production capability of the Anaconda Foundry.

The company answered the request for written information with a sixteen-page pamphlet entitled, *Four Ounces of Steel-A Revolution in the Mining World*.[3] These quickly became a scarce commodity. An abridged summary follows.

The Hawkesworth Drill Company was incorporated in 1922, under the laws of Delaware, to take over the patents owned by Arthur L. Hawkesworth in the United States and in foreign lands, covering his inventions of detachable drill bits and points. Substantial Butte mining and mechanical interests have subscribed for a considerable portion of the stock.

Plans have been completed for the erection of a manufacturing plant and an active campaign will be begun for the introduction of the Hawkesworth drill. Mr. Hawkesworth will have constant personal supervision of the manufacturing details, thus insuring the uniform delivery of a high-grade product.

Chapter Six

Second Eastern Trip

Now that Arthur had satisfied the foremost technical and practical Butte men in mining, he packed his old carpet bag, put in a spare collar and an extra box of smoking tobacco and boarded the train for New York and Connecticut along with Roy Alley.

Here he could experiment and perfect techniques needed for manufacturing the bit on a huge scale. For the twenty-four-hour shifts in all the mines of Butte it was estimated that a daily supply of 3,000 bits would be required as a minimum. More efficient machines were needed. The present equipment at the Anaconda Foundry could only turn out 1200 bits a day.

Back in the previous century the Anaconda foundry was one of Daly's coups. Its acquisition was a perfect example of a method he used to accumulate possessions. He needed a local reduction plant where the Butte ore could be smelted to metal. As Butte lacked water resources for such a plant, he went to Anaconda, twenty-six miles to the West. Abundant water was available from the Warm Springs Creek. The Tuttle Manufacturing and Supply Company was located nearby. Daly gained control of their stock. He next hand picked a new Board of Directors who later voted to transfer ownership to Amalgamated Copper for the sum of one dollar. This foundry, known locally as the Anaconda Smelter, became the largest in the state. The landmark stack rose 534 feet where its omissions polluted the atmosphere.[1]

Through conversations on the route to the east, Arthur learned some new uses for copper in a novel invention, the radio. The first commercial station had broadcast an address by President Warren T. Harding at the dedication of the Francis Scott Key Memorial in Baltimore, Maryland. His speech went by telephone to the station June 14, 1922.Even as they talked on October 28 the first football game was being aired between Princeton and the University of Chicago via long lines for the premiere time. Bits would be needed to mine copper ore for this new lucrative market as over five hundred stations had already been licensed including Butte with the call letters KFAP.[2]

From New York he wrote on October 31,1922 to Mamie.

I am sending Richard and Lawrence *Biff, Bang*. Mr. Alley and I went up to the top of the Woolworth Building. It was a great sight. Its top is 792 feet 1 inch high, the tallest in the world!

Alley is leaving today for Chicago. I will be here for a week longer getting prices on machinery. Will take about twenty days more before I get back. I am tired of New York City. Will be glad when I get home. I will have everything found out about making the drill machinery so we can go ahead. They are making dies at Ansonia.(Conn.) Going up there to see it work. I sent them a bar of steel from here. They figure they can make four per minute with one man working. With lots of love, Arthur. P.S. It cost 50 cents to go up the Building!

Local Connecticut folklore included a legend, believed by some and discounted by others, that brass workers were not allowed to emigrate from England until 1825. The Brass Workers Guild enjoyed Parliamentary protection which forbid these laborers to move elsewhere. But an enterprising Yankee journeyed to England on several occasions. Each trip he recruited up to six men, carefully concealed them in casks and rolled them aboard a ship bound for the colonies. Released from this confinement during the sea journey, these craftsmen once again entered their barrel, were tossed overboard the night before the official unloading and were floated to the mouth of the Naugatuck River where they washed ashore.[3]

These workers were not nomadic. Permanent brass mills were established along this river. The soil was not conducive for agriculture. ACM invaded this territory in 1922 through the acquisition of the American Brass company in Waterbury, Connecticut. This company was previously formed from the consolidation of five brass mills including Ansonia Brass and Copper Company, Waterbury Brass Company and Coe Brass Company.

By November when Arthur arrived, American Brass was the world's largest producer of copper goods. He had been encouraged to make contacts here.

Arthur wrote Nov. 9 to Roy Alley who had returned to Butte.

Finished here today. Everything is in good shape for making the machines and equipment. Have gone over it thoroughly and have agreed upon all sizes. They start immediately on the work. You will notice the new bits forged at Ansonia are a wonderful piece of work, saving in material, more made per minute with better machining and cutters. Hope you received the bits I sent you from Chicago.

Leaving here for Troy in the morning to get some dope for Mr. Earle. (The attorney who handled the legal issues with the ACM.) Sunday I will go to Syracuse, then Cleveland and Chicago.Each place I will take up the matter of furnaces.ALH.

Before leaving Hartford the earnest yet humble man thanked R.B. Hurlburt, machinery department manager of Pratt & Whitney, for the kindnesses and courtesies extended him while at their plant. He further wrote on Nov. 11:

"I find on my arrival here in Troy that the U.S. High Speed Co. are about on the rocks, not having been able to meet their pay-roll for the past five weeks and unless something turns up mighty soon they will be in a very embarrassing position.

There is one thing that I neglected to take up with you and that is a little special grinding machine for the re-sharpening of the bits when dull. No doubt there will be thousands of these machines required by the concerns who will use our bits. I think you understand about what kind of a machine will be necessary for this work and if you can gather some information on it now, it will facilitate matters greatly later on. Let me be advised as to what progress you make." ALH.

Later that day he wrote to Roy that the employees of U.S. High Speed planned a show down Monday of next week. He continued, "Met with Pratt and Whitney who are very confident that there will be no difficulty whatever in machining these bits with the outfit we propose to have. They want us to send them 500 or 1000 bits so they can machine them at their plant to ascertain whether everything is O.K. before shipment is made. No doubt we can make arrangements with the American Brass to forge some of these bits with the dies they already have. However, they won't need them before four or five weeks.

Pratt & Whitney were delighted also with the forgings we made in Ansonia as they will set in the jigs. (A devise used to maintain the steel in a correct position while the bit was being formed.) They hold more perfectly than the ones made in Butte. We will have to send them about a dozen shanks so they can try out the milling machines for them. There is plenty of time to take that up when I get back." ALH.

Operations went well at first with the steel companies in the East but suddenly some 'mysterious' influence began to manifest itself. The manufacturers didn't seem to 'understand' just what the specifications called for. Really they hoped to get out a bit of their own invention.

The detachable drill points (bits) were not looked on with favor by steel companies. There was an immense tonnage of their product used in the mining world. The "old" several foot long shank with a drill attached needed to be brought back to surface when dull. With this new bit the shank can remain in the work place eliminating fifty percent of needed stock. The miners are able to carry fifty bits in a canvas bag and never notice the weight. Before when they were affixed to the bit, this wasn't possible. Steel companies began to balk.

Disgusted with the annoying delays and the trivial excuses offered, Arthur came home. The ACM had decided to attempt to manufacture their own bits and a trial order of 8,500 were turned out with a twenty-five percent savings. Some machinery Arthur had selected was en route to the Anaconda foundry. He would take care of each detail in the manufacture process such as drop forging, milling, tempering (shaping by means of a rotary cutter)and treating.

The ACM agreement involving the transfer of rights was cleverly worded and stated that all the drills manufactured at their foundry department would be used exclusively in the ACM mines. No written records have been found to verify this arrangement except what was reported in *The Butte Miner Newspaper* which stated that "the ACM had secured the rights to manufacture the bit for use in its mines and then such Hawkesworth drills as will be used by other concerns will be manufactured in plants now being arranged for in Detroit, San Francisco and other places to be determined."[4]

Con Kelley Enters the Scene

Con Kelley wanted more than the rights to manufacture these bits for the Butte mines as seemingly was implied in the agreement. Kelley planned for the future. He wanted complete control of the bits and the rights to the machines Arthur was devising. No mention was made to Arthur that a purchase of the Chuquicamata Mine in Chile was in the negotiation stage by ACM where many bits would be needed. This huge purchase which was finalized in 1923 astounded Wall Street when ACM paid $77 million to the Gugenheim's for the Chile facility, a record transaction in the financial world.[5]

Arthur looked beyond mining. He had some other inventions in mind but would first see his factories constructed and proper machines installed. He smiled when he read in the *Mining Journal*:

"While the Hawkesworth drill will fill a long-felt want in mining work, it will find its greatest field in construction work in the larger cities. Some idea of what the demand will be for it in that field is evidenced in the report that more hard rock drills are used in construction work in New York City alone that in all the mines of Butte."[6]

Buck O'Donnell's cartoon drawn for Maurice. Miners wishing for the detachable bit!.

Chapter Seven

Lucid Explanations

Eagerly men of all ages filled the elaborate banquet room of the famous Anaconda Hotel. Almost 100 percent of the areas large Kiwanis club membership crowded together to hear Arthur on Feb.21, 1923. Nationally, this organization had 74,875 members that year. As the recognized inventor stood to begin, an expectant hush descended over the room.

Gentlemen: I want to state in the first place that I am a mechanic and not a talker so that you will not be disappointed. Since I was nineteen years of age, when I got my papers as a machinist, I have always followed that business, as a toolmaker and diemaker and as a machinist in the West. I suppose what you would be specially interested in would be something about what is now pretty generally known as the Hawkesworth detachable drill bit. Since 1885 when the first detachable drill bit or point was patented, the efforts of scores of inventors, mechanics and others have been directed toward devising some simple, practicable detachable drill bit for use in mining or in drilling any hard material. Dozens of them have been patented—all of them have been tried out and all, so far as I know, have been failures, with the exception I am very happy to say, of the one which I worked out after nearly twenty years of constant effort.

The average person hardly realizes the importance in industry of this little device. Of course, anyone who has ever had anything to do with mining, and has seen the hundreds of tons of drill steel going in endless round from shop to shaft and down into the depths of the mines knows the routine. Next it must go to the drilling machine away off in a drift or stope. It gets dulled after a foot or two of work. Then it must be laboriously transported back to the shop for redressing. This is an illogical, uneconomical and expensive proposition but at present the method used to handle steel. Two and one half hours per day are required in the Butte mines to lower sharp steel and hoist dull steel. Transporting it into the mines and out of the mines is a costly and oftentimes dangerous job. I am informed that since 1902, twenty-six men have been killed in the Butte district through handling steel. In one case six men were killed at one time. This does not include the damage to property.

Again, the proper dressing of drill steel is a delicate and difficult job, and the testimony of miners is that if they get three pieces out of every five which are properly dressed that is about all that can be expected. In other words, two fifths of the steel dressed gives little if any efficiency after it has been taken into the mines. This must be so from the very nature of the task with which a tool dresser is confronted. He must attempt to get a certain heat on the cutting face of the drill, and another very different heat on the shank, which is required to be tough, and not hard. With a solid piece of steel which is put into the furnace to be heated, he is up against a real proposition. About the best he can do, is average it up between the two heats required, and as a result breakage losses are very great and the mushrooming of steel an everyday occurrence.

When I first went into service in the mining business, I saw the wastefulness of the method of hauling steel and the great loss of time and money involved. It looked to me just about as reasonable to be handling the tremendous tonnages of drill steel the way it was done, as it would be to send an automobile every two or three months from Anaconda to Detroit to have the valves ground. So I started in experimenting and finally, a little more than two years ago, devised the bit which is making such a showing in Butte now. Also, it has been tried out in a dozen different mining districts all over the country.

This bit is very simple, as can be seen. In fact it is foolproof. It won't go on the shank except in one way and that is the right way. It won't come off until it is taken off. Then it comes off without any special effort. It will drill from 100 percent to 600 percent further than the present style mine steel and in much less time. With it there will be no danger in handling, and a miner can walk to the job with his steel in his jacket pocket. He won't be about all in when he gets to the job because he won't be lugging a lot of steel to his machine. A set of shanks will be at the drill site and he will be at work in a couple of minutes after he gets to the machine.

The job of distributing steel throughout the mines is a big job. A great deal of time is lost in doing so. Again miners often have to drill with steel that has become dulled. This results in lowered efficiency and also it necessitates much greater expense in maintaining and keeping in repair the drilling machines. With this new drill bit, miners always will be drilling with sharp steel and they will never be chasing around looking for steel.

The amount of drill steel used in the United States is very great. In the U.S. alone in the metal mines it is estimated that from seven to ten million pounds of drill steel are consumed every year. Add to this the drill steel used in the quarries, tunnels, coal mining, deep iron mining and so on and the total is startling. With this drill we claim we will save from 70 to 90 percent of the annual drill steel bill. We will speed up operations and very materially decrease the cost per ton of mining and all hard rock operations. In Butte during normal times from eleven to thirteen thousand pieces of steel are sharpened every day. The average efficiency of each piece of steel is about eighteen inches in average ground. With the Hawkesworth bit average footage or efficiency of from six to eight feet is obtained. The harder the ground the more significant the comparison in favor of the new system. The bit can be used on any type of steel and any kind of drilling machine or hand steel. It is adapted for use on axe blades and a score of other common tools in general use.

When the starter or larger size bit is dulled, it is quickly redressed at a nominal cost and used on the next longer shank. This is done four times or down to the inch and three-eighths in size. In other words there are five bits in the inch and seven-eighths bit, and each one of these five bits will give from 100 to 600 percent more footage than regular mine steel.

I want to express here the appreciation of myself and associates in this new enterprise for the helpfulness and assistance of the officials of the Anaconda Company, from John D. Ryan and C.F. Kelley, and from the mine officials at Butte, as well as the whole hearted and able work of Mr. Tanner, Mr. Blair, Mr. Bardon, Mr. Baglin and their assistance in developing and perfecting manufacturing tools and methods. Without the help of these men we would have had a long uphill fight to demonstrate the merits of this invention."

A standing ovation thundered through the air. This man was a winner.

Environmental Savings

From this speech, the aforementioned demonstrations, and the official response, it was easy to discern the environmental advantages, economic savings and increased safety procedures soon to be available.

1. Detachable Bit decreases amount of steel needed to mine.
2. Miners can use one-half to two-thirds less oil for lubrication.
3. Less powder is needed.
4. Compressed air usage is lessened.
5. Safety will be improved and labor less intensive.

The miners loved and respected the person who provided an easier life for them. They would not forget this in future years.

New Horizons for Maurice

Eighth grade graduation from Greeley provided a time to address Maurice's next level of education. Gonzaga Prep in Spokane, Washington, administered by the Jesuits, was chosen. For the past thirty-six years illustrious people benefitted from their teaching. Most famous at the moment was Bing Crosby who graduated in 1920.

Dressed in a striking new outfit, Maurice boarded the train a bit apprehensibly along with Pat McDonough, a student companion. "At fifteen this was a huge challenge to leave home", he once mentioned, "but my twenty-six-year-old brother Lee, who was home on vacation, encouraged me to venture forth into a world larger than Butte."

Lee was enthralled with his work in the movie studios in Los Angeles. Here he worked on an intriguing challenge. He was to design and make a miniature train set to be used in the movie, *Sergeant Grisha*, from a novel by Arnold Zweig.

While preparing to roll a cigarette, Lee fumbled with his paper and Bull Durham pouch. This, he knew, always fascinated Maurice. He further distracted the young boys from the impending separation by sharing the movie plot with them.

"A Russian sergeant escapes from the Germans in a train like the one I am creating. This petrified man is recaptured, tried and executed as a German deserter. Watch for the show to come out. I'll send you a picture of the train when I complete it."[1]

The anxious family waved until the Union Pacific disappeared from sight. Arthur comforted his weeping wife assuring her that when he was that age he gained maturity and received a better education when he left home for a distant school.

Maurice about to depart for Gonzaga in Spokane
gets word of encouragement from his mother.

Arkie Hawkesworth, left, banters with friends using
bits and shanks from the three cars they just loaded.

Miniature engine created by Lee Hawkesworth for the movie, *Sargent Grisha*.

Miniature German train of WWI vintage for *Sargent Grisha.*

The year passed quickly. It was a joyous moment when a self assured young man stepped from the train and greeted his parents. School had been a success but now he could bike, hike and be free of books. "One day a friend and I rented a tandem bike and we rode to Ramsey. The chain broke and one guy had to do all the pumping. I'll never forget that," he recounted in later years.

In July Maurice spent time at his aunt's spacious ranch which was located near Boulder. He expounded, "They owned half the Hamilton County. That was some ranch. I got to ride the range and made fifty cents a day helping out. The rest of my time I spent fishing. One day my uncle gave me a box of shells to shoot and that was special."

Next fall Maurice returned to Gonzaga and entered the tenth grade.C.F. Carroll, Dean, wrote to his parents on September 1,1923. "Glad to welcome Maurice back to Gonzaga."

Maurice, in turn, wrote of a new invention: a peanut butter and jelly sandwich. This made more impression on him than a bit invention.

After settling in, Maurice was excited to receive a letter dated Oct.5, 1923, from his father who was in Anaconda directing work at the Foundry where the bits were still being manufactured.

Dear Son,

I have just returned from Butte. Everyone is all right at home. Mother and I were to the Eastern Star dance last night at the Columbia Gardens. (At this time one of the grandest recreations parks in the West.) We had a nice time.

I read your letter and I was glad to know you are getting along so nicely. Glad to know you like your Music Teacher. That will make it easier for you to learn. So stay with it as we want one good musician in the Family. Also glad to hear you are doing so well on the football team. I didn't see Arkie last night but he is just the same, no better or no worse.(Later Arkie was diagnosed with diabetes.) Lawrence (eleven) is doing better in school. I got your letter all-right but it takes me a long time to answer one. I will get better the next time. I am feeling good only anxious to get through here and get started on our own factory. I don't know how long that will be for sure but I think about sixty days more.

We will send 6000 bits and 271 shanks to Butte next Tuesday. They will put them in the Emma Mine. Every thing is all right only it takes so long. I am going home Saturday night and coming back Sunday night. I will have more news next time. I got a new overcoat. Your Mother picked it out at Simons Store and now all the large stores' clerks are on a strike and have closed up. Well good-by and good luck. With love, Father.

Chapter Eight

Trip Number Three

"One phase in the history of the bit during this period is worth a mention. Attempts in forging were not satisfactory due primarily to the fact that proper equipment was not available in Butte or Anaconda. A cast bit seemed to be the solution to the problem. In order to determine the feasibility of this idea, 10,000 bits cast from alloy steel were ordered from an eastern manufacturer by the Anaconda company. The result was a disappointment. Fully fifty percent of the product showed serious casting defects, rendering the bits either unsuitable for drilling or unfit for further grinding. As a consequence of this experience, no further consideration was given to a cast bit."[1]

The HDC company needed a site location for a machine shop as the year 1924 began. The bit had been honed to perfection and Butte was the logical place to install their first plant. But first vital changes in the manufacturing machines themselves had to be made. Each particular step in making these machines and bits was a challenge. Many experiments were tried and discarded in ACM's Anaconda's Foundry. Above all a better heat treatment for the steel needed to be developed. This was as important to the success of the bit as any other manufacturing feature.

Arthur instinctively knew he had to return to the East where he could help in designing and testing the proper equipment. Hartford, Connecticut was America's manufacturing center for precision tools in the 1920s. It was known as the hardware Capitol of the world. Metal fabrications for the Colt and Springfield rifles, ammunition, jigs, fixtures of all kinds including weaving looms were created here.

Available water power at an ideal geographical location provided the right elements. Even into the next century thirty percent of the U.S. population and sixty percent of Canada's lived within some 500 miles of this city.[2]

His task became monumental taking nine months to accomplish but he never wavered in his resolve. Why did this take so long?

First, advancements in communications took a long time to catch up with the other basic needs of mankind. This skill lagged behind advancements in agriculture, clothing and shelter. In the 1920s the typewritten letter and the telegram were the fastest means to communicate from the East to Butte, Montana. Long distance telephone calls from New York to San Francisco began at this time and three minutes cost $16.50. The lines did not connect to Montana. Air transportation New York to San Francisco took over thirty-four hours. There was no Montana route. Arthur dictated letters and waited. One important letter was canceled, "Train Delay".

Second, subtle delay tactics were employed by the American Brass Company which was owned by the ACM who were desperately trying to invent their own bit.

Third, two board directors of the Hawkesworth Drill had other important full time jobs in the ACM, president of the bank and manager of the railroad!

Fourth, transportation of goods by rail was slow.

Fifth, Montana was isolated by geographic boundaries from the main areas of the country.

Arthur's main objective was to find companies that would produce the machines that he needed to manufacture the bits and shanks. These machines, in turn, would be sold to factory owners worldwide who would contract for them to produce the bits. With high hopes Arthur determinately set forth.

ACM on the other hand had hopes of their own. Ryan and Kelley pressured the infant research department to produce their own detachable bit and the machines to make them.

An Intrigue Enfolds
Main Characters

Anaconda Copper Mining Officials-ACM
Dan Ryan-Copper King from 1908 until 1933
Con Kelley-New York Office of the ACM; Chief Counselor of ACM beginning 1908 and CEO of the ACM after Ryan's death until 1955
Wm. Daly-Assistant, later General Manager of Mines for the ACM beginning 1922
Ed Borcherdt-Research Engineer
Chauncery Berrian-Supervisor of Mining
Hawkesworth Drill Board of Directors—HDC
Arthur Hawkesworth-General Manager.
Roy S. Alley-President.

Harry Gallwey-Vice-President and future President)also Manager of Butte, Anaconda and Pacific RR, owned by the ACM).

Ed J. Bowman-Treasurer (also manager of ACM's Daly Bank and Trust Co.

Jerry D. Murphy-Secretary.

Eastern Machinery Suppliers

Pratt & Whitney aka P&W-Jigs and fixtures through Mr. Hurlburt in Conn.

Taylor & Fenn aka T&F-Fixtures to grind bits in Conn.

Chicago Flexible Shaft Co.-Furnaces.

American Brass Company-Dies, jigs fixtures through Coe Brothers in Conn.

Strong Carlisle & Hammond-Furnaces.

Ajax-Shank machines in Cleveland.

The Bunch: l to r. front row-Geb Wertz, Al Waters, Will Bryant, Pat Murphy, Tom (Scotty) Hugh, John Duhurst, Cliff White, A.L. Hawkesworth. Back row: Otto Lundquist, Ed Trueworthy, Frances Catron, Henry Umhang, Frank Lynch, Bob Burton, Brown, Murphy.

Arthur's lengthy period of correspondence began in Chicago when he wrote to Roy Alley Jan.19,1924.

Have been with the Chicago Flexible Shaft Co. We hardened two of the bits in lead today. They came out good and hard on the cutting face and soft on the tongue side. It takes fifty-two seconds to harden holding them with tongs, with holders they figure about eight per minute.ALH.

To Maurice while lodged in Hotel Cleveland January 22.

It is cold here and the wind is blowing hard. How are you getting along in school? Stay with it. You will always be glad you did. I wish I had the chance at your age.

I am getting machinery to start our factory hoping you are well and will make good grades. Love, Father

A letter from Ajax Manufacturing dated the next day awaited Arthur at the hotel.

We are pleased to confirm our recommendation covering a one and one-fourth inch size Upsetting Machine for your drill shanks. We fully expect to be able to make this within three months from date. In fact, you will recall our General Foreman advised us he could build the machine in ten weeks. We are accordingly pleased to quote you:

One of one and a fourth inch New Model Heavy Duty Ajax Upsetting Forging Machine, Side Shear for cutting hot stock;

A special long three stud backstop to take care of your longest drill shanks which we understand are eight feet over all;

Annealed piping for carrying cooling water on dies and tools and all necessary wrenches.

Price : f.o.b. cars, Cleveland, Ohio was $4,850.00.

Hoping you will be able to follow your plan of calling here in about two weeks and placing formal order at that time. We remain very truly yours, H. D. Heman.

A letter from Butte indicated the Emma Mine was completely equipped with detachable steel bits. This mine produced an average of 550 tons of ore daily. Tests of the drill were to be on going under Borcherdt's supervision. The same correspondence annoyed Arthur. He immediately responded on January 24 to Bob Dias, one of the Bunch:

I just got a letter from Butte claiming the bits fit too high on shank, and that I ordered them to fit 1/8 in. high from the center. You remember in our talk when making the shank, we agreed 1/16 was about right. So far as that goes, if you are asked about it 1/16 will be right. That was my understanding all the time. If they appear too high, we can't help it now and if they send them back to be fixed, you can have Charlie draw the temper if it needs it and release the shank on the side so as bit will fit lower. This wouldn't be too much of a job, quicker than making new ones.ALH.

To Roy S. Alley, January 24:

Enclosed find copy of quotations from Ajax Mfg. Co. Note where it says upsetting shanks on the bevel, also with groove, that is—in the rough ready for milling. They claim that the machine will upset 125 to 150 per hour against seven per hour on the old drill sharpener, also claim that the seal upset this way the same as pressing out the bits, leaves the steel in better shape than any other way for forging.

Also, sending you quotations on furnaces and equipments from Strong Carlisle and Hammond Co. These men claim that lead hardening is the proper way for the bits. Mr. Parsons got the privilege for us to go through the Standard Twist Drill factory. It is an enormous plant, took nearly all afternoon yesterday. I saw them tempering hundreds of twist drills in lead, 24 in a holder, in fact all the hardening was heated in lead pots. The Superintendent, Mr. Wills, had one of his men harden three of the bits, heating them in lead and quenching them in water. All came out fine. Took about two minutes to each bit. They were a little slower than in Chicago but are just as good. The bits were held by tongs one at a time. They keep their hardening room dark. The only lights are electric lights with dark shades. This way the light keeps the same at all times. They also claim the lead hardening for the bits will be the proper method.

Nothing is here in the way of grinding machines. Leaving for Cincinnati tonight. Don't know just where I will stop. If I can get quick results, will be in Pittsburgh Monday. Send my mail to the Colonial Steel Co., Pittsburgh.

Now, about the shanks, the last order of shanks was made just the same as the ones used in the Badger mine. The ones we drilled with in the Neversweat mine were out of the same batch. The ones that Borcherdt drillled in the Anaconda mine were out of the same batch and in your telegram of the first day's drilling at the Emma mine were out of the same order. Everything was fine. No matter who says so, I never ordered bits to fit 1/8 high or disregarded any agreement in the fitting of bits. Will write as soon as I get a line on the grinding machines.I am feeling fine. Give my best regards to the bunch. ALH.

Arthur kept a notebook of sayings which sustained him at various periods of his life.

Do not turn your back on troubles, meet them squarely.

Most men would rather work someone than work for someone. ALH

Precious letters to "Dear Mamie" were not preserved but heart felt postcards were with pictures of the hotels Arthur endured and lovely gardens he cherished strolling while he reflected on daily challenges. These arrived steadily.

From Cleveland Jan.21:

Arrived here this morning. All trains late on account of cold weather, eight below and blowing. I did not mind it. Got around just the same. Got a good start on machining up furnaces and grinding machines. Feeling fine. Hope everything is all right at home. How are the boys? Will write soon. With love to all, Arthur.(All future letters were signed in this manner to his family.)

From Cincinnati Jan. 29:

I had to stay here two days longer than I expected. This outfit will have to design a machine for our purpose. What they have won't do. I went over it with them until 9:00 p.m. last night and all day today. Leaving for Pittsburgh tonight. It is raining today but not cold. Will write letter at Pittsburgh.

To Mr. Roy S Alley February 4:

Enclosed find quotations on steel. I got a lot of good information while in Pittsburgh, was at their plant all day Friday. Saw the steel made from start to finish. It looks like we will have to cut the steel ourselves into slugs. They have to inspect all the steel after it is rolled before they cut it up into slugs (sections that are cut from a circular steel rod into various bit sizes. These in turn are tumbled, heated and made ready for forging.). That means heating it again and cutting it hot. Cutting cold is too slow, and shipping slugs would cost us as much, as cutting them off the bar. So it looks like it will be up to us to cut them off. Steel has gone up about three cents a pound.

Mr. Brown had Mr. Procter take me to the *Mellon's Institute Research of Pittsburgh* No good came from this as a $5,000 donation had to be made prior to their sharing any information.

We next went to the U.S. Bureau of Mines, which I believe is the largest in the U.S., mostly pertaining to coal mines. It was very interesting. I found out that hundreds of Jack Hammers are used in coal mines around this district.

Saturday, I was also taken to one of the largest and best firms who do heat treatment for all kinds of tool steel, R.D. Nuttall and Co. Their head man, Mr. Emmett, of the Hardening Department gave me good advice on the lead heating. He thinks this heating will be the proper way to do them.

Interest from Oil Well Owners

I met a Mr. O.P. Hines, Manager of the Kentucky Glycerine Co., at Winchester, Ken. at the Gibson Hotel in Cincinnati. Mr. Hines is interested in the oil well drills; he said that was just what they wanted, and would order some right away if we had some for sale. I told him we had none as yet for the oil well drills, but would take that matter up just as soon as we could. He said he would keep in touch with us. I gave him a sample bit I had.

I just came from Mr. M. Daly's office. We had a nice visit. He told me that Bowman had not left for the east yet. I am leaving for Hartford today. Send all mail to Pratt & Whitney Co. ALH.

Next Arthur headed for Connecticut. During his long, circuitous train ride his inquisitive mind garnered a few facts from a traveling companion. Connecticut, named for an Indian word, "quinnehtuqut," meant "land along the long tidal river." This state had more than 200 mill towns. His interest was piqued as his father, whom he hardly remembered, was a superintendent of a sawmill in Bay City, Michigan. At that time the city was a lumber center and its nearby forests were a source of wood for the flourishing ship building trade.

Arthur heard of axe and machete mills, of clock and silk mills, of paper and textile mills, of saw and flour mills. The first woolen mill in the new country started here in 1788. Towns sprang up around these mills which were located on tangent rivers. The Connecticut River was too calm for mills and was a tidal river which flooded annually. During this era the river was great for transportation. The rich soil was a gift of glaciation as this land once was a large lake formed by a dam of glacial silt deposits before it collapsed.[3]

When the men lit up their pipes, tobacco became a topic. Broadleaf tobacco was a vibrant crop in Connecticut. This shade grown tobacco was used for the outer covering of a cigar and was considered the world's best.

To Harry (Gallwey) February 11:

This is no picnic of a job but feel that I am accomplishing something. Gathered lots of good information in heat treatments. Getting up a cheap grinding machine here, which will do for the mines and ourselves also. Going over the machines and fixtures with Pratt & Whitney Co. We will get better results by my coming here and explaining to them what we want. I have already shown them where they can change the fixtures for milling the shanks fourteen degrees which is about $300 to $500 cheaper than they quoted us.

I had dinner today with B.H. Blood, General Manager of Pratt & Whitney, his wife and her aunt at Mr. Hurlbert's home—very nice people. Mr. Blood brought me back to the Hotel Heublein where I am stopping.

I have not heard anything about the drills for some time. Hope everything is coming out all right with the ACM. It has worried me considerably but I know we will win sooner or later. Patience is holding on, perseverance is holding out, faith is holding up. We have all got that and we will win. It is snowing here today. It takes some time to thrash it all out.alh.

Instructs Pratt & Whitney Machinists

To Roy Alley, February 11:

I carefully went over the drawings with one of the Pratt & Whitney engineers and found out that they were wrong. I showed them how they could change the fixtures for less than $100 and be just as good as it was in the first place. It will get the same production they claimed at first. They agreed that I am right and it can be ordered that way with very little cost. They had the machine set up in the shop and ran it for me. We milled a few shanks. I liked it very much. Can mill about 30 per hour with one single change. The machine Anaconda(Foundry) has requires two changes.

Saturday we went into the matter of forming cutters, with Mr. Vokal, Superintendent of the Small Tool Dept. and to my surprise, he told me that the forming cutters would cost less, be stronger and easier to grind than the plain ones which they sent with the machines to Butte.

I took up the matter of getting a grinding machine for bits. Have been studying this out with the engineers and they are designing one to be solid and cheap that will give us a greater production. It will be a week or so before I get quotations on the same.

This week I will go into the fixtures for milling bits. Very little change necessary. I am satisfied with the bits forged in a screw press with the grooves on each side of the tongue making less stock to mill so that we can do away with the roughing machine.

Enter the Coe Brothers of American Brass

I will take up screw presses with the Coe Brothers as I understand they are the instigators of it. Expect to be with them in a week or so. George Coe was at the Pratt & Whitney Plant last Thursday. We had no time to talk as he had parties waiting for him. He just ran in to say hello to me.

Now the possibility of using an open hearth for bits instead of crucible steel. We will have to try it ourselves. Nobody in the steel game will recommend or admit that the open hearth steel for bits will take the place of a crucible for they don't know.It really depends on the steel company who is conscientious and reliable and has a reputation like the Colonial Steel Co.

I sincerely hope everything is looking better and the tests are coming along all right. I figure no news is good news. Expect to meet Bowman in Hartford. Will stay here as long as I can be of any good. The dies for the press will be the next thing.

The barriers are not yet erected which shut out aspiring talent
Keep your courage up and your temper down. ALH

Valentine wishes to Mamie were sent Feb. 11.

My whole affection is set upon you. Please say you like me a little bit too.

I am sending a few cards today. It is cold here and has been snowing. Not so pleasant to get around. Was at the works all day. Feel tired tonight sitting in my room all alone. Wish you were here—feeling kind of gloomy but not sick. Got lots to do getting all the orders together so Bowman can order them when he gets here. I expect him Thursday as he arrives Tuesday in New York. He will most likely be with M. Daly Wednesday and then come on here. Love to all, Arthur.

To Arthur from Wm. B. Daly Feb. 15.

Your letter of the eleventh congratulating me upon my recent promotion was duly received, and I desire at this time to thank you for the kind expressions contained therein.

It is a pleasure for me to receive a promotion of this kind, but it is by far a greater pleasure to know that my many friends throughout the country, as well as locally, are also pleased.

Again thanking you for your kind expressions, and with kindest personal regards, I am, Yours very truly Wm. B. Daly(signed personally).

Courtesy is to business and society what oil is to machinery.

An uphill journey early in life strengthens your staying power. ALH

Chapter Nine

Progress: Slow and Steady

I met Bowman at the Belmont Hotel in New York City Thursday, Arthur wrote to Roy on Feb. 18. He was all in a flurry to get back to Butte, of course, you know why. I just had about twenty minutes with him. He seemed to be all hopped up about the drills telling Hurlbert, Whitehead and myself that the Anaconda had to keep right on with the drills in order to keep the miners from quitting. They liked the drills so well. He was well pleased in every respect with the drills.

Mr. Hurlbert and Mr. Whitehead, chief designer, went down with me to New York to explain everything. They had all the drawings for a grinder and millers. We didn't get very far in twenty minutes as Bowman will tell you because he had to leave immediately for Butte. We all went to the station with him. We then got the six p.m. train for here. Ted, his son, came back with us as far as New Haven. Mr. Bowman said he would try and get back in ten days.

Pratt & Whitney sent the new quotations Saturday for the six items listed below. They did not have time to give me complete quotations being Saturday, as they close at noon. They only had enough blue prints to send to Butte, I will get mine Monday.

Item 1: Roughing Machine. I was in hopes of doing away with this machine in my letter to you written Feb.11 but after talking it over again here and feeling sure the Coe Brothers are for it, I feel as if I were taking too much responsibility to stand out alone on this and would say to order it as quoted.

Item 2: Fixture for finishing bits as quoted. This is $130 lower than before.

Item 3: Alterations fixtures for shanks.

Item 4: Special Hawkesworth Bit Grinders. Now this is the machine that has caused us lots of thinking and is wanted badly. To get a decent price on it we have to order five. To get a still lower price we would have to get twenty-five. And to get one alone would cost more than $2000. Now we must have some on hand for our customers and have at least two in our shop to start with. Maybe we could get Daly to order some for the Anaconda Mines. As yet, I don't know of any other way to get a grinder for our work. Of course, we will sell them for a little profit to our customers.

Item 5: Pratt Whitney Curvex Grinding-Machine for cutters. This is a cheap machine at $600, all the rest I have seen run more than $1,000. This should be ordered.

Item 6: Cinncinnati High-Speed Drilling Machine. This will do us to start off with. I expect to make fixtures and holders ourselves for holding the bits for drilling.

I had a long talk with Mr. A.H. D'Arcamble, the metallurgist for Pratt & Whitney. I took a shank with me and asked him what he thought of it. I told him it was a straight carbon steel eighty percent carbon. He said that is the wrong steel for that kind of work. He asked me what we hardened it in and I said, "Oil." He said it was not an oil hardening steel. He then asked me if we drew them and I said we did not. He said that all steel that was hardened no matter what way, should be drawn to relieve strains to keep it from breaking. He recommended S.A.E.6150, which he says will give us the required hardness and great toughness. This is an oil hardening steel and must be drawn to 650 deg. Far. He stated when we ordered steel to state that it must pass the Deep Etch Test, which means a disc cut from bars placed in 200 Deg. Far. Muriatic Bath and left there for three quarters of an hour. Taken out and washed off this will show any defects.

I hope to see Bowman soon so we can get the first orders placed, the ones that take the longest to get out West.

I went with O'Brien to a meeting of the *American Society for Steel Treating*. It was very interesting and instructive. The principal subject was *Roller Bearings* by L. Laning, Metallurgist for the New Departure Company. I took along my model and some bits. I met several of the boys who said the bit was a lead-heating proposition.

Rack Drillers

I also met a Mr. Stanton at the meeting whose father is a contractor who does a lot of rack drilling. He said his father had heard of the bits and wanted to know more about them as it cost him $700 to get seven drills sharpened last week.

A man's hardest competitor ought to be himself.

Not even genius compares with grit.

And a man can't lose if he will not quit. ALH

At the Emma Mine in Butte a method was being developed for distribution of the bits and shanks. Situated between the mine shaft and miner's changing rooms or dry house was a surface bit house around ten feet by sixteen feet in area. Here shanks and bits of various sizes and conditions, sharp and dull, were stored. The Bit House attendant received new equipment and returned dull steel to the Foundry. Records were kept. This mine and each subsequent one using the bits would have a different color painted on the shanks and bits for inventory control. The mine attendant reported to work at 10:00 a.m., filled the carriers, ordered materials, kept bit and shank records, signed for deliveries and took a monthly inventory.

The carrier the *Bunch* designed was a channel shaped sheet metal welded to a base. It had a cover and tubular handle. A four-compartment carrier held 16 bits and a five-compartment held twenty bits. Depending on the number of shanks needed and their lengths, they weighed between fifteen and seventeen and one-half pounds.

The attendant issued the carriers for the night shift; the boss tool man for the day shift. These carriers and shanks must be ready for the miner when he arrived. Each miner had a contract number and was accountable for his predetermined allotment.

Each level underground was required to have a Shank Locker for reserves. Here a broken shank could be exchanged. A nipper must maintain an adequate stock of new or repaired shanks in these underground lockers. He returns the damaged ones to the surface bit house. At the end of a shift, bits are separated and recorded as to dullness, damage or loss.

The degree of lost bits is dependent on the supervision of shift bosses. Loss manly occurs when bits fall into chutes or holes. Some of these are later recovered by magnets at the concentrator.

Shanks with Bits Attached.

Hawkesworth Drill Shop—Individual Bit Carriers

An encouraging handwritten letter from Harry Gallwey dated Feb.16 arrived.

Well, the Emma test is over and the boys are checking up today. We made an average footage of 7.2 feet per bit against 4.1 feet for old steel. It was extremely successful in every particular. All the men at the mine from foreman to Nipper are stuck on the bit and I doubt if the bits will ever be taken out of the mine. The miners finish drilling from 1:30 p.m. until 2:00 p.m. every day which is quite a savings in time. There were twenty-eight shanks battered or broken. Had some trouble at the start on account bits setting too high on shank but that was overcome when we changed back to original plans.

Run on the Banks

Mr. Bowman was East but I understand left for West Thursday night. We have been having runs on our Banks here. Tegan Bros. closed in Butte, Billings and Gardner. Their Anaconda Bank is still going but had quite a run yesterday. I think that is what hurried Mr. Bowman home. He will be here tonight or in morning and we will know what he did. Mason and Borchardt are at outs over Emma test. Mason is not with the boys on the figuring. Mike Loughran and Earl Lyford are for us and Borchardt and Sultzer for the ACM. Yesterday they got along fairly well together. Naturally, we all feel very jubilant over the results. It would seem to me that this test should suit the most particular.

Our weather has been glorious. No cold and very little snow. The bunch is all feeling fine and wish you all kinds of good luck. Kindly remember me to Mr. Hurlburt. I am yours most cordially, H.A. Gallwey.

To E.J Bowman Feb.18, 1924:

We were all sorry that you had to leave so suddenly; hope everything is all right in Montana. I talked to Pratt & Whitney people about Ted (his son). Everything is O.K. for him to start Monday. They will give him a good show. I explained to them that he wanted to learn all he could about shop practice, blue-print, reading heat treatment of steel, in fact, everything that would bring him in line with our business.

I am very glad that this thing came about, as it will give him a little advance knowledge before we start, as the manufacture of drills will be entirely a new thing. Great possibilities of expanding all over the country are assured. Eventually, new blood will have to take our place and if Ted likes it and sticks with it, I don't know of any better thing he could do. He was here with me today. We had dinner together, and I talked over the situation with him. He likes it and I am convinced he will make good. I am going to do all I can to help him.

The New York Central's water level route from NYC to Albany was a marvel of the century. Passengers could hear special radio broadcasts for the first time. Arthur heard tell of it while waiting for the train to Waterbury. On this particular cold dreary morning an earnest newsboy glanced at Arthur as he finished his conversation. "Paper, Mister?"

As he paid, a pang of homesickness struck him. Larry was about this boy's age. "What is your name young lad?"

"Jackie Coogar," (not he of cinema fame) came back the somewhat sad reply. Arthur paid, thanked him and looked for this boy on future trips. A few months later on Aug.26 Lewis Wickes, 1874-1940, took a famous photograph of Arthur's new little friend.[1]

To Harry Gallwey Feb.23:

Your most welcomed letter received. It did me good when I got it as I have never received a letter from any of the bunch. The test at the Emma was very gratifying. I have felt sanguine all the time about it. When we get going, we will be able to improve the shanks considerably. I have been talking with some very good men on steel, some of the best metallurgists in the country. All agreed that our shanks should be drawn after hardening. That was just what we did not do. But we will get this right before long. As Mr. August H. Landwere said, "A winner never quits and a quitter never wins." I went down to see the Coe brothers at Waterbury last Tuesday to commit them on several matters pertaining to the drills.

Grinders and Price Comparisons

Well, the price that Pratt & Whitney wanted to charge us for grinders got on my nerves so I made up my mind I would find someone who would do it cheaper and I have. Taylor & Fenn will make us a grinder that will grind just as fast with fixtures to hold bits. Five of them would cost $1250 while P & W wants $5,750 that will not grind any faster. You could hardly believe that there could be such a difference between two grinding machines. We will have a machine that we can easily sell to our customers at a profit. You see it pays to look around. It was snowing and half raining and sloppy when I made up my mind to go and find someone who would do it. That day was gloomy but by night I felt repaid for my efforts.

I got word from Mrs. H (Mamie) that J.P. O'Neill has resigned. Well, I expected it and was not surprised. Jack has been a good faithful servant to the company. I never knew him to do anything against them, always fighting for them. I was with him a whole lot for several years and know he had gone as far as he could and wasn't appreciated anymore. Ceasing to do new things and to think new thoughts-that is the real growing old. ALH

Family, Work and the Future

I must confess. I am not stuck on this job. I would rather be with my family. This is a lonesome job but I know it has to be done and will go through with it until I feel I have just cause to quit.

The other night I was drawing and sketching a new grinder and fixtures, not noticing the time. When I did look at my watch, it was 2:45 a.m. I don't mind that—it is interesting. I often do it. This saying I have remembered since a boy, "The heights that great men reached and kept were not obtained by sudden plight but were done while their companions slept and they toiled onward in the night." I would like to have a place where I could go on and work out my ideas. I have two good inventions thought of but don't intend to push them until we get the drills over the top.

I have been wondering what will be the next move with the Anaconda and what Borchardt is up to. It has not done him any good with our showing. I expect their report is completed by now.

The best way out of difficulty is through it.

A minute of keeping your mouth shut is worth an hour of explanations. ALH.

To Roy on Feb. 23:

I have found a place where we can get a cheap wet grinding machine. One that is good and strong and will give us the same production as the Pratt & Whitney design. This machine we can get for $160 and the fixtures will cost less than $100. In all about $250. They have them in stock. All they have to do is to make up fixtures and holders for them. This grinder will do the work and can be readily sold to our customers at a profit. The firm that makes them is Taylor and Fenn in Hartford. I have been with them the last three days getting up fixtures and holders. Mr. George S. Delaney, sales manager, and their chief designer had lunch with me at the Heublein Tuesday. We returned to my room, and discussed the fixtures for the grinding machines for more than two hours. Then we all went to the works.

I have never been satisfied with the P & W prices on grinding machines and fixtures. If we took five of their grinders at their price it would cost us $5,750 @ $1150 for each grinder with fixtures. This did not look good to me so I started to look elsewhere and found we can get a grinder that will do the same amount of work and is just as good for $250 each with fixtures or five for $1250, a savings of $4,500. I expect to have drawings and quotations on these Monday. Taylor and Fenn also make a high speed drill machine with two spindles, which means you can drill two bits at a time for $360. The Cincinnati high speed drill that was quoted by P & W Feb.15 has only one spindle, meaning you could drill only one at a time for $340.So you see by getting the Taylor & Fenn high speed drill for $20 more we get twice the production, and as far as the two machines compare, the Taylor& Fenn drill has it over the Cincinnati drill. I examined them both.

I expect a Mr. Olson at the hotel at about 2:00 p.m. today. He just called me up on the phone but I was at lunch. He is a steel man and wants to go over the steel for shanks. He claims he has a wonderful steel for that purpose. It is called Cycloid, made in Reading, Penn. I don't know much about it but will wait for him and find out.

Coes and Bowman

I went to Waterbury Tuesday, met both the Coes, who were very nice as ever. Got in there at 9:30 a.m. and left at 8:06 p.m. Nothing new. I went over the drawings of grinders and millers which they thought were all right. So did I, but the price, I told them was too high. We talked tempering shanks and bits but I did not get anything from them as they knew less than I did about it. They were just guessing at it. (They were fabricators and not machinists.)

A friend of yours, Gus Wenzel, came in while I was there. Had a letter from you to the Coes. We all went to lunch and after that they turned Mr. Wenzel over to someone who took him through the works while we talked over the drills all afternoon. They are for the Roughing machines. Also said that the latest thing in dies was no flash dies. I did not go into the making of dies as I will have to wait until Bowman gets here or some arrangements are made with them.

If you have some enemies you are to be congratulated, for no man ever amounted to much without arousing jealousy and erecting enemies. Your enemies are a very valuable asset as long as you refrain from striking back on them, because they keep you on the alert when you might otherwise become lazy. ALH

Opinions

To Roy Alley Feb. 27,1924:

Received your letter of Feb.20.Glad to hear from you and contents noted, especially the Borchardt part of it. We know he is not with us and no doubt Berrien is back of him. From the day Berrian said to me that he expected more stock than what he got, I knew right then he would not help much. And if any influence was brought to bear in opposition to us, he would turn that way. I think this has happened. He can't kill the(Emma) report but can delay it—that's what they want to do.

Borchardt figures delaying the report or cutting down the footage and misrepresenting other things are his only hope to get time enough to work out some of his ideas. We must walk away from that bunch (ACM) and forget them, get started. Other people will be glad to get the drills faster than we can make them.

There have been so many rough seas to this thing. When it gets rough and choppy, I just wait and float until it calms over and then row where I want to go with never fear of drowning. Otherwise, I would become too weak and exhausted to go on.

The Two Copper Kings

As Bowman had indicated, Mr. John Ryan and Con Kelley are not presently interested in investing financially in our drills. I cannot see where they are going to help much. The Butte team expects to come up with a detachable bit on their own. I feel sure this is the case. They haven't the ability to make a detachable bit or the machinery to produce them so this is no worry or problem for us.

I am sending you a list of material and machinery to order and my expenses for the first month for 31 days. I have just $81 left—all bills paid up to date so I will need $300 more to finish and to get back. I will have to return the same way, close up each deal, get the dies made right for shanking machines and for the screw press and a trimming press at Toledo.

A Little Gossip

Well, J.P.O'Neill has sent in his resignation to take place March 1. Of course, we all knew that was coming. He had no one back of him this time like the past, when you stood back of him. When a fellow stops to analyze it out, it shows some more of Chauncey Berrien's dirty work. I could see it when talking with him at different times that he hated Jack and has been after him for some time.

As he said one night when drunk that he could whip any man in the house but then dodged Larry Duggan when Larry told him the truth about himself and Mrs. B.ALH.

Handwritten to his "Dear Son, Maurice" Feb.27, 1924:

I received a letter from your mother and the bill from Gonzaga University for $190.45. Also your report card showing you were not doing so well. On the bill there were no charges for music showing that you are not taking any lessons.

It is a shame that you don't do better for it costs us so much money to try and give you an education. You know how much I want you to go on with your music for I know you have it in you. When years go by, it will be such a comfort for all of us. So take it up again even if you have to drop out of some of the athletics. You will be surprised what you can do if you try.

I am here in Hartford selecting material and machinery to start our factory. Have selected about $42,725 worth so far in Cleveland, Cincinnati, Pittsburgh and Hartford. Am not through yet. Will be home about March 20. Then we figure on putting a factory in San Francisco. I may come and see you on my way to California in about a month or so.

How are you feeling? I am feeling fine only it worries your mother and me when we find out you're not doing your best. So brace up and do better. I will need you in our factory some day. Get the education while you can. That is the kind of man we will want to take the lead. We can always get mechanics and laborers but this class of men can't take the high up jobs.

I have always regretted not having a college education. My father died when I was three years old. My mother was a widow with three children and couldn't afford to give me one. We were so poor. Your mother came from good people and on my side we are direct descendants of the famous Josiah Wedgwood of the great Wedgwood Pottery in England, known the world over. Some day the name Hawkesworth may be known all over if you try. Now is the time to start. Study whenever you can. Of course, you must have some fun but don't let it go too far. If the other fellows go too far, you quit, go practice and study. Show your will power and remember this saying: "The heights that great men reached and kept/ Were not obtained by sudden flight/But while their companions slept/ Were toiling onward in the night."

That meant the other fellows were too lazy or could not see any benefit studying or getting ahead. Now here is another saying I want you to pay attention to: A winner never quits and a quitter never wins.

Sunday I went around Harriet Beecher Stowe's House and looked in the windows. It was empty. A man by the name of Bond has bought it and expects to move in soon. Harriet Beecher Stowe is the woman who wrote *Uncle Tom's Cabin*. She wrote it while living in this house. I am sending postal of the house. Another famous resident, Mark Twain, lived in the same block, not more than 100 feet away. He is a great author and writer. I went into this house and saw lots of old things of his. One thing was a queer old piano like a grand but longer and slimmer than they make today. You get some of his books if they have them at the University.

Good luck to you and the boys. When you write, send it home as I will be leaving here most any day. Your loving father.

Chapter Ten

Grinding Machines and Prices

Tedious trials at varied locations, multiple hours of demonstrations, prodigious letters to board members, travels to cities and factories filled Arthur's days and nights. He wrote to Roy on the bonus day of this leap year.

Taylor & Fenn sent you quotations, drawings and circulars for the grinding machines, index fixtures and two-spindle drill presses.

The five grinding machines with fixtures and 20 inch wheels total $1870 compared to five of P&W grinding machines with fixtures and no wheels which total $5750. Both are hand operated and have the same production capability.

I don't expect the ACM will give us a report before they finish up all the shanks. It is certainly annoying. I wish we were through with them and our plant started. We will never get any where until we do. I imagine before this letter reaches you, I will know something. I realize you are having a hard time with that bunch of double deckers but the tide will turn and we will be on top and their stock will go down.

Tell Mr. Bowman that Ted is getting along fine running a lathe part of the time, grinding twist drills and lathe centers the rest of the time. He is taking a course in blue print reading.

When our orders are placed, arrangements will have to be made for shipping. I would like to get started on the dies for the screw press next with the American Brass.

Tomorrow I am going to see Carpenter Steel. They seem to do a large business around here. Both P & W and T & F say they have a good line and are a good outfit. ALH

J. O"Brien wrote Arthur a detailed letter March 2 on the subject, *Hardening of Drill Bits for Mining Purposes.* Next day a letter from Gallwey arrived for Al who was called this by a few close friends.

Your most welcome letter received and I enjoyed hearing from you. The boys gave Jack O"Neill a banquet on Saturday night. It was a fine affair.

Roy and I saw Bowman Friday and he agreed to write Mark (ACM accountant) right away. Expect to hear everything straightened out very soon. It would have been done long ago if Bowman could have stayed in New York. Now Mark is in Palm Beach. Mr. Bowman would go there to see him but doesn't want to leave here on account of the ticklish banking situation. We are all ready and raring to go. Hope we will have no more delays. The Emma report was turned in Friday. We haven't heard much about it only that it was favorable. Understand Eddie(Borchardt) put in several additions of his own labeled 'Readjustments'. Everyone at the Emma is stuck on the bit from the foreman to the nipper. We are all impatient at the delay and expect things will soon be fixed so we can get moving. All we are waiting for is Mark's signature to the contract and a check for their first payment.

Mrs. Gallwey is in the hospital with appendicitis. The rest of us are all well. Harry.

Arthur, a congenial person, with a perception for detail few have, little knew he was headed for six months additional "exile" on the East coast. Unknown to him, ACM was employing delay tactics such as stalling Bowman with extraneous projects which prevented him from following up on Arthur's orders and signing contracts promptly. They held back on test reports of the bit's efficacy at the Emma Mine. These tests had been ongoing for two years with ample positive results.

A March 6 letter from Bowman with a letterhead, Daly Bank and Trust Company of Anaconda, Capital and Surplus $200,000 arrived with an excuse.

I have delayed answering your letter of Feb.18, hoping to be able to tell you just when I could get back and take up the matters that you are working out. Roy and I have gone over the P&W proposal and the T&F. We should be absolutely certain that the fixtures made by P&W for holding the bits while milling will not permit the slightest movement and will always remain centered. The present construction sets the bit into an arched space on one side and is held in place on the other side by a straight bar forced in position by a wedge. I would suggest that you talk to Whitehead and Schram about the availability of making a fixture that will have a bearing on all four gage faces. I am not an engineer and this suggestion may sound foolish to them, but you know the necessity of having an accurate lock.

The drilling machines of the T&F look like the proper thing.

The grinding machines seem to be a more difficult problem. We think that it is very essential to work out one fixture that will grind all faces of the bit without changing the fixture or using two machines. Do you think it is possible or practical to grind the gage of the bit on either side of the grinding wheel? EB

On March 11 Arthur wrote to Roy.

Received your letter of March 5, which I was glad to get. I note what you say about grinding machines. Well, that just is what I have been trying to get to. It can't be done unless you run way up into the thousands which would be too expensive for small mines to have. As for grinding on the side of the wheel, it could not last any time and it would be no good for grinding the face of bits. I am still thinking and scheming on this and hope to get something better.

I am not surprised at all in having to wait for a report from the operating department on the Emma test. They know it is all right, for if it wasn't they would be glad to have told us right away, and show us why they can't use the bits. So the only thing they can do is to hold it up as long as possible. I only wish we were going on our own and not be dependent on the Anaconda Foundry so we could show them up. Do you know we could buy back the dull bits and pay ten cents per bit and make a large profit on them?

George Coe was here last Friday with two other men from Waterbury. I had them up in my room looking over the Taylor & Fenn drawings. Coe thinks they are all right. I will have things pretty well lined up by the time Bowman gets here. I got his letter and knew just how you fellows are looking at it and will do my best to better each thing or know why I can't.

The weather here is quite changeable like all March weather. Business seems to be picking up in all manufacturing lines here.

Politics

Mr. Hurlbert and I went to hear an address by former Governor Harkness of Vermont to the *American Society of Mechanical Engineers*. The Governor has been a tool maker and machinist like me. I got quite a kick out of it. When I first came here, everybody seemed to be for Coolidge but I notice it is dying out now. All have a good word for Walsh. ALH

A Sudden Knock

Late that night as Arthur wrestled with grinding machine challenges, a tentative knock resounded through the quiet room. There stood a middle-aged man who asked if he would like company. Taken aback Arthur realized several men had recently met with him in the privacy of his room. He had nodded to this effeminate man before on several occasions.

Suddenly realizing the situation Arthur replied gently, "No, thank you. I'm just finishing a letter to my wife and sons and am very tired." The customary nod sufficed in future encounters.

Safety Regulations

St. Patrick's Day he updated Roy.

Just a few lines to let you know how things are coming here. I have P&W and T&F engineers working on grinding machines to see if they can't get something that will be more suitable for us.

Most of the states have laws governing safety first on emery wheels. This includes California and Montana which already have rules for the safety boards to follow. They call it "Safety Standards" relating to the use and care of abrasive wheels. It states grinding on flat side of straight wheels is often hazardous and should not be allowed on such operations when the sides of the wheel are appreciably worn thereby, or any considerable or sudden pressure is brought to bear against the side of the wheel.

In designing grinding machines one has to be guided by these rules. Anyway it is not economical and is not practicable to grind on the side of wheels as the wheels will not last half as long and are more liable to break. We will have to use two or more wheels on one grinding machine to grind bits in one operation, or two machines doing one operation each.

The fixtures for the milling machines look all right and should hold the bit. There are fewer moving parts to these fixtures than the one Anaconda uses which is in our favor.

I took up the steel question with D'Arcamble and J J Fischbeck, metallurgists. They are of the opinion that the Universal steel quoted to us on Mar 3 at 18 cents per lb. will stand up longer than the Colonial No.7. As they put it, the highest price is not always the best and the chromium in the Universal Steel will make the bit wear longer and stand up as good as the Colonial #7. They say we should try it. The analysis of Universal is .80 carbon, .50 chromium, .15 vanadium. Nobody around here uses the Colonial steel. They haven't even an office here.

I hope Bowman gets in New York City today as I would like to get home. There is much to be done yet and I am anxious to get it finished. The weather is extremely cold here.

Man never reaches above his habitual thought.

The art of pleasing is the art of rising in the world. ALH.

Another Brainstorm

To Roy Alley March 20, 1924:

I just discovered a new way to grind bits cheaply. It came to me last Monday night. I made a sketch of it, took it over to T & F the next day. Their chief mechanical engineer, S.M. Mathias, and I went over it together. He agrees it is a better way and it will cost less than what has been proposed.

The holders and fixtures are easy to make, will be able to grind bits for one to two cents each by taking the T &F grinding machines, putting the bit on a holder and let them feed by gravity. That is, the weight of the bit and holder will rest on the wheel. When the bit is ground enough, it comes to a stop. Then the operator changes it around to the next groove, and the same thing is done to the side of the wings only in a different holder.

Now one operator can run four to eight machines. He will grind one every two minutes with four machines or one every minute with eight machines at a cost of one cent per minute. There will be no danger of grinding the bit hot which would draw the temper, as the pressure will be regulated by the weight in the holder and will always be the same; not like the operator would sometimes do, to bear too heavy, get the bit too hot and take the hardening out of it.

After the operator places one bit for grinding, he leaves it alone, goes to the next machine, does the same and the next and so on until he gets back to the first one which will be ready to change again. It makes it easy for him. He doesn't have to do any grinding himself—just change the position of the bit.

You can readily see that the P & W machines are not what we want. An operator has to be on the job at all times, moving the bit forth and back under the wheel. Only at the time the bit is in contact with the wheel is the bit being ground. Every time it passes by the wheel at each end of the stroke, it is not grinding, and on its return stroke it can't grind any, to speak of, as it has already ground it on the forward stroke. Every time the operator slows up, gets lazy or has any other thing to do with the machine, the bit is not being ground. You can't grind cheap that way or get quantity production.

Remember, to grind fast you must keep the bit right on the wheel at all times with just enough pressure applied so it will grind and not get too hot.

The T & F design is the same way as the P & W as to its operation. The operator has to do all the grinding himself which would be a tiresome job for anyone. You would not get much efficiency that way.

I have learned to believe in small machines to make a unit instead of a large complicated machine by itself doing the same amount of work. If something goes wrong with the large machine, your whole work is stopped or crippled. If something goes wrong with one of your small machines, the rest are going right along.

Grinding Machine for Drill Bits—1924.

Henry Ford's Experience

Now Ford found this out. He had a large complicated machine built for $65,000. This machine took the place of sixteen small ones he had in his plant. After two months he scrapped it. He found out it didn't pay because when any part went wrong or if cutters needed to be changed the whole unit had to be stopped. It was the same as shutting down 16 of the small machines at once. He went back to the small machines. When one was down, the other 15 were working.

I have not received the bits yet but hope they will be here by Friday at the latest. You said you were mailing under separate cover a copy of a chart showing in condensed form the history of the Emma test. I haven't as yet received it. Would like to get it.

Quarry Visit

A welcomed diversion presented itself one clear but chilly March day as Arthur waited for Bowman's arrival. He accompanied a colleague to one of the largest quarry faces in the world, a traprock quarry cut into the Totoket Mountain of the Metacomet Ridge near New Haven.

This fascinating site elicited further discussion about the state's venture into iron mining and of its demise last year. The ravages of deforestation reminded Arthur of Butte. Much acreage had been cleared to convert wood into the charcoal necessary to keep the furnaces operating. Quartz mining still existed along with some granite and green marble.

Arthur later wrote to Mamie that the natives boasted that some granite was used in the Brooklyn Bridge Construction and some green marble for the Statue of Liberty Monument.[1] He concluded that every square foot of this formerly nicknamed *Provisions State* seemed to be or has been used in some way. It was so small compared to Montana.

To Roy March 29, 1924:

Received the patent papers, filled out statement, sent it on to Beims. Bowman is in New York City. (A month delayed.) Going down to meet him Saturday afternoon. I expect Bowman will come back here Monday with me.

Opinions

Glad to get your telegram saying that the Emma report was favorable, as far as the manufacturing end. ACM couldn't commit to it as they don't know how to start a thing like this. That whole mechanical bunch is way behind the times. We could make the bits for the ACM for 25 cents and give them 10 cents for each drill bit needing regrinding, regrind them, sell them again for 25 cents and make a large profit and the bit would cost them only 15 cents a bit.

Con Kelley Negotiates

To Roy April 1, 1924:

I went down to New York City Saturday night and had a conference with Bowman. Got back here Monday morning. Everything is looking good.

Con Kelley and Thayer are now very interested in the bits. Bowman was to meet them Monday to have lunch and talk drills. I have not heard yet what they did. No doubt you will have word before you get this letter. If we make the drills in Butte for them {ACM), it will cost from .01 to .015 more per bit on account of higher wages and union conditions. Even at that, I think it would be a good thing for us all around and hope it works out that way to start.

If we charge them thirty cents for a new bit and grind the dull ones for ten cents each, it will cost them sixty cents for four bits or fifteen cents per bit.

To make them in Butte, it shouldn't cost us any more than twenty-eight cents overall making us a profit of 32 cents on the four bits, which would be 100% profit or over.

Pratt & Whitney are through tempering and annealing the 125 bits we gave them. I expect to ship them to you about Thursday. The metallurgist is examining them now. Will get a report on them this week. ALH.

Bowman's Faith

To Roy Alley April 7, 1924:

Bowman and I went all over the machines both at Pratt & Whitney and Taylor & Fenn. We were well pleased. The grinding machines at T & F look good. Will get this grinding down to less than one cent per bit.

The action of the ACM has been very disappointing but not surprising to both of us. Bowman has lots of faith in the drills and confident that everything will come out all right. He went down to see Mark Saturday afternoon. Has a meeting with Con Kelley Monday, but he doesn't expect anything but the worst of it from him. I am to wait here until I hear from him which will be about Wednesday. All depends what Mark does. Bowman intends to give him a good talk.

I know these bits are harder than those done by Anaconda. Bowman was well pleased with the lead tempering. I had O'Brien temper one while he could watch. He took it with him. I sent back 111 bits all heated in lead to 1050 degrees F for three minutes, then heated in another pot to 1525 degrees F and 54 bits drawn to 350 degrees F and 57 bits drawn to 400 F.

I am sending a cost sheet per bit based on Eastern and California wages which cover nearly everything with twenty-seven cent steel which we would get for twenty-four cents in quantity.

Did you know that Mr. Leonard of the Denver Rock Drill called on Mark weeks before the report got down to the ACM office and told him that the ACM would not report favorably? There is something wrong somewhere.

Kelley says if we could make bits for .15 and grind them for .088 cents per bit it would pay. Of course, I know that his talk was part of the game. That way would cost them .414 cents for 4 bits or.1035 per bit. Now we can sell them one bit for .30 cents, grind three times for six cents which would be in all .36 for 4 bits or.09 per bit. I suppose if he knew that he would cut it down still smaller. Anyway Bowman and Mark know that I showed Kelley this and also convinced him we can grind for one cent instead of two cents. We could sell the ACM. bits for 25 cents and grind 3 bits for two cents at a good profit. Making it cost them .31 per bit or .0775 per bit against .1035 their prices. They are fighting hard against us but we will win.

No doubt before you receive this letter you will know more from Bowman. It seems that Berrien and others had juggled the report to their own liking after leaving Butte, but it won't stand. ALH.

Arthur wrote to Bowman who was at the Belmont Hotel in New York City, April 7. He informed him of his price talks with Con Kelley.

Gallwey wrote a handwritten letter on Butte, Anaconda, & Pacific Railroad stationery, Office of the General Manager, April 10.

Received your very welcome letter and enjoyed your poetry about the Tea Pot Dome. Suppose Mr. Bowman has told you all about our report. We are now having it checked up and from present indications we will show up any number of the ACM's inconsistencies and rank injustices, but with it all they acknowledge it is all right in every way from an operating standpoint. The way the manufacturing costs must be reduced, that is no news to us. We knew that all the time. We are not discouraged at the report. We are more disgusted at the deal. However, we are going to keep plugging away and hope Bowman comes back with the dough. If he does, the rest of it will be easy.

Dien Kilroy(a former ACM employee) is in Seattle and I understand is going to San Francisco to work for the Hearst people. I wish we were in San Francisco right now turning out a few shanks and bits. We are all well and happy and hope you are the same. Harry.

Home in Two Weeks?

To Roy Alley April 12, 1924:

Enclosed find copies of cost to make bits, shanks and regrind bits. I gave Bowman the original last Thursday. He was up here from Waterbury and left for New York City that night. He had an appointment with Kelley for Friday. I don't know what happened, but I do feel that things are looking better. He expects to meet Mark next Monday, then he will get in touch with me. I expect Waterbury will be my next move to make arrangements for the dies, then Cleveland and home. It will take about two weeks more.

You will notice I raised the price per hour on operators and helpers. Also, added 6 % on money invested for machinery and equipment. We are going to come to the Red Star Vanadius steel for bits at fifteen cents per pound with reduction off by Carlbad Tools. This will bring it around thirteen cents per pound, making the bit cost around eleven cents per bit. I have been talking with O'Brien on this subject and he thinks the same as I do—that the Red Star steel will be all right for bits and give just as good results.

You will find a price copy enclosed from T&F for Bowman. He wants to have one machine of each made up and tried out before we order the lot of ten. It will cost more than $300 to do this. I think myself it is a waste of money for these fixtures are so simple and the operation is so plain. Any mechanic can see what it can do. We will be making these fixtures later on. There is no better method for regrinding. I still learn something every day. Hope to get back soon. ALH

It was a productive two weeks but Con Kelley still wanted his research department to come up with a bit grinding machine and a detachable bit of their own design. In the meantime more delays were planned to deter Arthur. The ACM research team was gasping their last breathe of air. American Brass would attempt some delay tactics.

To Roy Alley April 14:

Glad to hear that the lead tempering bits I sent are standing up. I never doubted but that they would, but in grinding them the man will have to be careful not to grind the temper out. This is such an easy matter to do. No one would know except the one who did the grinding. If he grinds them so hot that they turn blue, they will be soft. He could grind off the blue in the next couple of seconds. They will appear like they had never been hot but with a file test would show soft. You would not know if they had a deep hardening or not. These lead heated bits show a much deeper hardening than the ones hardened in Anaconda. Another thing in our favor is they come out alike, no soft ones. Now to the grind of the bits. I have kept that in mind all the time that they must not be ground soft and if an operator grinds them by hand or by a lever, he is bound to grind some soft. That is why the T & F grinding machines can't be beat. You get just the proper pressure on the bit against the wheel that is required to grind and maintain your hardness.

J. R. Coe promised to call me and let me know if they could make the dies for us at the American Brass. He told Bowman and me that he would have to take it up with their president and then let me know. A week has passed and no word, so I called Coe this morning to know what they were going to do about it and that we were anxious to get started. He said he had not seen the president,

Mr. Coe his brother, yet but expected to get in touch with him Friday or Saturday. Then would let me know. You can't hurry these fellows up down here. They all take their time.

I had Mr. McDonald and Mr. Brembick come from Boston to see me on the steel question. Had them in my room for three hours. Then we all went to dinner. Will have their bids and proposal in a few days regarding the use of the Swedish Steel for bits that I wrote to you about. I am going to Billings & Spence, large forging plants here in the morning. I want to see if the cut of the flash is cold or hot and a lot of other things pertaining to annealing and heating.

Pratt & Whitney are going right ahead with all our work. I want to get the dies made so as to have bits for them when they are ready to try out the cutters and holders.

If American Brass does not have the time to make our dies, I have got to look up some other place to get it done. I am on the lookout right now. I know of a couple of places that I will see here in Hartford if it comes to that.

T & F are getting along fine on the grinders. I was there today. I am watching the slug matter closely and everything seems to be shaping all right with but one exception, that is the cutting off. If we don't get the Ajax forging machine, we will have to find something to cut off the slugs from the bar. J.R.Coe says cut them off with a saw. Well, that is a joke. I have seen every style of saw known in operation here and they are all too slow. You could cut them off by hand quicker. I will find something that will do, and do it fast before many days. I hope to get through here before long. Will be glad when I can get home. ALH

Chapter Eleven

Potpourri

Old friends, new information, a lonesome family, Butte elections and ACM shenanigans instilled in Arthur a deep longing to be home but he trudged forward as seen in his correspondence.

To Mr. Tom. M. Hamilton in Los Angeles April 19.(A mining engineer who had worked in South America with Eugene Braden for a long time.)

Just received your letter and was glad to hear from you after so many years. Have sent it to our office at Butte. Mr. Roy S. Alley, our president, will inform you of all the particulars and data pertaining to the drills which I have not with me. I can say, however, that ACM has used the bits for the past two years in the hardest ground that could be found, and also under the severest conditions known. They have pronounced them O.K. The results were wonderful and surprising. They will drill faster and last longer than the old steel, besides other advantages too numerous to mention.

I have been here for several months getting machinery and equipment to manufacture them on a large scale. Of course, this is an entirely new thing. One has to go carefully and slowly to avoid mistakes in selecting same.

We expect to be going by September 1 in Butte. Our plan is first to supply the ACM, then the Butte district, followed by a plant in Northern California. Other places including Canada will follow just as soon as possible. Our agencies have not been decided on yet as we will have plenty of time to take that matter up later on. I expect to be home in three or four weeks. ALH.

Highway Routes

Roads were precarious in 1924 especially the East-West routes. Connecticut was one of the first states to color code routes using the telegraph poles. Red colored bands on the poles indicated E-W routes while blue designated N-S directions. Diagonal and secondary roads exhibited yellow bands. Arthur became very familiar with these markings in his travels. The present US highway marking system was two years into the future.[1]

Fixtures Started!

To Roy April 19,the day before Easter.

We were going some last Tuesday. I left Bowman in New Haven about nine p.m. We covered a lot of ground. First we went to P & W and got them started on the fixtures. Then we went on to T and F and got them started on the grinding machines. Ted, his boy, got a car and we three went to Waterbury.

Coes Delay Again

Saw J. Coe and went over the making of the dies with him. He is going to take this up with the President of the American Brass(his brother) and let me know. Then I am to go down there and see that they get every thing right. We went to Ansonia to see the press at the Farrell Foundry Co. It is some press. I liked the looks of it and I think it will do more bits than I figured on. I have to get a knock-out put on it to knock out bits. I expect to go down there next week and attend to that or sooner if I hear from Coe.

I have been with P & W the past four days going all over the drawings for the cutters and changes in the jigs and fixtures. We completed them yesterday and they have sent you a letter telling just what they want back and the sooner it gets here the better.

The dies are very important and must be made before I can get back home. Next about 1000 bits have to be forged up for P & W to test with the machines and holders. I suggest that we make the bits out of eighty percent straight carbon steel, the same as used in the drills today, with either the Swedish steel or the Red Star made by Colonial. Then try them out while we are waiting for and installing our machinery. This steel will be laid down in Butte for twelve cents to thirteen cents per pound. The Swedish steel can be shipped to Seattle from Sweden and then to Butte. I expect to get in touch with them next week and will know more about it.

Now here is my opinion of straight carbon steel. Saying a bit with flash weighs ten ounces, the steel in the bit would cost seven and one-half cents and about eleven cents will pay for the making and the steel. The Swedish and Norwegian iron has been known for years as the best iron and I don't think they would send to this country anything but their best goods. That is the best iron in their steel which forms the base. They are competing with large manufacturers in the steel game over here which must be very keen. Neither would American steel concerns dare send a poor grade of steel abroad and expect to compete with steel companies in their country. This is worth looking into.

To Maurice from Mother

Day after Easter, April 21.Arthur has been away four and one-half months.

I rec'd your letter, picture and program of the play, *Gogotha*. I was glad you were in the choir. Pa is not home yet and Lawrence seems lots better. I hope he keeps so. It's trying to get warm here but having a hard time. I bet you miss the family. Did you get your Easter box O.K.? Mollie sent you the cake. I want you to write and thank her for it.

Maurice, I would rather you didn't play football. I worry so that you might get hurt, but as long as you are playing you may as well have the shoes. You can put them on the bill.

I have a terrible cold and sore throat today. We were up to Duggans for supper Saturday night. I had Houlihans and Ed McGovern to dinner Easter. Then we played cards and had a really nice eve.

When will your school be out? It will be out here in six weeks. I guess Dad will be home in about 10 days. My, I surely hope so. This has been a terrible lonely winter for me and besides that I have all the chores to do as Lawrence cannot do a thing. I let him out to play Sunday with a kite and he took a terrible nose bleed—poor kid. Aunt May gave him a lovely mouth organ that will hold him for a while.

Well, dear boy, I want to give this to the mailman. Good by with love from Mother. P.S. Did I tell you Aunt Sarah died? I got a new grey coat.

A card arrived from Gonzaga. Mamie was notified that the cast had received a special invite to dinner in the Marie Antoinette Room of the Davenport Hotel and that Maurice attended.

Canals

Delays, Arthur realized were beyond his control. Now that spring emerged, he would explore some sites instead of worrying about the dies for a day. Twelve miles north of Hartford the last canal erected on the Connecticut River years ago, the Enfield, was prominently situated. It connected with Springfield, Massachusetts, only thirty miles away, as well as other main business centers. A jaunt to tour the four locks was arranged. The curious machinist studied the mechanisms which controlled the six-mile long enterprise. Boats up to seventy tons could be handled. A team of horses previously pulled up to a 1200 pound wagon while now a team of mules could manage a fifty-ton canal barge.[2] "In the Butte mines all mules with two exceptions had been replaced last year by 200 four-ton locomotives," he remarked to his companion.

During a previous jaunt he had toured the five and one-half mile Windsor Lock Canal. Both of these canals were as essential to the river valley commerce as were Britain's canals in the days of his ancestor, Josiah Wedgwood.

Arthur shared this of his heritage. Back in Burslem, England in 1767, Josiah was an influential proponent of creating a Canal System. Pottery breakage diminished greatly when the canal opened and transportation by mules or by wagon over muddy, rutted dirty roads was eliminated. One of the principal factors hampering the expansion of industry in Staffordshire 150 years ago was the state of communications with London. Josiah became prominently involved in a scheme for the construction of the Trent and Mersey Canal. This ninety-four-mile passageway had cost 300,000 pounds.[3]

Arthur mused on his return to the hotel, "If only there had been an inland passageway across America for Lewis and Clark to discover, I might not have had to experience these interminable rail delays and transfers."

Seeds of discontent will take root on any soil.

Waiting to be a somebody will make you a nobody. ALH.

An ACM Proposition

Three weeks later, May 13, a handwritten letter to "My dear Hawk" arrives from Gallwey.

Enjoyed your song and poetry very much. We went after the Emma report in good shape about ten days ago up in Mr. Hobbin's office. Roy just got fairly started criticizing it, when Billy Daly said he didn't expect anything like that at this meeting and said he was not prepared with his figures to take up the matter at that time and suggested that Roy write him a letter embodying all our objections which Roy did.

I saw Chauncey (Berrian) Saturday night and he told me he had been working hard all day Saturday checking up the report and that a meeting will be held this week. He said he was making some adjustments in their report. I told him before we could do any business with the Company we must have their exact costs. He understands that. Mr. Marc Thayer is in town and we are anxious to settle it while he is here.

As I understand the proposition, (from the ACM) the Hawkesworth Drill Co. is to install a unit in Butte and we are to have the privilege of using any of the ACM machinery and any of their buildings which may be suitable for us. We are to manufacture bits for ACM; they are to pay us a reasonable profit. We can sell any surplus drills to other companies, here or elsewhere.

We must have accurate costs from ACM in order for us to make them a price. This cost must be low enough to enable the ACM to operate as cheaply as they are now doing. We have always claimed we could do this. I feel we will be given a chance to prove it. Our meetings have all been very friendly and we are anxious to get going, which I think we will now be able to do.

You have had quite a visit in the effete East, 'spose you are tired of it and anxious to get home. We will be glad when you do. Kindest regards and best wishes, Harry.

A letter goes to Alley the same day from Arthur.

The bits you sent me tested out and I find them to be good and hard. Gave them the oscilloscope test which showed 85 average. We hammered on it and couldn't break it. In fact it left large groove marks in the face of two hammers. Then we took a round punch, drove it in the well until it broke. It showed a tough hardness on the face that goes next to the shank.

T & F are about ready to grind the bits. They are waiting for the emery wheels to come from Norton Emery Wheel Company. Expect them this week. The only thing that seems to be held up is the work at P & W. They are waiting for the chuck and the parts to be shipped from Butte. I expect you can't send them until you get your understanding with the ACM.

I have not heard from Coe again but expect to most any day.

I went over to Billings & Spence Drop Forge Co. and saw them dropping all kinds of forgings and dies. It was very interesting but all I saw were mild steel like wrenches. They case carbonize them for mild steel but this method wouldn't do for high carbon steel like we use for our bits unless it was subsequently annealed. Going to call on Firth Sterling Steel and get bids from them. They sell lots of steel around here.

I wish things were going faster. I can hardly wait until we get started. Mrs. Hawkesworth is feeling a little uneasy because I have been away so long and I feel the same. I would like to get home but feel that it is my duty to do anything you fellows think best to get this thing going. I realize how hard you are working on it and feel confident everything will come out all right, so here's hoping to hear good news soon. ALH.

Feelings Shared With Maurice

One day while in New Haven Arthur explored Yale, the third oldest university in America founded in 1701. Noah Webster and Eli Whitney were graduates and the engineering school was well developed.[4] He wrote to his son at Gonzaga May 14.

Well, I am here in Hartford yet. Things have taken so long to shape up that it has and will take lots longer than I anticipated. I wanted to be home long before this. It looks like you will be home before I am.

I am sick of staying away so long and will be glad when I get back. I went over to the Hawkesworth's (an uncle) last night and Harry just received your letter. He was tickled to death to get it. I read it over and it was a nice letter describing the mines and the ranches. They all got quite a kick out of it. I noticed where you were playing third base on the ball team. Glad to hear it and hope you make good for that is the game I like and hope I have a Son who will be a star at it some day.

I got a letter from Mother and she sent me a couple of your letters with it where you say you are getting tired of school and want to get home. Well, I expect it does get tiresome and it won't be long before you get the vacation, but never give up getting your education. I hope to put you through a college like Yale some day but it takes pluck and staying qualities to do it. You may not see it now but when you grow older you will feel so much better and be so glad that you stuck to it.

No one likes a quitter, now look at the drills. Who would have thought that it would take me five years to get only this far? Well, it has and I have been getting them better right along. It is conceded by all as an absolute success. While a year or so ago most of them doubted it, but all are for them now. Before long we will be going in good shape. There were times I felt like throwing up the sponge but wouldn't dare do it, for I hate a quitter. Well, Maurice, answer this letter at Hartford in care of Pratt & Whitney Co., as I get my mail there. Am writing to Mother today. With lots of love from Dad. P.S. Sending a pamphlet showing the Heublein Hotel where I have stopped for three months. My room is where you see the X marked. The air line pamphlet shows the Elton Hotel where I stopped when in Waterbury.

Promises to Mamie

The separation continued taking its toil on Mamie. Arthur made her a promise. "The oldest carpet weaving Company in America, the Bigelow, is here where the first power loom revolutionized weaving. I will order an elegant carpet for you once our business is on its way."

Mamie produced delicate crochet work. She would appreciate the knotted counterpane designs and the elegant wool. Production at America's first woolen mill had started here in 1788. "There is nothing manufactured like this in Montana," he continued. "Since 1884 our U.S. Presidents have worn suits made from cloths woven here."[5]

ACM Antics

To Roy Alley May 16:
Received your very welcome letter and was glad to learn you had a meeting with Daly and Hobbins. I know you have them up against a hard proposition. If this Emma report of theirs was on the square, they would have no trouble in upholding it and could argue it right there and then. But they have got to do some

hard figuring and make false statements to substantiate their claim. That will take more time than they have now without continuing to alter reports.

No doubt Borcherdt and Sultzer are working night and day with Daly and Berrien's help to juggle the figures. It will be hard for Daly and Barrien to give in that they are wrong for that will show the higher officials that they don't know their business or that they are a pair of crooks. That is unless the officials over them are standing in on it too.

If they aren't, I expect to see them censured for it. No doubt, if it comes to a show down like that, the buck will be passed on to Borcherdt and Sultzer who are about as dirty and crooked as they make them. The report was changed so much before it got down to the New York office that I bet Berrien didn't recognize it when he showed it to Con Kelley. I only hope the higher officials are not in on it.

I just came from T & F. They made two of the holders wrong and are going to remake them the way I want. The emery wheels are expected today and by the middle of next week, we expect to be grinding bits.

You say the town is improving—that helps some. I am anxious to learn how the election came out. I know all my friends like Larry Duggan and Bill Horigan must have been deeply interested in it. I would have voted against the Klans and that Maple Tree Bunch if I had been home.

I went to see two different picture shows. One was *Thief of Bagdad* with Douglas Fairbanks and Rachel Walsh. Each time President Coolidge's picture was shown at the newsreel there was not a single applause from the audience. I see no one around here who is enthusiastic about him.

I haven't heard from Coe yet and don't like to volunteer going down there until I get word from you. But if he calls me to come, I will go right away and hurry things up.

Well, I hope by the time this letter gets to you, things will be ironed out but it is going to be hard for those fellows to give in. ALH.

National Political Convention

Dinner conversations at the Heublein Hotel became lively with the approach of the Democratic National Convention which was to be held at Madison Square Garden. John William Davis(1873-1953) was nominated for President with Charles W. Bryan from Nebraska as Vice President. (On November 4 Calvin Coolidge, Republican, was elected much to Arthur's chagrin.)

Grinding Away

The letter to Roy May 28 indicated that Arthur had been grinding bits.

The grinding machines are doing better than we had figured. They work fine, can grind one bit per minute using six machines with one operator. Ted and I have two machines set up in the shop at T & F, one for grinding the groove and one to grind the side. We grind a bit complete in two and one-half minutes and have enough time to spare to handle four more machines. I have been making slight changes in the fixtures and holders. Today everything is working fine. It is an absolute success. This is the very best job and cheap.

Now we can do one bit per minute with six machines at a cost in Butte of one and one-half cents per bit and no doubt will get it down to one cent later on.

Haven't met with ACM yet? Been looking for a telegram telling me about it, and word to hurry up at this end. It has been raining nearly every day this month. Have had a bad cold for a week. ALH.

Late May Arthur procured a rare copy of *First Impressions*, a crossword puzzle book. This latest craze he found out about one day as he read *The New York World*. This fifty full-page book was the first of its kind. What a fun indulgence for a man cooped up in what was becoming a stifling environment.

Hope never wavered in Arthur. But Kelley appeared to be setting the hardworking inventor up letting him do all the creative and grueling work, while he schemed to pounce at an opportune time when the machines were finished.

Hawkesworth Drill Shop- View of Grinding Machines

Layout of Hawkesworth Drill Shop.

Maurice Readies Shanks for Distribution

Chapter Twelve

A Plant

Energizing news arrived for Arthur suddenly June 2. He rejoiced because his company finally acquired its own location, three buildings at the Anaconda Company's West Grey Rock mine yard. This site included 9300 square feet of floor space. Despite some building irregularities, his company was ready to install their newly invented machinery and equipment to the best advantage. By the time Arthur's custom designed machines would arrive, the "Bunch" could proceed to manufacture bits and shanks on a scale larger than had ever before been attempted. Demand promised to be greater than even they could supply.

Arthur responded jubilantly to Roy by return mail.

The West Grey Rock is about as good a place as I know. I have been there several times. Will be glad when we get all the fixtures in place and start work in earnest.

I am well pleased with the way the grinding machines perform. You can't beat them. I hope satisfactory arrangements will be finished soon, so we can fly at it. I am raring to go.

Political Connections

Senator B. K. Wheeler, in Washington, D.C., was the next to receive a letter from Arthur written June 4. He knew the Senator and Roy Alley didn't like each other when they served together in the Montana Legislature but he also realized that it was important to stay in contact with politicians.

My dear Senator:

Just a few words and a few clippings. Glad to know you are doing so well in Washington. I take great interest in what you and Senator Walsh accomplish. I have been in Hartford, Connecticut nearly five months getting machinery made here to manufacture the drills. Of course, being from Montana, I am asked nearly every day about you and Senator Walsh. Everyone around here that I meet thinks well of you both. I was hoping to get down to see you before Congress adjourned but couldn't make it—too busy here.

Expect to be back in Butte about the last of July. Enclosing a couple of poems on the political situation.

Give my kindest regards to Senator Walsh and with best wishes and success to you both.

Arthur confided in his last letter to his son the next day.

Glad to hear from you and to know that you're running along smoothly. The drills and grinding machines are coming along all right but slow. You can't seem to rush people. Have been delayed considerably by getting down to some agreement with the Anaconda Company. That is about all straightened out and I hope to go along much faster from now on. We expect to start in Butte first. Would surely like to get home soon.

I'm glad you take an interest in baseball and are holding down third base. I expect to see some of the big leagues play before I get back. It has been cold here and raining for a month. I am quite proud of your writing. I think you do well. You will come out fine if you just stick with it. This takes will power. I wrote a poem on this subject which I am sending, also a song on Montana. When I get home, I am going to have you compose the music for it. I hope this letter gets to you before you leave for Butte. I figure it will just about make it. Mother and Larry will be glad to see you. I hope you get something to do after you get through visiting. It is awful the way Arkie lays around and doesn't do more for himself. I have been hoping and expecting to see him change for the better. I expect he will wake up some day and see what a rut he is in for it is never too late to mend. Well, I will have to close, so write soon. With lots of love, Dad.

Informs Alley of Address Change

I have moved to 99 Elm Street which is about two blocks from the Hotel. Have a nice large front room facing Bushnell Park. Couldn't stand the Hotel life, especially the food, any longer. It got on my nerves. I am feeling in good shape and hope to see you all soon.

No man is as perfect as he would have his neighbors be. ALH.

Connecticut

Connecticut was associated with many nicknames over the years. *The Land of Steady Habits, The Nutmeg State, The Arsenal of Democracy* were invoked before it officially became *The Constitution State* thirty-five years after Arthur's sojourn in its heart. This state was the first in many instances for ideas, inventions and literary greatness even though it was the third smallest in geographical area.

One first was Hartford's Bushnell Park where Arthur enjoyed part of each of his last days away from home. This was America's first public park whose heritage could boast it was conceived, voted, built and paid for by the people. Reverend Horace Bushnell spearheaded the movement and saw it to fruition.

Frederick Olmstead, a local resident, had designed the grounds for Central Park in New York. He recommended Jacob Weidenmann be commissioned to oversee Hartford's park as Olmstead himself was too preoccupied in New York at the time to take on an additional project.

Weidenmann's site selection was controversial. But forty-one acres consisting of two leather tanneries, ugly pigsties, a foul-smelling garbage dump, crowded tenements with their outhouses disappeared once the area was approved for the project.

More than 157 variety of trees shimmered in the defused light along the route leading to the stately Civil War Memorial Arch when the park reached its completion. Park River ran through the complex but was subsequently covered. A carousel was added in later years by Olmstead's son.[1]

Arthur relished a walk through its peaceful grounds. Gardening had been an advocation since his youth. Someday when his business boomed he would build a park in his neighborhood to emulate this one. Butte had only Columbia Gardens and to enjoy it required a streetcar trip out of town. There was nothing for the people in any residential area. Butte could learn from Hartford's choice of land and clean up some of its mine debris substituting parks.

At his new brick residence he savored the excellent kielbasa and the local robust cheddar. Meals were indeed better than the hotel menu but not as good as he experienced in Butte. Mamie told him of a new eating place that served "John's Original Pork Chop Sandwiches." Arthur could hardly wait for a change in diet. His thoughts meandered homeward more frequently these last busy days.

Grinding Machines Finally Finished

Arthur firmly believed everyone should be kept informed about his progress, laborious as it sometimes seemed to him. He wrote to Bowman on June 12. "Ted and I took a ride in his car last Thursday evening. The mechanic did a good job on it at Buffalo. He has started home."

Then diplomatically let it be known that he wished Bowman would hurry up with the things from his end including the payments! He continued saying, "The grinding machines work fine. Had Ted over grinding. I am having T & F figure on making the indexing fixtures automatic which can be done for a very little additional cost. I found out by grinding a couple of days that an operator would have to go some to keep six machines going. He couldn't keep it up for you see, he would have to be at each machine four times in three minutes. That would make it twenty-four times on six machines changing the bit around four times to grind out each groove and wing or gauge. Besides putting the bit on and off the holder and grinding at the rate of one bit per minute with six machines.

Now by having the fixtures index automatically, an operator has to be at each machine once in three minutes putting in and taking out bits. That would make it only six times instead of 24 times on 6 machines. In 3 minutes the operator could tend to 8 or 12 machines.

I am having the holders made interchangeable. That is you can grind both ways without taking the bit off the holder. Just slip the holder with the bit on, out of one fixture into the other.

American Brass

I went over to American Brass and saw what they were using on their press. Didn't see any of the Coes as they were at Waterbury. Expect to go down there next week about the dies.

I have been expecting blue prints and specifications every day from Butte. Until I get them, I can't start on the dies. I hope things will speed up. Would like to get home.

The next day he responds to Roy:

Received your telegram. I went over to the American Brass with Mr. Osborn, sales manager of Farrell Foundry, to see how they had the knock off devises on their presses and to look up the die proposition. The press has not been shipped to Butte nor have they had any orders to do so. I don't know who is taking care of that. I suppose Dan Welch at the New York Office?

Broken Piece, Other Delays

While I was at American Brass, I got a look at the one die—the one made over. They had broken a piece out of the top die and had to make a new one in its place. Was just hardening it when I arrived. I couldn't do anything about the rest of the dies until I see what is on the ACM blue prints which haven't come yet. In talking to their boss tool maker, Mr. Pollard, he said that George Coe first told him that they were going to make about 12 sets. Then the other day Coe came around and said he didn't think they would make 12 sets; just finish up the one they were working on. I asked Wilkinson if they had time to make our dies and he said they had all kinds of time as they were short of work. So we will see what the Coe's say when the order is placed.

I went to lunch at the Ansonia Manufacturer's Club with Mr. Osborn and while there met C.E. Nighman, superintendent of the Phosphate Mines, Berrien's friend.

About cutting off slugs. We can cut them off with our screw press about 20 per minute hot. Just remove the bit dies and put cutting off dies on the press and cut up enough to last a week for one man. Later on we can get a press for that purpose. Not a screw press but an eccentric press like the one at Anaconda for trimming bits, only a little larger. Any second hand one will do for that work. I looked the second-hand warehouses over around here but they had none. I am sure I can pick one up in Buffalo, Cleveland or Chicago on my way back. That is what the American Brass uses for cutting off their round and bronze rods up to 1 ½.

Notes Due At Home

To E. S. Shields in Butte June 16:
Received your most welcome letter on my return from Ansonia and Waterbury this last week. I was looking after machinery that we are getting made.

Time has slipped by so fast I had forgotten about the notes due. I will take care of it just as soon as I can get back which will be about the latter part of next month. You see I installed a furnace in the house last year which cost me around $400 and my expenses have been considerably higher of late on account of having been away from home so much. But everything is coming along fine and I will be able to take care of things as soon as I get back.

I am bringing into Butte about $50,000 worth of machinery. We will make the drills for the ACM and other companies right in Butte.

The ACM has turned over machinery that we can use. We expect to get started just as soon as we can get all the machinery, which has been ordered, finished here and shipped.

Copper Demand High

Butte is bound to get better. I expect to see a boom in copper industry in the next year. The industry today eats up copper at a rate of more than 100% over two years ago. This consumption is growing in volume rather than falling off as indicated by the figures recently made public. In March deliveries of copper totaled 271,000,000 pounds, necessitating so substantial a cut into reserves that today stocks represent only about one month supply of the metal.

Butte may be dull and slack right now, but I fail to see it any different from wherever I have been in the last five months. The factories here are complaining of no business and I know it is so, as I go into them nearly every day and see it. ALH

A Respite

Arthur wasn't enthused when a friend loaned him a mystery book one evening. Learning that this first time author, Agatha Christie, was of British birth, he decided to give *The Mysterious Affair at Stiles* a glance. When he became engrossed in the plot, his need of just a few hours sleep per night proved an asset. He returned the book with warm thanks at their next meeting and further encouraged Mamie to read the same.

A Letter from Arthur's Mother

Julia encouraged her son, "Enduring contributions in history take tenacity, hard work and dedication. Your great uncle Egerton Ryerson spent eighteen months in Europe working to get a charter of incorporation and a government grant to start what became Victoria College in Ontario. Subsequently, he became Chief Superintendent of Education and founder of the public school system of Education in Ontario, Canada. He remained at this post for thirty years. Your future lays before you and you will succeed."

To Roy after the reception of a letter on July 9.

I am sorry you have so much trouble getting contracts settled up with the Company. I know it must get on your nerves, but worrying never helps any and when we get going, we won't have time to worry. That's when I'll feel good. I also feel that it won't be long before we will be getting down to business.

The jigs and fixtures arrived at P & W on the first. I saw Hurlbert and they won't touch them until they get an order from Bowman. I told him he would be here soon and take care of it.

I noticed where you say that the bits fit altogether too tight at the Pittsmont. They must be using heavy hitting machines in hard ground. If they were using jack hammers in medium ground, I don't think they would be any too tight. Anyway, I would rather hear of them tight than loose. It is a whole lot in our favor and will give more life to the shanks and they can easily be adjusted to fit correctly.

Everything is about the same here. We must get our orders placed before we can do more. P & W put half their works on a four-day week. Things are awful dull in manufacturing. Hope Bowman gets here soon. I am feeling good but it is so hot. I hope Harry is improving. ALH.

To J.D. Murphy July 18.

Received your most welcome letter and it did me lots of good. I like to hear from any of the bunch. I have had a long session of it here. Never dreamed I would be away from home so long and will be glad to get back. There is very little I can do now until we get the various orders placed. I expected Bowman by now but as yet have had no word of his coming.

It is very gratifying to hear how the drills are doing in the East Butte Mine. It is too bad we are not in shape to supply bits right along. It has taken time to get where we are now. Lots of patience on the part of all of us but we can't lose. It looks better every day. When we get to make bits with the new method of hardening, we will still do better. I am very confident, since I came East that we can manufacture them cheaper and use a cheaper steel and get greater results than ever before.

Primary Elections in Butte

I hope I'll get back in time for the Primary Election. If I don't, send me about 20 absentee vote ballots. Have Fair Trile mark them but don't let him hypothecate them. I want to vote twenty times or more for Wally and some more of my friends. I see where Wheeler has bolted to the head of the ticket. Well, he is as high as he will ever get and too high to suit me. I am off him forever, for I think we have a good ticket and will win.

Baseball

Glad to hear that the baseball is good this year and sorry I couldn't have seen a game. May get in on the last of it. If I ever get in a city where the big games are played, I will go and see one or more as I really like this sport.

Enclosed is a poem for the inner circle. Give one to Roy and keep the others.

OUTLAWS

Say! What's all that scandal I hear
There's something gone wrong I confess,
I haven't paid much attention
Since I went away out West.
Thirty-five years ago
Things were working fine;
When I left for Butte, Montana
To work down in the mine.

I saw many bad men in the West,
Who held up railroads and banks
But you couldn't compare those fellows
With some of these Washington pranks.
We had bad men on the ranges,
Who stole cattle and horses too,
But never so slick and cunning
As these political grafters do.ALH.

To Roy Alley on July 23:

Went to Boston with the Elks. Came right back thinking Bowman might arrive while I was away. Now I wonder what has caused his delay. I know so many different things can happen. Hope our troubles will soon be over.

I have been talking with G. Coe over the phone. They are ready to go ahead with our dies and want me to come down and let them know what to do. I told him that I expected Bowman every day and couldn't go ahead with the dies until I get the blue prints on them from Butte. He wants me to call him up in a day or so.

I think I got the steel treating man and metallurgist about worn out answering my questions during the trip. Met a couple of the Elks who were very interesting. They all agreed that the bits should be heated in lead and that the electric furnace is still in the experimental stage. I learned that the term "hardness" is ambiguous and is rather indefinite in its meaning. Certain hardness tests show some materials to be hard, yet they can be filed or machined. High speed steel, for instance, by testing is found to be hard and yet soft to the file. Manganese steel can be sheared but cannot be machined.

Work around here is awful dull. Most of the factories work four days a week and are going to shut down for two weeks in the near future including P & W commencing the first of August. I hope we get our orders placed before that.

How is Pipestone Springs (located between Butte and Whitehall) and the ranch this year? I expect you are enjoying yourself out there by this time. I would like to be there myself. It has been so hot here. ALH.

Maurice and Lawrence

Thinking about his boys, he told Mamie about Erector Sets which had been invented in this area a dozen of years ago by a man named Gilbert. He decided to procure one for his lads. Some day he would also purchase a Seth Thomas Clock for the family as he had stopped by their factory in Ansonia. Delayed gratification was a necessity at this time but his financial future appeared to be bright.

Received your letter, Roy, on the 29th. Bowman has not arrived but expect him some time today. Will then get busy immediately.

Glad to hear the good news from Myhre how well the drills did at the Pittsmont but sorry to learn of their closing down. He said they intend to do some development work.

Confidential Mysterious Information

No new arrangements on stock or new deal of any kind to be tolerated. You can rely on my standing pat. Your letter will be kept strictly confidential.

I will be glad to get started and realize the sooner the better as the 22 months will slip by before we know it. We will have to do everything in our power to speed up the orders here and get them to Butte. (What are the 22 months he mentions, which would be to May 1926 and what was the confidential information? No answers are available for these two items.)

Will keep you fully informed as we close up matters. I have picked up lots of good information in manufacturing and handling steel. This will save us lots of money and time.

With best wishes to the bunch and hope to be back with you soon. ALH.

Homeward Bound

A week later the machine orders were placed. He wrote a last time to Roy Aug. 18.

Everything has been taken care of. There was a lot to do after the orders were placed just as I had expected. I have been jumping some since I left Cleveland, between Taylor & Fenn, Pratt & Whitney, Waterbury and Ansonia and the steel order.

Went over the forming cutters at P & W which we checked up carefully with the drawings and sample bits. This was a very particular piece of business as some of the drawings that Bowman brought with him showed up several mistakes. One example: a special arbor had to be made to grind the bits in gangs on the curvex grinder instead of grinding them single. The cutters were started Wednesday and the jigs and fixtures today.

Saw the two Coes at Waterbury. Went over the making of dies with them. They sent me to Ansonia to get what I wanted and to order the dies. I had to get holders to hold them in the screw press. Gave them an order, a copy of which I am enclosing to you. I tried to get die stock from them but they would not let us have any. Will get it from some of the other steel concerns, probably in Chicago.

Will take up the cutting off of slugs at Beloit, Wisconsin. I expect to leave today if the draft comes.

Car Accident

I had a first class toolmaker, Mr. Fred Larson, from P & W who was not working, drive me in his car to Waterbury and Ansonia. We got along fine. Left Ansonia at 6:30 p.m. and were on our way home between New Haven and Meriden when we were struck head on by another car which was going at full speed. We were badly shaken up. I got cut on the forehead and nose by the flying glass from the windshield. Got my pants torn and hip cut. Lost my glasses and a book that had data in it. Am stiff and sore but nothing too seriously. Larson was badly shaken up—just the two of us in the car. I thought the car was going to turn over. It turned half way, then settled down on the wheels. We were both very lucky. It could have been worse. I barely could move the next day.

Needs Money Once Again

Enclosed find expense account from July 14 to Aug. 15 for $272.42.

I am through here and want to get back but haven't enough money. I telegraphed to Bowman on the 12th but haven't got any reply or money. He told me to let him know by Wednesday which I did. If it doesn't come today, I will send a night letter to you tonight.

Everybody is doing their best to get things shipped with all possible speed. I am more then anxious to get back and every little delay gets on my nerves. ALH

Trip Ends, Questions Flourish

So ends seven months of incessant delays and intense labor away from his family, friends and factory. What was ACM's plan to get hold of this equipment? How intricate was the plot? Did ACM delay Bowman in Anaconda at their bank? Did they instruct the Coe Brothers to use all sorts of tactics? Did they delay and manipulate the Emma Test? Now that they knew the machines were perfected did they arrange for the car accident?

All these methods were indicative of ACM when they wanted something. No written records to answer these specific issues definitively have been discovered. For certain, one of the purposes of the delays was to give their research department time to come up with their own invention. That didn't work.

Arthur started back to Butte his feat accomplished. He meticulously had supervised and brought to fruition the best machinery possible and had selected the best quality of steel for use in his future factories throughout the world. His perseverance was amazing. His machines endured and during the life of the bit were never excelled.

Arthur and Mamie on the side of their Argyle home, May 1925.

Chapter Thirteen

Butte, A Welcomed Sight

Arthur jerked awake. His heart leaped. He recognized the rugged but beautiful terrain. The abundant Ponderosa Pine trees, a few bright yellow chested and throat Meadowlark birds flew into view. After the porter adroitly applied his whiskbroom to his pressed suit, Arthur opened the window for a breath of mountain air. The train's barber had previously groomed him and the porter had given an extra polish to his shoes the previous night.

In a few moments he would discern the dozens of Gallows Frames outlining the Butte Hill. The train slowed near Pipestone Springs where Alley had a home and started to descend the steep Woodville Hill. He ached to see his family, his friends, his home and the garden which Mamie had planted. How he wanted to have been home in time to plant. He remembered the year he won a prize for his potatoes at the State Fair in Helena. Last year he had used carbide from the mines for fertilizer. So much catching up to accomplish. What would we have for dinner even entered his thoughts after months of restaurant and hotel meals.

Great joy! Mamie, Maurice, Lawrence and many friends greeted his triumphant return. All was in place for a glorious future. He knew that he had accomplished his very best, a maxim that directed his life. "When you do your very best he told his children happiness will follow."

A pleasant aroma greeted him at home, "Ah, a pastie". Mamie received yet another embrace. His bed would be warm tonight.

Arthur's vision was worldwide and he felt even though the detachable drill bit had its origin in a mining city that its future use would be more in construction work. Mining was a cyclical business, good when metals were needed and found, poor when the demand was low. As Felix Wormser stated in the *Engineering and Mining Journal*:

"Building construction, railroad work, highways and the thousand and one operations that require the drilling of rock for their accomplishment are a fertile field for the use of the Hawkesworth Drill . . . a field much larger than mining."[1]

By November 1924 the new machinery had arrived and was in full operation. The Bunch produced 1200 new bits, 60 shanks, 2500 reground bits, 120 repaired shanks per eight hour shift. ACM and many worldwide orders kept the machinists working around the clock six days a week. Arthur began to plan for a Detroit and a San Francisco factory in earnest. Expansion was desperately needed.

Gradually, his health began to fail. He attributed it to hard work and stress but gall bladder was the diagnosis. Diet didn't help. Doctors and friends convinced him to take a respite and to undergo surgery. Work was on an even keel, relationships with the ACM seem to be working satisfactorily. Arthur entered St. James Hospital and Dr. Shields, a well-respected surgeon, performed the surgery.

Tragedy

Unexpected tragedy struck just as he was at his greatest triumph. Arthur's life flickered out. The man, whose hopes had never wavered, was suddenly gone. His picture and work accomplishments were on the front pages of all the local papers.

The *Butte Daily Post* reported on June 14, 1925:

"It's 8 o'clock, Roy, and I have never been late for work. The dies are all set." With these words and with a smile upon his lips, the spirit of "Al" Hawkesworth, the Butte inventor, passed out into the beyond at 8:00 yesterday morning while the mine whistles were calling the men to work.

His mind was on his work at the foundry while the death angel beckoned yesterday, and he went out of life with his waning thoughts fixed on his factory at the Grey Rock, where his dream of years is being realized.

All his life Arthur had been an inventor. Standing in the front ranks as a machinist, his active mind was constantly engaged with plans to improve the mechanisms upon which he was employed. He invented improvements for oil pumps and numerous other devices which are now freely used in machine shops and factories.

The darling of his dreams was the detachable drill point. Night and day he labored on his plans, made models, scrapped them, made others, tested them, found defects and tried again.

One by one the difficulties that had barred success to others gave way before, the keen mind and unflagging application of this Butte machinist until at last he saw the happy day, May *18,1922, when the best minds of the Butte mining world assembled at the St. Lawrence mine to watch the experiment and at its conclusion placed on the Hawkesworth detachable drill bit the seal of their approval.*

A company was organized and a factory established at the Grey Rock mine. A press that turns out 10 bits a minute was installed to supply the demand that began to pour in from Arizona, Utah, Montana, Australia and Africa. The Badger mine had just put in a full equipment of the bits. Other hill mines were doing likewise.

Planned For Ease

"I've worked pretty hard on this thing," Hawkesworth said recently, "and I think I can see my way to take it pretty easy before long." The fates willed otherwise and Hawkesworth died in the harness, loved, respected and admired by those who knew him best and particularly his associates in the enterprise that has given to the world a device that means increased safety to the worker and decreased cost to the operator."

A large picture and headline, "Loved Inventor Called By Death As Fame is Won", preceded the article.

The *Anaconda Standard* on June 17, 1925 disclosed some particulars:

"Mr. Hawkesworth had been suffering from gall trouble for some years. The disease was making progress and he reluctantly consented to give up his work at the factory, which he had founded at the Grey Rock mine, and submit himself to a surgical operation on June 2.

The operation was successful and the patient was in excellent condition for a time, but kidney complications arose and he steadily grew weaker until the end came on June 13."

The smile on his face reflected the glory of the past, the acceptance of the present and the vision of the future. What a special way to die.

Death ultimately occurred from empyema of the gall bladder and gall stones with acute suppression of urine as the secondary cause. A bit of humor emerged from the actual death certificate as it stated in error "emphysema" of the gall bladder.

Two renowned doctors commented eighty years later after examining his death certificate. "He had a severe infection involving his biliary tract. Also the bacteria involved most likely was in the blood stream (septicemia) and led to multiple organ failures and death with the kidneys failing to do their job because of the infection ending with renal failure. He had to be one sick guy."

A wake held at the home was followed by High Mass at 9:30 at his St. Ann's parish. This church would later be the site where his children and grandchildren would worship and celebrate the sacraments on a happier occasion. Interment was in Holy Cross Cemetery in a newly purchased family plot that would have a copper headstone. It was one month shy of the couple's thirtieth wedding anniversary.

Family In Shock

Mamie, his four sons, his mother, aged 81, who resided in San Diego, California, his brother, Frank, founder and present member of one of the states oldest foundries, Caird & Hawkesworth, and his sister Lulu in Michigan were in shock. This man had not mentioned being sick last year except for a cold during his seven months in the East. Two weeks before his death a healthy looking man had a photographer come and take a picture of the couple by their home. It was to be their last. He had not been one to complain of health problems but he had them most certainly because ten months after his return he is dead.

Being perfected in a short time, he fulfilled long years; for his soul was pleasing to the Lord, therefore he took him quickly from the midst of wickedness. Wisdom 4:13-14.

Chapter Fourteen

Pre-Depression Days

It was coincidental that William Clark and Arthur Hawkesworth died two months apart. Clark expired in a fifteen-million-dollar New York mansion on Fifth Avenue with its one hundred and twenty-one rooms and thirty-one baths at age 86. Because of him hundreds had become millionaires, thousands had been employed, thousands had been exploited.

Arthur died at St. James Hospital, revered but just beginning to make his mark at age fifty-five. His legacies to the world would be safer working conditions for thousands of workers and an increase in production for mining and construction companies with the use of his detachable bit along with his effective ventilator and oil pumps.

Both men made a huge contribution to the mining world. One was remembered in the history of the city, the other mostly forgotten.

What conditions existed in Butte and Montana after the death of these two men? For fifty-miles in every direction, this *Richest Hill on Earth* had its ancient evergreen forests logged and stripped for the benefit of the ACM mines which were hot, gaseous and dangerous. Fumes from the smelters ravaged thousands of individuals of all ages. Disease was rampant. Life expectancy was shortened by silicosis, Miner's Con, influenza, or tuberculosis. Hundreds of miners were buried either in the 2,700 miles of tunnels or in the 10,000 miles of underground passages, virtual catacombs, or in one of the cities six cemeteries. The mines' lethal acidic waters flowed abundantly to Silver Bow Creek, an ugly orange color contaminated water, better known as "Shit Creek." to adults. Even the children knew better than to approach the foul looking "Halloween Creek."

In contrast the *Roaring Twenties* sparkled in Butte. Columbia Gardens rocked to the Charleston, Fox Trot and Shimmy. Business was brisk in Pleasure Alley.

Tunnels connected some businesses around the area to a famous brothel. A person of distinction could arrive undetected, climb some musty stairs and be ushered into elaborate above ground accommodations which could be locked from the inside. A revolving tray conveniently provided drinks and other items for the amorous couple. This thoroughfare also led to a network of tiny underground one-room cubicles or "cribs.[1]

The philosophy of the ACM was to encourage recreation and entertainment of all types. This kept the local economy booming and provided outlets for the miners other than union meetings. Restaurants in Meaderville and other ethnic districts thrived and gambling was an acceptable activity in this wide-open town. The infamous Chinese lottery reached as far as San Francisco. America's version of today's popular Keno game originated in Butte's Chinatown where more than 1,250 Chinese lived in a cluster group around six square blocks. Horse racing, dice, roulette, poker and panguingue kept the miner's occupied.[2]

Most livelihoods were dependent on the mines. At this time over two-thirds of the state's population was employed by the ACM. Someone decried this situation and erected a billboard on a twenty by twenty-foot plot of land in the third largest state in the union. It flared out, "This is Montana, not owned by the ACM." At times the city boundary lines ran to the mine fences, swerved around their perimeters and that way ACM avoided city property taxes.

The Company's tentacles reached into everything. This corporation with its all encompassing power provoked fear and submission Their lawyers were brilliant. Unions were fought. Politics were corrupt. Corporate greed was rampant. As passed word of mouth through Butte, "Con Kelley is the man whose skill the murderer will seek before he begins to kill".[3]

The Hawkesworth family went forward without their leader into this milieu. Friends surrounded Mamie, Maurice and Lawrence. Lee at age twenty-seven had a contract to fulfill at the Los Angeles Studios. Arkie's health was unpredictable. Alley, Gallwey, Bowman, Murphy and Riley assured the bereft family all was stable with the company. Contracts, patents, business agreements would continue to be honored in normal fashion.

For the HDC business continued briskly. As more mines inaugurated the detachable drill bits, production expanded. The first year of its use, 1922, ACM's ore traffic reached more than 2,334,000 tons. Each year as more mines transferred to the exclusive use of the drill, BA&P's capacity incrementally increased until one year it hauled 3,310,000 tons of ore to the smelter. Ore production and BA&P tonnage remained at or above these levels through 1929.[4] Gallwey as President of the BA &P had to be pleased with these results.

ACM controlled all aspects of mining up to and including sales. Eliminating competition was the logical outcome of *Gilded Age Capitalism*.

Ore Processing

The process of extracting copper from the ore that arrived at the smelter in Anaconda included four operations.

1. Milling: the ore was pulverized to powder which was mixed with water.
2. Concentrating: light rock was separated from heavy copper.
3. Smelting: the copper was heated to a point where the waste rose to the top and was sent to a slag pile. Now the copper was 98 percent pure.
4. Refining: accomplished by electrolysis.

Bit Distributions and Manufacturing Methods

The distribution system for the Hawkesworth drill bits and shanks took on a routine.

1. New bits and shanks were manufactured at the HDC's central plant.
2. Trucks distributed these items to the mine bit houses. Miners took them to the working faces of the mines.
3. Each miner returned the worn bits and damaged shanks to the mine bit houses. These items were trucked back to the Hawkesworth Drill Company.
4. Next the damaged shanks and dull bits were reground and put through a heat treatment process.
5. These were reissued now a smaller size with each re-grinding. Repaired shanks were returned to the mines.

New bits were manufactured in the following manner using one 1/4" cruciform carbon steel bars.

1. Steel bars heated 1800 to 2000-deg. F.
2. Bits cut, pressed and trimmed to one 7/8" in Ajax forging machine.
3. Bits annealed in lots of 5000 in an electric furnace, taking five hours to reach 1450 deg. F. Held at this temperature for six hours, then cooled in furnace for 24 hours.
4. Bits tumbled to remove scale.
5. Bits slotted and faced ground in special automatic machines.
6. Bits then hardened by:

   A. Preheating in bath of molten lead at 1100 deg. F.
   B. Heating in fused salt bath at 1475 deg. F.

C. Cutting face cooled by water spray.

D. Annealed in boiling water to relieve hardening strains.

The bit faces had a Rockwell hardness of 68 to 70, and the depth of hardening was 1/8 to 1/4".

Shanks were made from hollow octagon carbon steel in five standard lengths, 38,56,74,92,110 inches and some longer for special drilling operations. For each shank the machinists had to saw to correct length, forge ends, cool in air, anneal at 1450 degrees F., cool in quicklime, grind, slot, heat to 1500 deg. F., and finally quench them in oil.

All heat operations were closely controlled by recording pyrometers.

The original 1 7/8" bit was reground four times, producing successively smaller sizes beginning with 1 3/4" to 1 5/8" to 1 ½" to 1 3/8". The last sized bit when it became dulled by use was sent to the scrap bin or to the concentrator ball mill where it was used in place of pebbles or steel balls.

ACM's Profits

During the remainder of 1925 and into 1926 the Badger State Mine was completely equipped with the detachable steel where an average of 1200 tons of ore was mined daily. ACM's net profit for 1925 was $17,540,532 nearly two-thirds greater than in 1924. The company was among the top twenty favorites of Wall Street.

In 1926 the Butte mines reached the 5000' level. At this time Anaconda and its subsidiaries, including the Chile Chuquicumata Mine had an outstanding total bonded debt of $249,000,000.[5]

Family Decisions

New family decisions ensued. Maurice would return to Butte to finish his last two years of high school, 1925-1927. Mamie enrolled him in the Irish Christian Brothers but after only one day Maurice enrolled himself in Butte High. The Brothers were not favorably compared to the Jesuits in his mind. He reflected in his retirement years, "They were unjust to several his first day and he was not about to become a future victim after one beating across the knuckles for something he hadn't done."

The feisty lad showed an inner strength along with wise decision making skills and a sense of justice that followed him from that moment forward. His grief-stricken mother did not learn of this unusual event until the first report card period. She wisely respected his choice and reasons and let him remain.

The school's music department recruited Maurice to be part of their vocal class. With them he represented Butte High School at the "Montana Interscholastic Music Meet" in Livingston, March 23, 1927 soon after he met the love of his life, Tecla Davis, in a law class.

Their long courtship began March 4, a date he never forgot. As seniors they went to a B Sweater Dance at the Wintergarden. Tecla's mother was a chaperone and looked the young man over closely. The rest of the year a group of six shared their delightful days together skating, and attending picnics at the reservoir. Both were thrilled when they came in second at a dance contest at the Odd Fellows Ball.

For a high school graduation gift Maurice and Tecla reveled in their first air flight to Helena. The sixty-five-mile trip took 35 minutes. "We flew on a Falkner six passenger plane which took longer to get up to its flying altitude than it did to reach our destination. Western Airlines was just a year old and formerly was called National Park. We were presented with a box of stationery and Tec left her camera on the plane. It was mailed back to us. Oh, yes, we had to call our mothers to let them know we were safe. We did come back on the train as we could only afford one way," Maurice fondly reflected later in life.

Lindbergh had flown to Butte earlier that year and a desire to fly had been instilled in Maurice. Next year he and Tecla were among those gathered to witness the excitement of the first air mail arrival from Salt Lake City. Strong intuitions guided Maurice all his life. He confided in Tecla that somehow flying would play a major role in his future.

In the fall Maurice enrolled in the Montana School of Mines. Once a degree was earned, he would enter the family business. After a brief period of work with the Butte Credit Union, Tecla was offered two positions. One was in the Bureau of Mines office at the University of Montana in Missoula where her older brother attended. The second was as private secretary to Dr. Thompson, President of the School of Mines. She chose the later to be close to Maurice. Until her father died, she kept her own money and bought her own clothes. As her wages were fifty cents an hour, a lot of money to a young woman who worked four hours a day, she was able to help her widowed mother and younger sister at that time.

Tecla was eligible to enroll in classes and attended for two years. Both young adults enjoyed participating in the annual painting of the big "M" on the hill beside the school. This seventy-foot wide block emblem needed a yearly coat of whitewash. A bucket brigade of students and faculty were dwarfed by its immensity but it gave the city a distinctive landmark when they completed the task.

Annual "Big M" White Washing Day by students of Montana School of Mines.

Davis Family Residence: Tom, Tecla, Tom, Jr.,Tecla D. and Lenor.

Roy Alley continued to assure Mamie all was in order. He promised that she would begin to receive the payments which had been deferred from the sale of the patents to the HDC. In the meantime a contract was drawn up. Alley was to sell her stock at $5.00 a share to cover her immediate expenses. In Mamie's handwriting she recorded in 1925, "Received $500 from Alley for selling 100 shares @ $5.00 each." In 1926 she recorded, "Received $2272.29 from Alley for selling 455 shares @ $5.00 each." No royalties or lump sum payments were received. She meticulously itemized every expenditure.

In 1927 an additional agreement was drawn up with her brother-in-law, John Myhre, who had become a board member. Mamie records in her hand writing: "Received $8454 from John Myhre for selling 2000 shares @ $5.00 each." This was the portion actually received from a $10,000 sale of 2,000 stocks dated April 13, 1927.

Next a contract was drawn up with Roy Alley:

Mary W. Hawkesworth hereby gives and grants unto the said Roy S. Alley, an exclusive option to purchase 8,000 shares of the capital stock of the said Hawkesworth Drill Company of Delaware, or any part of the said 8,000 shares of said stock so owned by said Mary W. Hawkesworth at a price of not less than $5.00 per share; said option to date from the first day of January 1928, and to continue in full force . . . provided Roy S. Alley shall, beginning with January 1, 1928, pay the undersigned each month not less than the sum of $200 per month on the said purchase price of said stock . . . Dated Dec. 19, 1927, i.e., $40,000 total payable over eight years.

Roy signed the contract which was placed in the powder box, the depository for the families' important documents.

It was at this period of history that a crucial error in judgment was made by Dan Ryan, the present Copper King. He sold the Montana Power Company to the American Power and Light for $85 million in stock in 1928.

Chapter Fifteen

A Mysterious Purchase

Chauncey Berrian reported in the local paper that the ACM bought the Butte plant of the Hawkesworth Drill Company June of 1928 and procured the rights to manufacture the drills and shanks for the Butte Hill. The detachable steel would be used immediately beginning in the Mountain Consolidate, Belmont, Otisco, Elm Orlu, Original and Steward mines. As soon as this agreement was concluded, the Hawkesworth Drill would take subscriptions for more stock financing and begin their plants in other sections of the country.

Mamie Hawkesworth and her family received nothing from this transaction. No official mention of this sale was mentioned in any preserved HDC records or mention found in the Butte or State Archives in Helena. How much did the ACM pay and to whom for those rights?

The mystery began to deepen just like a mine. Many levels became involved with many dead ends.

Late in the year of 1928 the Butte and Superior Company, not owned yet by the ACM, installed detachable steel in the Black Rock Mine. One by one the mines of the city transferred to the exclusive use of the detachable bit. When the Mountain View Mine completely equipped its miners with the detachable steel, the full capacity of the HDC shop was reached with 140,000 bits per month along with the required shanks being produced.

The year 1929 began with no HDC shops being built elsewhere. Delays continued. Without HDC's creative leader, investors were hesitant to finance new operations. Who would oversee the expansions? Maurice at twenty-one wasn't quite ready to assume the leadership.

Estate Settled

Arthur's estate was settled in the District Court of the Second Judicial District of the state of Montana in and for the County of Silver Bow on Feb. 2. Mamie was to inherit:

Item 1. Cash on hand, no/100 dollars. (0.00).

Item 2. Lots 5,6,7,8 and 9 in Block 11 of the Daly addition.

Item 3. Lot 4 in Block 147 of Aberdeen Townsite, Bingham County, Idaho.

Item 4. Trustee of 15,478 shares of the capital stock of the HDC.

Mamie sold her Idaho property almost immediately.

(This location was located near one of the largest natural water reservoirs in the country. The environment was conducive to the potato industry of today. Alley had land holdings, as well, in this Blackfoot area near present day Pocatello and Twin Falls. The men knew of its geothermal springs, actually the third highest number in the continental United States. Why they actually invested here remains another mystery. Most likely it was due to the availability of lumber for the mines. By the year 2000, Idaho had the highest per capita water consumption in the country.)

The year continued. No financial statements for the HDC have been discovered for this period. ACM issued new stock to buy some speculative companies. Copper was 18 cents a pound.

Another intrigue developed when a keynote address was given by Chauncey Berrien on October 5, 1929, to the *Western Mining Congress* held in Spokane, Washington. It was documented in *The Montana Standard*. Almost two entire pages, sized 18" x 21½" in those days, was devoted to the speech under a large bold headline.

C. L. BERRIAN GIVES INTERESTING PAPER BEFORE WESTERN MINING CONVENTION ON DEVELOPMENT IN BUTTE OF THE HAWKESWORTH BIT.

A financial fact was revealed in the address. "Considering 50,000,000 cubic feet as the average total annual cubic feet excavation of ore and waste, the ACM will save $140,450 per year by the use of the Hawkesworth Drill bits. However, with reduced manufacturing costs, improvements in distribution, control of loss in mines and other factors, we feel that the above savings will be materially increased."

The unfair distribution of wealth in the 20's was about to produce a cataclysmic shockwave throughout America. While the employee class of people saw more than a forty-one percent increase in wealth, wages had risen only two percent for its workers.[1]

Twenty-four days later on October 29 the stock market crashed. Dan Ryan lost a fortune. The stock he received from the sale of his Montana Power fell from $175 a share to $4.00. Life began to change in Butte and America.

Chapter Sixteen

The Great Depression

In 1930 during the Great Depression the ACM constructed a new detachable drill steel plant with a capacity of 225,000 bits and 1,500 shanks per month to supply the Butte mines. The HDC did not expand as Arthur planned. Alley abruptly stopped payments to Mamie for the stocks he purportedly sold for her. He disappeared from the company. His name was not mentioned again by Maurice or Mamie. Gallwey took over as President.

A provocative notice was sent to stockholders.

"A special meeting of the Stockholders of Hawkesworth Drill Company will be held at the office of the Company at 309-10 Lewisohn Building, on Monday, April 21,1930, at the hour of eight o'clock p.m.

This meeting is called in pursuance to a written request signed by directors E. J. Bowman, H.A. Gallwey and John S. Myhre constituting a majority of the Board of Directors of the Hawkesworth Drill Company, for the purpose of full considering certain proposals submitted to the Company, covering in brief the following purposes:

Proposal of H. R. Van Wagenen of Los Angeles, California, which if accepted, would increase the Capital stock of this corporation to 200,000 shares; also contemplates the optioning, for a two-year period, of certain shares of the corporation after the capitalization has been increased; the appointment of Van Wagenen as General Manager of the Corporation, at a salary of $500.00 per month and reasonable expenses; the drafting of a contract between the Hawkesworth Company and Van Wagenen for the future promotion of Hawkesworth Company.

Proposal of Sullivan Valve and Engineering Company of Butte, which, if accepted, would sell to Sullivan Company 15,000 shares of the stock of the

Hawkesworth Company for $150,000.00; payable $50,000.00 in cash installments, and $100,000.00 representing the plant of the Great Falls Iron Works which would be turned in on deal; contemplates the manufacture of bits at Great Falls; sale of bits, shanks, etc. by Sullivan Company, and the future promotion and building of plants in this country by sale of additional treasury stock, and the appointment of Mr. T. J. Sullivan, President of the Sullivan Company, as General Manager of the HDC.

Proposal of Mr. Carl J. Trauerman, President of the Montana Stock and Bond Company, of Butte, which if accepted, contemplates the sale of the treasury stock of the Hawkesworth Company for $15.00 per share, allowing the Montana Stock and Bond Corporation 20% commission for handling stock sale; or contemplates the sale of the Hawkesworth Company outright to certain large interests which Mr. Trauerman purports to represent.

In addition to considering the above propositions, this meeting is called for the purpose of transacting such other business as may legally and properly come before the said meeting. This meeting is of vital importance to all stockholders, and if you are unable to be present in person your proxy should be returned immediately in the enclosed addressed envelope to the secretary of this company. Butte, MT, the 10th day of April, A.D. 1930 J.D. Murphy, Secretary."

Here was an opportunity for financial infusions which would enable new plants to be developed during the depression. Why was there no record of the outcome of this meeting? Interesting that one company would pay fifteen dollars a share at this crucial financial period.

The financial records of this company were obliterated. Mamie received very little remuneration, if any, from the HDC from this moment forward. Maurice was forced to leave school as he could not afford the tuition. He reflected prior to his entry into the work force on Nov.10, 1930:

Life is just a big gamble
A vast game of chance.
And we keep striving forward
To do our very best.
Into our heart creeps sunshine
Then dreary days appear.
We grow tired and weary
Wonder how to endure.
Then out of a mystical magic
A blessing of some great hand
Seems to smooth all the restless feeling
And makes us all understand.

As we look o'er nature's beauties
Its magic lakes, rivers and dells
It puts our brain in a whirlwind
And creates a beautiful spell.

He assiduously started to learn the business from the ground up alternating work periods in the various departments of the HDC shop from 1930 through 1932. He made a positive impression on the "Bunch." Friendships made by Hoxie lasted a lifetime.

Tecla's Background

Thomas Lewis Davis, Tecla's father, was born in Merthyr Tydfil, Wales Oct.30, 1863. He entered Montana Territory like Arthur prior to its statehood in 1888.

Tom flourished employed by the Great Northern Railroad, first as a pile driver during the building of the Great Salt Lake Causeway and then as a veteran engineer in Butte. One occasion he helped save the railroad during a Missouri River flood. Another time as a Push Engineer, he adroitly uncoupled President Harding's train without a jerk at the top of the Woodville Hill near Elk Park. He and Maurice were fond of each other and worked on home projects together.

In time Tom's seniority entitled him to the job of switch engineer at the nearby yards where he could "switch off on the fly." Daily, he arrived home for lunch with a fringe benefit under each arm, a lump of coal. Many times during the Depression this cherished commodity was a gift to the local Methodist minister. The yard hands appreciated Tom's stopping the engine just at the right spot. The tracks for the coal car had been deliberately slanted a bit so a few remaining lumps could be emptied out furtively each day.

Her mother, Tecla Olivia Erickson, was born in Linkoping, Sweden, June 25,1875. Her mother, Clara, had died during childbirth and the newborn Alfreda and Tecla along with their father, Eric Adolph Erickson, emigrated to Carlsend, Michigan. Tecla Olivia was raised near Arthur but the two never met.

Tom and Tecla were married in the Lutheran Church in Great Falls. Tom was 42 years of age and Tecla 30. Both their names were inscribed on Ellis Island's "American Immigrant Wall of Honor" and in later years they were listed among the *First Settlers of Montana.*"[1]

Thomas and Tecla's children, Thomas, Jr., Tecla and Lenor, were all born in Butte. Their mother did not like Butte because the city was too dirty. She had been raised in a spotlessly clean Swedish environment and was an excellent housekeeper, seamstress and cook.

Tecla reflected, "My father really did enjoy his home, but he would have no phone and insisted on his privilege of having a "call boy" awaken him each day. He valued education, loved raising chickens and watering his garden. When his son, Tom, played high school football, he never missed a single game. He was a wonderful father and I was the only one who received a kiss just before he died in our home, a victim of the great flu epidemic in 1930."

Tecla Olivia Erickson Davis and Thomas Davis—Tecla Delores' parents.

Veteran Engineer Tom Davis with his engine number 1327.

Maurice slowly became accepted by Tecla's mother during their four-year courtship. Both were ecstatic when their mothers granted a long wished for engagement approval. This was a tumultuous moment, a Catholic and a Protestant, getting married in Butte, not in a church but in St. Ann's Convent privately. To the disgust of Maurice the priest, Father English, concluded the ceremony with, "That will be five dollars!" Maurice had a twenty in his pocket but turned to his mother and asked for five. So began on September 12, 1931, a wonderful fifty-three years together. Their children would inherit a Swedish, Welsh, English, Irish and Canadian background.

A wedding reception and dinner were celebrated in the still quite elegant four story Anaconda Hotel where Arthur had given his first address to the Kiwanis Club. Tecla later laughed, "The funniest thing that happened to me during our precious honeymoon was that I caught my first fish at Echo Lake!"

Tecla continued on as secretary to Dr. Thompson. She had the family Chandler car to drive. Her father never drove as he had enough running Engine 1327. Tecla was properly trained by Roy Evans, a neighbor employed in the summer to drive the coaches through Yellowstone Park. Few women attended college and few women drove during the 1920s. The Davis-Hawkesworth women began then and remain today ahead of their times.

Mining Amidst Depression

The depression hit Butte very hard that same year. Mining was one of the last industries to be affected during this depression. Copper fell to eight cents a pound.

An interesting phenomenon occurred in the steel industry. The retained workers produced one third more steel per hour than before the depression. The output per man had risen twenty-two percent. A company could lay off unproductive workers and hire only the best workers without fear of union reprisals. But as the depression lingered on, only fifteen percent of the steel industry's productive capacity was operating by 1932 and into 1933.[2]

Unemployment nationwide fell to 24.9 percent. The market demand for steel bits decreased at this same period.

Lawrence, now called Larry, began an apprenticeship with the HDC. Mamie mortgaged her well-kept home. No money was ever again paid by Alley to Mamie. He took 10,000 of Mamie's stock for which she was only partially paid and laid it aside selling off his own instead. Alley had informed her that 9,070 shares from the estate as notarized on Feb. 2, 1929 when she had 15,478shares had been sold and he was "watching over her affairs."

Tecla's "Honeymoon Fish".

Lawrence Hawkesworth's High School Graduation Picture.

ACM had obtained 50,000 shares of optioned HDC treasury stock by 1932 and had control of the board. Many needed money during the depression and ACM could afford to buy up their stock and gain control of the Board. A list of stock holders as of January 4, 1932, was in the powder box. Forty-nine individuals were listed plus the Daly Bank and Trust Co. Notable investors of the 100,000 shares were:

Alley, Roy S.	1570
Berrien, C, L.	325
Bowman, E.J.	3200
Daly, W.B.	1250
Daily Bank	50000 (not paid for but optioned treasury stock)
Daily Bank	10000 (Optioned by several individuals)
Daly, Marcus	5000 c/o Bowman
Gallwey, H.A.	1900
Hawkesworth, Mary	6,408
Hawkesworth, M. W.	2000
Myhre, J.S.	150
Murphy, J.D.	1600
Riley, J.J.	3300

During 1932 Maurice worked underground conducting further tests in conjunction with the ACM's Engineering Research Department. Marcosson wrote, "ACM's present Research Department at Butte had its beginning many years ago with the inauguration of experimental investigation in rock drills and detachable bits . . . in charge of E. R Borcherdt. Its objectives were greater efficiency in mine operation, safety and reduction of costs."[3] (Prior to this title it was known as the Efficiency Department and later as the Rock Drill Department.)

No mention is made in his book of Arthur or the Hawkesworth Drill. Marcossan was a very pro-Anaconda advocate.

Family Expands—HDC Does Not

A daughter, Montel Lenor, was born at 12:05 a.m. April 12, 1932. While waiting in the quiet and deserted Murray Hospital hallway, the nervous father received a summons from Dr. McDonald. "Maurice, come on in and watch the birth of your first child. You've seen more bloody events in the mines than a birth."

The Hawkesworth families were thrilled to have a girl. The exuberant parents lived with Tecla's mother on Second Street as this was closer to work. Maurice occasionally walked to save the five-cent fare. Butte families suffered financially from reduced payrolls. Many were faced with delinquent tax payments. Employment in the mines dropped sixteen percent. Chinese laundries no longer found it worthwhile to "mine" their wash water for profits as they had in the past.

Chapter Seventeen

Maurice Aims For Gold

Times continue hard for the country. The HDC Board was not effective. No strong leader emerged after Arthur's death. Financial sources did not surface to build new shops. Maurice contemplated the future and went before the board on Jan. 16,1933, with a possible solution.

Today we are being confronted with two great difficulties, and to neglect either one, the HDC will be jeopardizing all possible chances of advancement. The time has come that requires every ounce of our energy and concentrated thought to be put into action. The HDC has conquered many obstacles, no doubt, but the last and most important one still hangs in the balance, and our ultimate goal is yet far from us.

First: How long will our patents be protected? We find the bits now being manufactured were patented in 1922 and 1923. Therefore, the basic patent will expire in 1939. This, as you will note, leaves us only seven years to establish the Hawkesworth Detachable Drill on a manufacturing basis, whereby the stockholders can hope to reap any profit. Do you realize, if we do get someone to furnish the capital to build a manufacturing plant, that it will take a considerable amount of time to establish a plant? Although we have a model plant to copy from, it will take at least a year to equip a plant. Allowing for this, and the fact that we haven't anyone with capital interested yet, it is easy to see that we haven't such a long time left for patent protection, and if the next few years are like the last, other manufacturers will be gathering the harvest that should rightfully belong to the HDC's stockholders.

Second: Many large manufacturers are realizing the great possibilities of a detachable bit, and are entering the mining fields with their own detachable bits. This is plainly shown us by the article published in the November issue of the *Engineering and Mining Journal* on detachable drill bits. There is no doubt but that we have by far the best detachable mining drill so far invented, but when you take into consideration the amount of money backing the other detachable drills it is easy to realize that a great deal of harm can come from such sources. If something tangible cannot be done soon, our HDC will be a thing of the past. We cannot afford to wait for someone to come along and discover that we have a valuable thing which can be made to pay dividends, but we must be the aggressor by working day and night to develop a plan that will promote our drill.

While I realize present business conditions are far from satisfactory in most mining fields, there are, however, a few large mining fields operating at full capacity, in which we are fully protected by patents. I believe if we do not start negotiations with some of these mining fields we will be jeopardized as far as promoting the HDB (Hawkesworth Drill Bit).

I have information from Mr. G. C. Bateman, secretary of the Ontario Mining Association, Canada, stating there are companies in the Ontario mining fields with other detachable bits; but Anaconda's experience would, no doubt, be an important factor in helping us introduce the HDB into Canadian fields. It is our duty not to let other detachable bit companies get ahead of us.

In Ontario, Canada, are located some of the world's largest gold fields, and today they are operating at full capacity. The Province of Ontario is now the third largest producer of gold among the countries of the world. Some of their mines rank with the great gold mines of South Africa, both in the amount of gold produced and the tonnage treated. Owing to the youthfulness of the mines in operation, the increase in tonnage and ore reserves in many properties, the opening up of new mines, and the extensive areas still not prospected, it can be asserted with confidence that the gold production of Ontario will continue to increase for some years to come.

The two foremost gold bearing areas are located in the Porcupine and Kirkland Lake districts. Rouyn, Quebec is the newest of all gold fields. It is in the midst of a gold boom and is situated only sixty miles from Kirkland Lake.

The centers of the world's greatest nickel mines are located in Sudbury, Ontario. The mines at Sudbury owned chiefly by the International Nickel Company are producing nickel, copper, and appreciable quantities of gold, silver and platinum. The Sudbury district contributes the third largest annual supply of platinum being surpassed only by Russia and Colombia.

In order to show the tremendous amount of mining going on in this field, I have gathered a few statistics.

Porcupine District

Hollinger.................Mines 4,200 tons daily. They paid an extra five cent dividend above the regular five cents a month dividend in 1932.

McIntyre ....Mines 2,000 tons daily—In 1931 produced 229,413 oz.
of gold. They pan to sink a shaft to 6,750 feet and it will
become the deepest mine in Canada.

Dome ....Mines 500 tons daily. In 1931 they produced 169,686
oz. of gold.

Coneaun ....Mines in 1931 produced 36,278 oz. of gold.

Kirkland Lake District

Teck Hughes .... Mined 1,250 tons daily in 1931 and produced 294,422 oz.
gold. They showed an average recovery of $12.52 gold per
ton for the year ending Aug.1, 1932. Total operating cost
ave. $5.60 per ton. Ore reserves are valued at $7,931,338.
As of August 31,1932, they had cash and high grade
bonds totaling $3,164,931. Mine is 6,700 feet deep.

Lake Shore...............2,500 tons mined daily.

Wright Hargreaves... 700 tons daily. In 1931 produced 140,520 oz. gold.

Sylvanite ....Produced 43,477 oz. gold in 1931.K

Kirkland Lake..........Produced 28,000 oz. gold in 1931.

Norando Company... 3,000 tons daily in 1931 produced 253,363oz. gold.
Reported good values to 1,000 ft. and declared a dividend
of 60 cents a share last June."

Maurice continued with a more detailed cost analysis and concluded with these comparisons:

"Anaconda estimated they excavated 50,000,000 cubic feet in 1929 compared with the two Canadian Districts 69,560,400 cubic feet the same year. Berrien reported a net savings of .002809 per cu. ft. excavated. Therefore, a net savings to all Canadian mines per cu. ft. excavated would save $195,325.16 based on ACM experience in this operation alone. There would be a $134, 940.00 per year net savings due to the increased capacity of hoisting by use of the Hawkesworth drill. If a central plant were built to supply the bits and shanks, the total profits in the manufacturing aspect would be $330,643.53 for a year."

Maurice concludes, "I wish to state that Mr.E. R. Borcherdt, research engineer of the ACM has checked my report, and he found it conservatively estimated.

(By default this shows the money the ACM saved by manufacturing their own Hawkesworth Drill Bits. Maurice submitted a proposal to the HDC Board.)

1. I will be given the title of general manager.
2. Regular monthly meetings of the directors are to be held.
3. I will obtain a salary of $150 a month for a period of nine months.
4. My expenses will be paid.

My plan is to go up into the gold mining districts of Ontario and gather data which is vital in considering any estimate of probable profits and also to present the operators with the facts relating to the savings possible by equipping their mines with the HDB.

Data which is necessary in preparing an intelligent report to prospective users includes information on methods and costs of distribution of present steel, number and cost of steel dulled per day, conditions of rock to be drilled for comparison with proven records in Butte, besides a study of the geographical location of the various mines with respect to the location of a central plant.

Due to the tremendous savings, I should be able to interest a group of mining men there to enter into a manufacturing plan with us. With such a large undeveloped field the advantages of the drill should be readily seen, and should result in a successful enterprise.

I hope you will judge my proposition fairly and conscientiously and trust you can see the advantages of my plan."

This was the first new leadership to challenge the board. They accepted his proposal. He would survey the mine fields of Ontario, Canada, and attempt to interest the mining companies in the Hawkesworth Drill Bit.

Maurice shared the good news with Tecla and her mother. A brisk walk to Argyle Street ensued. His mother felt optimistic for the HDC's future. Maurice waltzed with her to the piano. He sorted out some of their growing sheet music collection and played for his mother, *Always, Ain't She Sweet,* made up spontaneous words to *I'll Get By* to his today's version, *We'll Get By* and ended with an Irish favorite, *McNamara's Band.*

Copper King Dies

The price of copper fell to five cents a pound in 1933. Dan Ryan died nearly bankrupt February 10 though he was buried in a copper casket. Had he exploited the HDC trying to recoup loses from his failed power stocks? Had someone in the HDC sold out to him? Corruption was occurring, but this will never be solved satisfactorily as all HDC records except those in the old powder box were expunged.

Work pace slowed in Butte. E. R. Borcherdt arranged to accompany Maurice or "Hoxie" as he now was called in the mining world to Canada. As a result of Borcherdt's diligent and meticulous testing, he had become a strong proponent of the bit and was eager to extol its value. A life long working arrangement and friendship began between the two men.

Arthur had known there was a double-decker somewhere in the loop. He thought Borcherdt was involved but his fears never materialized in regard to Ed. Betrayal occurred but not through Ed. Anaconda's endorsement of the bit carried weight around the world. Borcherdt had multiple connections and Maurice hoped he would be an asset on this trip.

Many of the mine operators in Canada had worked for the ACM or had attended the Montana School of Mines. More questions to ponder floated to the surface as the two men prepared to depart. Did the ACM have a hidden agenda and want first hand knowledge of Ontario's mining operations and maybe gain a foothold in them by having additional information? Did the ACM want to prevent the HDC from expanding before they could gain complete control? Had they already secured all the rights needed along with royalties? Would Borcherdt supply some of these answers in a seemingly innocent way for the ACM?

Chapter Eighteen

A Duo In Canada

Maurice's personal notebook gives a glimpse of his first international travel adventure accompanied by Borcherdt during February and March 1933. It began on a journey to the Porcupine Mine District situated 25 mi. NE of Timmins, Ontario. This site was famous for its nickel and gold mines.

They met with John Knox, General Manager, of the Hollinger Mine February 5. Borcherdt had known him in Houghton, Michigan. This gold mine had increased daily ore production to 6500 tons.

Succinct notes materialized in his notebook. "Brief interview—showed much interest and seemed to be quite enthusiastic. We are meeting him again tomorrow afternoon."

At this mine "much time required to hoist and lower steel—in wintertime it takes six men, three at the level to pull steel cars off and three on top. Time could be saved using the Hawkesworth Bit and in turn better spent in lowering timber. The underground motors could be used for something else."

"Mr. Knox seems to be very aggressive in his actions with a keen mind to the saving possibilities of our bit. Acted as though they would like to have a plant of their own and include the Dome and McIntyre with them. He asked for written facts."

Borcherdt compiled a short temporary report and also included an addendum regarding their methods of mining. He offered them suggestions and possible changes which would make their Canadian mining methods more productive. This last comment was negatively received with "much ill-feeling toward Borcherdt. I wish he would have just stuck with the bit factors," Maurice concluded.

"Met J.H. Stovel, General Manager, of Dome Mine Tues. Feb.14. Presented him with facts relating to Hawkesworth Drill. He showed enthusiasm and is very much interested. He is willing to put an engineer on to study existing conditions relating to savings made possible through the use of our drill. They move 1500 tons per day presently. Taking us underground again on Thurs. morning."

"Went underground with Mr. Stovel Feb. 16. Mine conditions very adaptable for the use of our drill. Went to his house for lunch. Very nice gentlemen."

Other mines in this district included the McIntyre, Vipound, Consolidated West Dome Lake, Coneaurm, Ankerite, March and Paymaster. All of which they visited.

Maurice sent Tecla a picture of his skiing in this area labeling the persons as Mr. Martin, a surveyor at the McIntyre and Mr. Caty, in charge of the Hawkesworth Drill test at Hollinger and "yours forever next in line."

Kirkland Lake Gold Mine District

"Met with L. B. Smith, underground Superintendent of Wright Hargrave Mine which averages 700 tons per day."

Other mines in this area: Teck Hughes averaging 1250 tons per day, Lake Shore, 2500 tons per day, Sylvanite, Tough Oakes, Burnsides and the Kirkland Lake Gold Mine. This last mine operates today. In 2003, 50,000 to 70,000 oz. of gold was produced and it is scheduled to yield until at least 2008.

Rouyn, Quebec Mine District

He met with Mr. Roscoe, General Manager, and others at the Norando Mines Feb. 20. In 1934 they mined 3000 tons per day. The mine produced six valid minerals: gold, Chalcopyrite, pyrite, pyrrhotite, quartz, and sphalerite. It continues to operate in the twenty-first century.

Borcherdt's Report

To: John Knox, General Manager, Hollinger Gold Mining Co., Timmins, Ontario, Mar. 16, 1933.

I am of the opinion that the application of the HDB should be entirely practicable and should result in material ton cost reductions in the Hollinger Mine.

The ACM's use of this bit has covered a period of years in which it has definitely proven its reliability as a dependable mining tool for a large operation and has demonstrated conclusively that mining costs can be lowered by its use. In addition to the direct savings there are many intangible savings which are of unquestionable value in improving efficiency but are difficult of determination in dollars and cents value but which are helpful . . . reduction of accidents, maintenance of shafts, hoisting and lowering great weights of steel, availability of cages for handling men and other mine supplies, which becomes increasingly important as greater mining depths are reached, imposition of less rotational strain on the rock drills by the use of sharp steel free from binding and rubbing in the hole and reduced powder consumption.

The paramount advantage lies in simplification of the costly problem of distributing large amounts of regular steel to difficult working places. Its use permits the miner to increase his effective period of drilling, which after all is the duty for which he is hired, and which results in a direct saving to the mining company. Instead of requiring him to spend from one to two hours per shift in getting his drilling tools to the working face of the stope and limiting his output in terms of drilling and breaking by a large percentage of this total time the detachable bit permits him to begin drilling as soon as he can set up his machine.

Our miners realize what a tremendous time and energy saving device the Hawkesworth bit has been and we would be confronted with serious difficulties if we were to go a step backward and return to the use of the old style regular drill steel.

A comparison of the costs of regular drill steel and detachable must be based on total steel costs and distribution costs. Regular drill steel to include labor and supply cost of the actual sharpening operation plus the maintenance cost of sharpener equipment, plus new steel replacement cost, plus handling or distribution cost of sharp steel to the various mine levels. plus miners time expended in getting sharp steel from the shaft station to the working place, plus the nippers time in collecting dull steel from the workings and transporting it to the stations, plus labor in hoisting dull steel and returning it to the sharpening shop and sorting it for sharpening.

Borcherdt continues with a cost comparison for labor, supplies and distribution and concludes by saying their Canadian engineers have agreed their figures are on the conservative side. The concluding paragraph is most revealing.

ACM's cost per ton of ore milled for all detachable drill steel costs noted above and including distribution averages between $0.05 and $0.06. I have assumed an average cost of $0.0555 for convenience in calculating which gives a cost difference of $0.13 per ton in favor of the detachable steel. This amounts to $16,957.59 per period, or $220, 448.67 for the year. This is most certainly an item of saving which no mining company can afford to overlook, although it must be understood that royalty charges and a certain amount of plant amortization are not included which would reduce this figure. This also presupposes that operating conditions at the Hollinger and the Anaconda Mines are identical. This must be determined by tests which I will arrange to conduct in the next four to six weeks. After which, if acceptable to your Board of Directors, I will arrange a meeting with the Hawkesworth Drill Company representative and yourself to discuss terms of royalty, time contracts, plant construction, etc. As soon as possible, I will forward you an estimate of the Canadian delivered prices of necessary equipment for a complete manufacturing plant of 250,000 bits and necessary shanks per month.

For your perusal in the interim I am enclosing a list of the costs of the principal items of equipment for a plant of this capacity which we purchased in boom times and which can be duplicated today at far lower costs. Respectfully submitted, E. R. Borcherdt.

During August and September of 1933 Borcherdt and O'Neill his assistant research engineer ran a test at the three Canadian mines but no plant was planned.

Maurice at the Empire Hotel in Timmons, Ontario.

Maurice and Foreman Lang at the McIntyre Mine in Ontario.

Three Months Later

Recorded in *Montel's Baby Book* for Jan. 24, 1934 were the words: "Daddy all gone bye, bye, toot, toot, Canada." For 162 days Maurice revisited the same sites as he had on his first trip.

Canada was now in the throes of the Great Depression. Mining slowed considerably but Maurice ran extensive tests and innumerable demonstrations. An account of his expenses for about a six month period and a detailed order for the machinery needed to start a manufacturing company was found in his frayed black notebook.

Machinery needed for bit manufacturing:
$750 for Bit Forge Furnace
$8000 for Ajaz bit forge
$280 for Motor
$200 for a Bit Conveyor
$1700 for Trimming Press
$837.72 for two Annexing Furnaces
$400 for one Bit Tumbler
$15,660 for three Bit Millers
$22,589 for six Bit Regrinding Machines
$5,978 for two Bit Hardening Furnaces
$100 for Quenching Tanks
$80 for Stress Relief Tanks

Total= $64,154.72

Equipment Needed for Manufacturing Shanks
$400 for one Shank Hack Saw
$150 for one Upsetting Furnace
$5850 for one Ajax Shank Forge
$250 for miscellaneous forging equipment
$300 for two Annealing and Hardening Furnaces
$60 for two Lime Bins
$150 for one Oil Quenching Tank
$150 for two Shank Grinders
$10,080 for fiv e Shank Millers
$368 for other miscellany Equipment
$400 for two Shank Drillers

Total= $18,158

MAINTENANCE NEEDS
$1000 for two Die Furnaces
$250 for one Drawing Furnace
$50 for one Oil Quenching Tank
$5,500 for two Lathes
$785 for one Shaper
$3000 for a Universal Miller
$1500 for one Vertical Miller
$2000 for two Cutter Grinders
$1200 for one Drill Press
$100 for one Tool Grinder

AUXILIARY EQUIPMENT
$1200 for Piping
$1000 for Heating
$1000 for Tanks
$1000 for Trolley supports
$1800 for Shafting, hangars,& belting
$1770 for Oil supply equipment, tanks pumps and compressor
$4800 for Transformer, wiring & Shop Motor
$500 for Benches, vices, etc

$50 for Mauals

TOTALS
Bit Equipment.............. 64,154.72
Shank Equipment 18,158
Maintenance Equip...... 15,385
Auxiliary Equip......... $13,020
Accumulative Costs:=$110,717.72
Shipping Machinery from Butte to Toronto was $2.38 per hundred car load and $2.83 per hundred for bag of steel and $4.16 per hundred for finished bits.

Maurice's Expenses from January 25,1934 to July 6,1934:

Butte to Chicago, Toronto, Timmins, Toronto, Chicago, Butte

Pullman=$49.26+Fare=$157.12 for a total of $206.38.

Hotel bills, medical attention, meals, entertainment, tips, etc. 162 days @10.01=$1621.62.

Total Expenses $206.38 +1621.62=$1828. Money Received by Maurice was $1828.

During this foreign expedition, one letter gives an insight into Maurice's marriage and family life. From the Empire Hotel in Timmins, Ontario, the warm, devoted, emotional Irishman wrote on May 11, 1934:

My dearest Tecla,

Well, it seems I've lost all track of the time and Mother's Day is Sunday. As a matter of fact I thought I would have a letter reach you on this day telling you what a wonderful Mother you are.

It seems rather strange the way events have taken their course and now you're a Mother and your daughter and hubby think you are a most wonderful Mother, too. We both love and think so much of you and wish you a most happy Mother's Day.

I am still flying around like a chicken with its head cut off and the days don't seem to be long enough for what I have to do. I get terribly lonesome and I am anxious to be with you soon. As I told you before, the test has not been going as well as it should, but I will have a definite idea within a few days.

Well, my darling wife, your baby and I wish you a most pleasant Mother's Day.

Yours forever, Montel and Maurice Xxx and Ooo."

By early July a new infusion of business seemed to be in the HDC's grasp. Maurice departed Canada with hope in his heart.

A week after Maurice's departure on July 15, 1934, R. R. Rice recommended a Hawkesworth Drill Shop be built in Canada. His fourteen page analysis to his mine superintendent of the McIntyre Porcupine Mines, D. E. Kealy concluded:

"While a trial run on 436 bits can hardly serve as a definite indication on long time practice in the use of detachable steel, the present writer's opinion, it has been demonstrated that, with intelligent cooperation between the mines and manufacturers, the drilling tools of the Hawkesworth Drill Company offer considerable possibilities, which merit further and wider investigation.

In this respect, during the present series, the miners have been more favourably impressed than in past tests, have become more conscious of the advantages offered by the use of a successful bit, and are now in a highly receptive mood to the education necessary to bring about efficient operation.

It has been tentatively proposed that the Hawkesworth Company install a small manufacturing unit in Canada, thus enabling them to supply larger quantities of their product, to use a better grade of steel, and to experiment on various proposals made to them which suggest advantages in meeting conditions in the Porcupine District. In this event, it is recommended that tests be carried out on a sufficiently large number of bits and shanks to give a wider indication, and that the mines cooperate, both among themselves and with the Hawkesworth Drill Company, in such an investigation."[1]

Chapter Nineteen

High and Low Levels

A momentous occasion loomed when Tecla planned to meet Maurice in Chicago on his return trip home. The two grandmothers loved the thought of taking care of Montel while Tecla traveled. In turn the young mother looked forward to the train trip. During her childhood Tecla's family had packed a well-stocked trunk and vacationed for a month each summer either in Michigan, Minnesota or California. Her close—knit family was entitled to one courtesy pass a year on the railroad. In the past the thought of beauty, clean air, new experiences had sustained Grandma Tecla. Presently, she was happy for her oldest daughter to have a trip.

This time Tecla purchased a ticket. She had budgeted the couple's expenses carefully since the start of their marriage and money for leisure was always set aside. She enjoyed being Dr. Thompson's secretary and knew Maurice's work bought satisfaction to him. Together their meaningful employment provided the means to spend some vacation time together even in the throes of the country's depression.

The deeply devoted couple attended the magical Chicago World's Fair, *A Century of Progress*, which had opened a year ago in May. Together they explored more than 400 acres of fascinating exhibits after paying the twenty-five-cent entrance fee. Maurice became engrossed in the fair's stated goal, "To attempt to demonstrate to an international audience the nature and significance of scientific discoveries, the methods of achieving them and the changes which their application has wrought in industry and in living conditions."[1]

The earnest, hard working, young man envisioned future uses for the drill bit. Little did he realize where this dream would actually take him as he gazed at the Goodyear Blimp against the city horizon.

When Tecla saw the exhibit, "Living Babies in Incubators", she spoke of having another child. A loving look passed between them and they knew they were ready to add to their family. While viewing the new streamlined train, she then ardently wished her father were alive to witness such a marvel.

Sally Rand's Burlesque performance was taken in stride by Maurice. Tecla wasn't so enthralled but she was aware of such features in Butte theaters.

After experiencing the thrill of the Sky ride and a Coca Cola dispensed from the first automatic fountain dispenser, both knew this fair was even better than their honeymoon. Before departing this vibrant metropolis, pictures were taken on a ferry boat of the smiling couple, Maurice with his white Panama hat and spats; Tecla with a stylish hat. Newly purchased piano sheet music, *My Happiness* and *Blue Moon* found room in Arthur's old travel bag.

The couple's spirit sank shortly after their return to Butte. A strike began. It was to become Butte's fourth longest mining strike not ending until six weeks later on September 20. The copper supply on hand was enough to meet the nation's present demand. As historians have stated, "There never was a strike the ACM didn't want." Bit production slowed. No action was taken on a Canadian venture by the board members.

One crisp fall day Maurice added to his notebook. "By chance I slept in today and accidentally ran into an afternoon meeting of the HDC. Those present were Gallwey, Murphy, Bowman and Borcherdt. I had to wait outside nearly an hour before I was admitted and when I did go in everything had been decided. They asked me if it would be agreeable to give Borcherdt and Bowman authority to go to Canada and close any kind of a deal. They wondered if my Mother would be agreeable. I told them to ask her. I also told Gallwey and Murphy not to send Borcherdt because of the ill feeling toward him at the Hollinger. I also told them this upon my return from Canada. They paid no attention to it. I did say, however, that I was in favor of Gallwey going instead of Bowman."

A formal meeting of the of the HDC board was called for December 26, 1934. Present were Gallwey, V.P. Lentz, Murphy, John Kelly, Borcherdt and Maurice. The main topic centered around what could be done about the Canadian business.

Maurice chided the board for "their negligence in pushing things." He felt the Hollinger and Dome officials were more than willing to invest in the bits if they were approached with the proper attitude and in a spirit of cooperation. He sensed Borcherdt had not established a good relationship.

"It was decided that Borcherdt should write to the Hollinger, McIntyre and Dome officials to see what could be done. I argued that I did not fear the results of the tests, but that with careful handling a deal could be completed between the mines there."

Another meeting was called January 6, 1935, for the stock holders and for the election of officers. Gallwey, Lentz, Murphy, and Bowman were reelected. John Kelly and Maurice were voted new members. Maurice realized new ideas and more energy was needed to get business moving. Gallwey was sixty-nine. The older members seemed lethargic, or worn out with negotiations. Their working years were coming to an end.

His notes included, "I gave a talk covering details of the tests in Canada and explained that if things were handled rightly they would have no trouble manufacturing in Canada."

A Dr. Thompson who was present offered a suggestion. He wanted the Canadian rights and would pay the HDC one-half cent royalty on each bit used until the patents expired.

Despite all this it was decided that we should wait until we heard from the letters Borcherdt wrote before taking further action. The meeting closed.

Two days later on January 8, letters were received from the Hollinger and Dome.

"Received your letter of December 30 and showed it to John Knox. He will be willing to meet with Borcherdt should he be here when you come up."

The Dome letter indicated, "Received your letter of December 30. We will be willing to meet you and discuss a proposition. As a matter of fact, I told you that in the last letter I wrote you of which I never had a reply!" Maurice never did learn who had that letter or what happened to it. Was it lost in the mail or did some board member misplace it deliberately or did a director with an aging memory mislay the document? A question with no answer.

Despite what Maurice recommended, "Borcherdt and Bowman made the trip to Canada leaving on January 26, 1935. Borcherdt returned home February 11, a journey of seventeen days. He made a trip to Timmins, Sudbury and New York during this time. No plant was established.

The depression worsened on both sides of the border. Maurice personally heard no further word from Canada not realizing a communication had been sent to someone. He continued working with "The Bunch".

A hoped for son, Maurice William (Bill), arrived in Butte May 26,1935. The family rented their first home on Harvard Avenue across the street from Tecla's sister, Lenor, who just had her first child, Earl, two days prior.

ACM decided to lift spirits in the morose town with a Miner's Union Day Celebration June 13 at the Columbia Gardens. The planned event was a bit somber.

More excitement was evident when the federal government promised food for the Butte area. This jubilant mood tapered off when the method of food distribution became known. Only two dozen out of three hundred small grocery stores were chosen by the ACM to allocate the food. The soon to be mayor, Charles Hauswirth, was one of a few people brave enough to attack the company and survive. He uttered, "What sort of a country is it when Uncle Sam puts out money for relief purposes and then we have a bunch of ACM swivel artists dictate who will get the business and who will not."[2]

The subterfuge operations of the ACM were intricate. Power and greed prevailed for the present. Butte citizens had no idea how much the Company was decreasing its debt during these lean years. That would be revealed later.

On the brighter side the WPA program actually began in October. This was a mammoth boon for the starving city. Improvements sprouted everywhere as $35,000,000 was spent in the Butte Zone. Eighteen miles of new sewer lines were installed and 298 blocks were improved with blacktop sidewalks. "Beef Trail", the new ski club, made great strides with improved trails and a ski lodge.These proud results were born of laborers who knew how to produce. This was one of the few times Butte received any monetary remittance from a nation to whom she had contributed so munificently.

Even the airport with its new upgrades became an attraction where spectators could enjoy with eager anticipation the arrival of an airplane. Maurice and Tecla had a favorite "observation" location. They remembered when nearly 100,000 had assembled here to see Lindbergh arrive during their graduation year. Frequently, after watching the enchanting landings, they slowly drove up to the spring on the Harding Way. Daddy instructed Montel and his newborn son, "Take ten deep breaths and a good drink of pure water to help you sleep well and stay healthy." This became a family ritual.

Arthur's brother, Frank, died from paralyzes and heart failure in Tonapah, Nevada Oct.24, 1935. The disease's onset began eleven years prior when he learned of his brother's sudden death.

Earthquakes

In November a series of earthquakes rocked the state. The epicenters were in or near Helena. On the twenty-eighth the most devastating 6.5 on the Richter Scale affected Maurice's aunt, Lizzie Hawks. She arrived, visibly shaken, to stay with Mamie until order could be restored in the Capitol City. Her deceased husband, Daniel Hawks, had been the caretaker of the Broadwater Hotel and Swimming Resort when Maurice and Tecla had visited them after their first airplane flight. The family were distraught to learn it was severely damaged.

Here the world's largest swimming pool had been frequented by the ACM millionaires. It was fed by a natural hot springs. The elaborate hotel finished in antique oak had velvet carpets and beveled plate-glass bay windows. Eight to ten course meals were in vogue. The nearby artificial lake provided boats for pleasure parties. Saddle horses and autohacks could be rented by the hour or the day. The *Broadwater* would never be the same but the family kept a wonderful brochure and some postcards and most of all happy memories of the days spent in its pool.[3]

Death Strikes Again

Arthur's son, Arkie, died a year later from diabetes and alcoholic coma Sept. 23, 1936. Standard syringes for insulin injections were eight years into the future.

A question was answered. Neither Frank nor Arkie were physically able to take over the company upon Arthur's death. Maurice was next in line but "just a little too young" as Tecla mused sixty years later.

Julia commented in a letter written to Lee her oldest grandson, January 27, 1937. My thoughts centered on my son, Frank, and my grandson, Arkie, who were released from a restless misunderstanding condition of earthly life, in the same little town and the same environment of brain sickness. Never fear. They will be cared for, The Creative Intelligence, The Supreme Being, The Soul of the Universe, commonly called God, never created anything for destruction."

Chapter Twenty

Pivotal Events

An ominous absence of mail from Canada propelled Maurice to tackle a new challenge. He felt a need to obtain more knowledge about types of steel so he enrolled in the School of Mines Metallurgy Department in 1937. The course, "Alloy and Straight Carbon Steel" would keep him abreast of advancements in the use of steel. Education was a necessity for him if he were to gain the respect of the top echelon in the mining world. This would have to come through practical experience and occasional courses as he had to support his family.

At the same period he embarked on a new adventure and commenced work in the capacity of an underground engineer in conjunction with the engineering research department of the ACM. New mining methods intrigued him beyond that of drilling.

Brotherhood

To Maurice and Tecla's delight an Ecumenical Banquet at the elegant Finlen Hotel was planned and they attended. This nine-story copper shingled building, designed after the Hotel Astor in New York City, had welcomed people of many faiths. Lindberg, William Jennings Bryan, Teddy Roosevelt and Charles Russell could be counted among its former guests.

Butte Protestants, Catholics and Jews were encouraged to participate. This one time event was not applauded by many. In a predominant Catholic community, Maurice and especially Tecla wanted their children to see the good in every religion. Their parent's had bequeathed a Catholic, Universalist, Methodist and Lutheran background to them. In turn they wanted their children to attend public schools and go to catechism classes to ensure an exposure to other religions.

A New Birth

Maurice brought his mother and his two children uptown, parked the car and told them to "stay put" while he went inside to get them something special September 7, 1937. After an agonizing wait he returned to proclaim, "You have a new baby sister, Lynn Delores. You can come in and see her for just a moment." All the Irish genes shone through this beautiful dark curly hair and blue-eyed baby. The family was now complete.

Friendships

Friendships were another component of life in Butte. Wholesome, dedicated hard-working family men provided a more permanent work force than did itinerant single men. Without some stability in the population, Butte never would have survived the Depression. Friends supported and trusted one another in difficult moments.

Good friends of Tecla and Maurice since high school days, Gwen and Milt Brown, purchased a home across from the School of Mines on Granite Street. Milt had become the Registrar for the prestigious school. He and Maurice planned a Saturday to bowl. The two women had played bridge earlier in the day.

Much to everyone's amazement, Milt needed one final strike for a perfect game. Without warning he collapsed after a successful last crucial release of the ball. Maurice had become involved with safety issues in the mines and realized Milt required expertise care. He rushed his friend to the nearby hospital. Diagnosed with a bleeding ulcer, Milt needed an infusion of blood. Maurice volunteered and a person to person transfusion began. Fortunate for all involved, Maurice had type O negative blood. Upon his friend's recovery Maurice informed Milt in an Irish brogue, "You just needed some good Irish blood in ye!" On St. Patrick's day for the next fifty years a card arrived from the "Irish Blood Cousins."

When Red Cross blood donation drives began officially, Maurice led the way. His children, too, when they reached adulthood responded munificently as had the Ryersons before them.

Once a month the families alternated sharing a Sunday meal together. Nonie and Marcia were best of friends with Montel, Billy and Lynn. A never forgotten quote emanated from the sagacious young boy one meal, "Daddy, we're saving money tonight aren't we?"

Fort Peck Dam

Many single miners found it a necessity to move on to obtain work. The Fort Peck Dam project was a common destination. Between 1933 to 1940 the world's second largest earthen dam in its day was built with 10,000 workers employed for fifty cents to $1.20 an hour in wages. The four-mile long, 220' deep structure with its 1600 miles of shoreline provided much needed water to eastern Montana.[1]

City, ACM and Family Economics

By early spring of 1937 only two thousand eight hundred were employed in the mines and by mid-summer this dropped to 800. Wages were $5.25 a day. Initiation of a five-day work week acutely demoralized the city. Men accustomed to six days of pay now lost thirty-two hours of wages per month. Businesses collapsed and Butte spent a period in bankruptcy. Hard liquor by the drink finally became legal in the bars, not that anyone noticed.[2]

ACM continued to reduce its loan, its main thrust during the depression. Their contribution to Butte during this dreadful period was "Clark's Park," a minor league baseball facility in the summer which was transformed into a skating rink in the winter. Secondly, they capitulated to miners demands and installed a Group Insurance Plan. That was basically it!

Mamie was forced to sell the Argyle home April 30 for $4,234.69. Even this posed a problem, as the title had to be cleared. It was discovered the Marcus Daly Estate owned the underground rights to all the property in the Daly Addition.

Maurice at the Argyle home with "For Sale" sign on pillar.

Her sad thoughts turned toward a positive upcoming event. Tecla and Maurice decided to have her three grandchildren baptized. Monsignor Michael English, whose influence over the Catholic population was similar to Kelley's control over the ACM, had transferred to another parish. The new priest at St. Ann's met the family approval.

Gar, as she henceforth was affectionately called since Montel coined the name, had fretted about the delay. Many years later she confided to Montel, "You choked on a chicken bone when your parents were in Chicago. I took you over to the sink and baptized you. Your grandfather once told me of two miners. One was baptized and one was not. A horrible accident occurred in the mines and the unbaptized man was near death. His partner emptied his lunch bucket, filled it with copper water and baptized him just before he died. He told his friends that no one should have to spend an eternity in a place as hot as the one they had been in."

Gar's sister, Margaret and nephew, Richard, became sponsors for the children May 25. Father D. Harrington performed the ceremony in the sanctuary where their grandfather had laid.

September 1938, Montel was about to begin first grade. At the Whittier school entrance Maurice was informed by his self confident six year old, "You can go home now, Daddy. I know my way back."

Nell Coughlin, the first grade teacher, instilled a life long love for learning in the Hawkesworth as well as many other Butte children. "A good teacher was more important than the subjects taught," Tecla felt. Sixty-seven years later the wooden spool doll made in the first grade at Christmas time still adorns a family tree. Lynn's care of family artifacts over the years was reminiscent of the family's saving of important letters and documents.

For eight years the Hawkesworth children walked the four blocks alone to school. Every noon Tecla had lunch for them. Not once were they driven to or from school even when the weather got in double digits below zero. Not once did they experience a weather holiday. Not once did they eat at school other then the daily spoonful of Cod Liver Oil during the long winter months.

Children were safe in and around Butte. They also knew how to brave the elements. On the negative side no parks, playgrounds or swimming pools were built other than the Columbia Gardens for the neighborhood children. Arthur's life was too short for a dream of parks within the city to come a reality.

One bright event the Company had established was "Children's Day" at the Columbia Gardens during summer vacation. Bus or trolley fare was free and supervision was provided by the public school elementary teachers every Thursday. This was the highlight of most children's summer days. The musical merry-go-round with the elegant hand carved horses cost a nickel to ride. The twirling bi-plane attraction fueled young imaginations of air travel and the fearful roller coaster where every dip was anticipated with glee cost ten cents apiece. Ice cream, popcorn and arcade games were five cents. Each Hawkesworth child received fifteen cents and their biggest decision each week was how to allocate this amount. The prices never changed.

An unwritten Miner's Code in regard to children was respected. The men presently had their block long, brick lined Venus Alley filled with cribs. This led to the infamous Dumas Brothel where a white light shone over the inviting entrance Gambling parlors, saloons, picture shows, restaurants or cafes complemented their diversions. ACM's philosophy was at work: Give the miners adequate recreation of all kinds and plenty of good places to eat. Labor issues will then simmer and not boil."

ACM and Its Debt Reduction

Behind the scenes during this cruel depression Anaconda and its subsidiaries continued their debt reduction, unconcerned about nickels and dimes. At the end of 1932 the debt, including bonds and the bank loans, had been reduced to $105,815,000. By the end of 1933, this had been reduced to $102,561,000 and by the end of 1941, the debt under Kelley's guidance, had been reduced to $20,935,000. As of December 1942, all indebtedness of the company and its subsidiaries had been paid.[3]

In sixteen years since the introduction of the bit with twelve of those years coming in the height of the depression their debt was completely reduced $249,000,000 to zero!

Did ACM take profits from the sale and use of the Hawkesworth Drill Bit help to bring down the debt along with work stoppage at the mines and depreciation of inventory?

Butte people starved during ACM's depreciation of their debt. On multiple occasions Maurice, Fred Wagner and Buck O'Donnell traveled to their favorite trout fishing spot on the Big Hole to help out during this severe crisis. The animated men remarked, "We caught interesting limits of rainbow, cutthroat and black-spotted trout." Slyly they continued, "We saw to it that the fish warden was adequately supplied."

Widows and the unemployed in their neighborhoods watched for them to return and were never disappointed. The friends had heard of the Donner Party and reasoned, "We can alleviate some starvation pain."

September and October of 1938 saw the reopening of five mines which had been closed for several months, the Belmont, Leonard, Mt. Con, Stewart and St. Lawrence.

Stock Infusion

A mysterious certificate #172 for five thousand two hundred HDC shares inexplicably appeared in Mamie's name Dec.29, 1938. Stock manipulation was in full swing as she had firmly stated she wanted no more stock payments, only cash deposited into her account. Where did this stock come from? Something wasn't right. A crucial year for the family was about to begin.

137

Chapter Twenty-One

1939

Montana celebrated 50 years as a state. Copper rose to twelve cents a pound and wages increased to $5.75 a day. Production was on an upswing just prior to World War II. The HDC produced and sold more bits and shanks. Maurice worked along with the Bunch and ACM focusing on underground research.

A three-bedroom home came on the market at 2324 Yale Avenue for $1500. It was two blocks away from the present Harvard Avenue rental. Maurice and Tecla obtained a mortgage with a monthly payment of twenty dollars plus eight percent interest, and became first time home owners. Lynn, nearly two, entered and amused everyone when she walked into the large fireplace to view the new environment. Gar gave Montel the beloved family piano and lessons began in earnest from Margaret McHale, her mother's former teacher. Maurice never went a day without playing. The Irish tenor enjoyed creating songs to amuse his family such as:

> Oh, I know a girl who lived down the lane
> People use to say she was insane.
> She sprinkled gold dust all over her bed
> Woke up one morning
> Found her ownself dead.
> Oh, I know a girl whose name's Maureen
> Don't know why the girl's so lean
> She won't take a bath
> Not even a scrub
> For fear she'll slip through
> The hole in the tub.

Neighborhood children gravitated to the spacious Hawkesworth yard which contained multiple poplar trees perfect for a quick climb. Many times a knock would resound on the back door and a child would query, "Mrs. Hawkesworth, can your husband come out and play with us or can we come in and hear a song?" Mom always encouraged friends to be around. Her psychology was, "If you know who your children's friends were and how they played together, very few problems would arise that couldn't be solved."

Lynn, Bill, cousin Freddie Wagner, friend Robert Cotter.
Fence in the background was made with old trolley car ties;
swing rope and poles were "gifts" from the mine yards.

An Unsolved Problem

To compound matters in their search for financial backing, the aging directors of the HDC knew by 1939 that capital investments nationwide were only sixty percent of the 1929 levels.[1] Venture capitalists, as the financiers are known today, did not come forth during these depressed times. The reasons for this could be multiple, many coming from outside the mining world. Farming, geography and communication challenges were among the predominant factors.

Historically, with the arrival of the railroads, it was natural for settlers who had the moniker, "honyockers" or "scissorbills," to enter Eastern Montana. The Northern Pacific beginning back in 1864 was given twenty miles of land on either side of their main line tracks. This amounted to more than fifteen percent of the vast Montana territory. They advertised furiously to entice Easterners. Come they did and by 1922 the newcomers occupied more than forty percent of the state, about 93,000,000 acres. These people also known as "sod busters, chicken chasers or "homesteaders" were not liked by the cattle ranchers who had previously roamed freely through the plains.[2]

At first abundant success with wheat farming sprouted. Ferocious winds, hungry grasshoppers and terrible fires followed these first few favorable years. One out of every two farmers soon lost their family land. By 1925 there were 20,000 foreclosures. Then in 1929 a ten-year drought cycle began along with the depression.

Geographically, Montana was not strategically located. Eastern Montana was more inclined to favor the Midwest. Western Montana was more oriented to the Pacific Northwest. The Continental Divide on the Rocky Mountains sliced these two areas. On the Western side the rivers flowed to the Columbia ending in the Pacific Ocean. On the Eastern side three meandering rivers merged at Three Forks, the Gallatin, Madison and Jefferson. They became the Missouri River which was one of the headwaters forming the great Mississippi.

Travel favored the north/south route to Salt Lake City, Reno or San Francisco. Spokane to the West was a much shorter distance than Chicago to the East. Butte was physically isolated with mining at a standstill.

Long distance telephone calls were a rarity and astronomical in cost. Communications reached Butte by mail and telegraph until its first radio station, KGIR, founded by Ed Craney went on the air in November of 1929. This media was a local godsend. Periodically, events from a far away world were broadcast when a connection was made with KSL in Salt Lake City. Housewives were enthralled. Tedious days were livened up for idled men.

No Eastern bankers emerged to invest in a Hawkesworth Drill Factory. ACM's iron grip could be deadly in so many diverse and seemingly unrelated ways. Their corporate offices in New York had a great influence on Wall Street.

A combination of all these factors, geography, agriculture, communications, aging board members and above all the power of the ACM influenced the investment world's attitude toward the HDC.

An End

Early in June Maurice realized the ACM had outwitted and had maneuvered the family to gain majority control of the stock, board and company. He tried one last time to salvage a part of his father's work. The HDC was the owner of patent No. 1,627,983 for Arthur's bit grinding machine. Maurice asked the board if he could "acquire the sole and exclusive right and license to manufacture, sell and otherwise dispose of the bit grinding machines." He would buy these back from the company and also pay a percentage of the profits made by him to the HDC when he marketed them to other sources. The board refused.

The Hawkesworth Drill Company survived through all of this. Then fourteen years after Arthur's death, everything came to a rapid finale on June 19, 1939. This was five and a half months after the additional stock had been issued to Mamie.

Fifty years hence Tecla broke a long silence and shared with Montel, "Alley was a crook, a double-decker. He substituted and sold his stock instead of your grandmothers when the price was high. He took the money and left. When your father cleared out the HDC office, there was not a single piece of correspondence there from Alley. The contracts signed by him were found in Arthur's effects at home. But, honey, life is more than fame or money or even power. Your family had the love of each other.

Your dad and I decided never to speak about the causes for the dissolution of the HDC and the loss of its fortunes. He quoted his father's favorite saying, 'A winner never quits and a quitter never wins.' We will make it through this he told me and we did. Now let us talk about something nicer."

What part did Alley play in the company's demise other than stock manipulation? One hopes that after all the trust given to Alley only a possible loss of his fortunes in the depression led him to this and nothing else. Had he been surrounded by unethical ACM leaders to the point where their morals engulfed him into their intricate web? Fourteen months after the stock discovery The *Fallon County Times* reported that Alley died on Aug. 29, 1940, at Pipestone Springs at age 64 from diabetic complications. *The Montana Standard* stated he "served as personal representative in Butte for the late John D. Ryan from 1905 until 1922 when he retired."[3]

No mention of his many years as President of the HDC was mentioned. Retired in 1922 when the HDC was beginning? Why did his family need bodyguards in 1938 when Ryan had been dead five years, sixteen years after Alley retired and Con Kelley had become the head of the ACM?[4] No answers can be found to these questions in any city or state archives or literature.

The Hawkesworth family knew the company was betrayed. Stock manipulation played a part but how did ACM actually acquire all the patents and rights? Why did a Canadian plant never come into existence? Why did Mamie never receive any recompense? These questions most likely will never be known but ACM's history in similar cases was well documented in the "The War of the Copper Kings" and other publications.

Arthur worried about Borchardt and Berrian. Both these men were in middle management and were always good to and friends with Maurice throughout the ensuing years.

Final Moment

From: Hawkesworth Drill Company, P. O. Box 1971, Butte, Montana
To: Mary Hawkesworth at 2324 Yale Avenue, Butte, Montana

Dear Madam:

At a special meeting of the stockholders of the Hawkesworth Drill company, held on the 19th day of June 1939, the following resolution was adopted by a vote of 42,770 shares, representing more than 85% of the issued and outstanding capital stock of the Company:

"Resolved, that a liquidating dividend of Twelve Cents (12 cents) a share on all the issued and outstanding stock of the corporation be declared and that the officers and directors of this corporation distribute the said dividend to the stockholders entitled thereto and administer the property and assets of the corporation after the dissolution."

Pursuant to this resolution, there is enclosed herewith check for $1,374.96, which represents 12 cents a share on 11,458 shares standing in your name.

A small balance is still in the treasury which is being kept for the purpose of meeting any further emergency expenses.

The corporation is in process of a dissolution, and the officers will conduct its affairs for an additional three year period and will distribute any further assets which may come into their hands after payment of all debts and liabilities.

Yours very truly, J.D. Murphy, Secretary.

The Metals Bank and Trust Company

Mamie slowly entered the Metals Bank with her last check from the HDC. The couple's dreams were down to a piece of paper. A wistful smile passed over her Irish countenance as she realized where she was: 13 South Main, the former site of Butte's Theatre Comique. Here until the turn of the century was the heart of Butte's entertainment. Vaudeville and burlesque shows, legal prostitution and gambling occurred on this actual site. In the past this foundation had supported a garishly ornate facade structure with a sawdust floor. Its life had been fleeting like that of the HDC.

"Yes," Mamie reflected, "Our family, too, has a foundation even though our walls have crumpled. Something solid like this bank can emerge from Arthur's legacy. Our Hawkesworth creativity can be passed on to future generations."

With peace in her heart, she walked bravely to the bank teller and deposited on July 8, 1939, $1,374.96, the start of a new beginning. (Four years later on May 8, 1943, Mamie Hawkesworth received an additional $343.74, the final liquidating dividend.)

Mamie now known as "Gar" with grandchildren,
Lynn, Bill and Montel at her home on Yale Avenue in the 40's.

Board Members and Their Future

The Bowman name became prominent in Montana history: Bowman Airfield in Anaconda, Bowman Lane in Whitehall, Bowman Dam, Bowman County and

Bowman Gray School of Medicine to name a few. Ed Bowman's, Harry Galwey's and E. Murphy's names were found in Hoxie's address book of later years.

Gallwey, the expert in figures, the jovial Irishman, Montana's No.1 citizen in popularity died at age seventy-six Dec.27, 1942, three and one-half years after the dissolution of the HDC. His fairness, his manliness, his love of people was extolled by the Elks. They eulogized, "Wouldn't this world be better if folks we meet would say: I know something good about you and treat you just that way. Wouldn't we all be happy if the good that's in us all were the only thing about us that folks bothered to recall?"[5]

Harry died after a long illness. His age and health a possible factor lessening his contribution to the HDC board toward its end. Five columns in the Montana Standard elaborated his contributions to the states of Montana and Nevada. No mention of his fourteen years with the HDC, several as its President, was mentioned in the tightly controlled ACM paper.

J.D. Murphy was elected in January 1946, for a third term as President of the Butte Country Club, Montana's oldest and finest. *The Butte Daily* Post of January 28, 1946 reported that a rousing ovation greeted him after his report of clubhouse improvements, the new lockers, dining room space, condition of the golf greens and excellent financial condition of the club. Ironically, this news clip ran adjacent to Arthur's granddaughter Montel's picture for winning a city ski championship. No mention of his nearly twenty years with the HDC.

The ACM newspapers seldom mentioned Arthur's name after the week of his death. Even the Mining Museum in present day Butte has only a small, dusty bit displayed with a misspelled Hawkesworth name. The family tried multiple times to correct this error.

Small companies did not survive the ACM but memories linger. Yes, Anaconda was a good name for this company. It came from a Civil War Veteran who quoted Horace Greeley as saying Grant's army "encircled Lee's forces like a giant Anaconda."[6] Arthur Lee Hawkesworth's company was encircled. Life was cheap on the hill when Anaconda wanted something.

Final Unanswered Questions About the Hawkesworth Drill Bit

1. Why are no official records of this company, financial or otherwise, available in the Butte or State Archives except for a listing in the Butte phone directory for two years?
2. Why weren't other Hawkesworth Drill factories built?
3. Where did the profits go? Not to his widow or sons.
4. Why was the Hawkesworth Drill Company dissolved?

The year continued with its sorrows. Julia, Arthur's mother, was buried under her favorite tree after ninety-six years, one month and eleven days of vibrant life. Pneumonia after a cerebral hemorrhage which was preceded by three years of chronic nephritis ended her brilliant life on February 24. Her grandson, Dr. Maurice Miller, had made her later years comfortable in his home back in Bay City where Arthur's life began.

Maurice's brother, Lee, arrived from California after an emotional experience of finding his much loved wife, Elva, with another man. He quit his job, never remarried and remained in Butte.

After her stomach surgery was unsuccessful, Tecla's mother died November 13. A premonition, on her death bed elicited one of her last comments to her daughter, "Take my diamond ring. This is for Montel unless she enters the service of the Catholic Church."

Tecla O. Davis at Harding Way Spring, April 8, 1932.
Enjoying fresh air and spring water four days before Montel's birth.

Julia Clark Hawkesworth-86 years old in 1929.

Chapter Twenty-Two

A Family Challenge

For the rest of his life Maurice refused to talk much about the Hawkesworth Drill Company. He was bitterly disappointed and momentarily angry that the family company was betrayed and sold out from under them. Both he and Tecla knew they were outmaneuvered and wronged but they put the past behind them. They determined to make the world a better place to live in and they began. Their philosophy was to learn from their past, look to the future and live the present moment. The past was over. The future could be better. Maurice would have to deal with the ACM for the present as all his training was in mining and research. This was a one industry city and state in the throes of a depression.

Early fall of 1939, the thirty-two-year-old father aggressively entered the office of the vice-president of the Butte Mining operations, E. McGlone. He blurted out, "You won our company and the least you can do is to give me a job, even by God, if it's only that of a contract miner!"

Though available jobs were few, McGlone peered at this young, animated man and replied, "You will always be given work. Go see Borcherdt." Maurice turned to leave and impulsively replied, "And you damn well better take care of my mother. You know she has been wronged!"

His spirit ignited a spark deep within him and he would make it glow. He was willing to bide his time, the same as ACM had, but in the future he would come out the winner. He felt that deep in his heart.

Maurice, from then on known in the mining world as "Hoxie", commenced work for the ACM. He had been initiated into the Miner's Union #1 on Nov.12, 1934. His dues were stamped paid through Feb.3, 1936, but now he was on his own. He was hired as a contract miner. These workers did not belong to the Miner's Union but negotiated with the Company to produce a certain amount of work above the amount assigned to a union miner. Their pay scale had to be at least a union wage but they usually made more by producing more. In 1940, eighty percent of the miners worked on contracts.

A minuscule, pencil written diary had found its way into the crowded powder box. The fragile two-by-four inch pocket book held a record of daily occurrences in his life beginning with New Year's Eve, December 31, 1939 and ending October 19,1940, three days after he registered with the Selective Service.

Hoxie worked one-half of a shift at the Anselmo and interesting enough he was invited to the ACM's Research Department's New Year's Eve Party. He began his diary, "Party was a flop. Didn't have the old research spirit—oh, yes, made whoopee, in the dog house at least 24 hrs."

He had to work the night shift New Year's Day. Butte mines usually had three shifts: day from 8:00 a.m. to 4:00 p.m.; night from 4:00 p.m. to midnight and graveyard from midnight to 8:00 a.m. Hoxie worked one week day alternating with one week night during the year.

Butte miners, now with Hoxie one of them, arrived at the Dry House where they changed into work clothes. Next they joined their partner for the ride down the shaft to the level assigned. Many mine cages had four decks and could move up to thirty-two men at once. On a single deck cage seven ton skips were suspended below the deck for the ore removal.

Off from the main level men drilled and blasted ore in an area called a stope. These were adjacent to or above the main passage where ore veins were located. Some stopes became the size of a large room. The rock was sent down chutes to waiting ore cars. Other times raises were mined. These were vertical tunnels and footholds had to be cut into the rocks to enable passage upwards. Drifts were tunnels following an ore vein. All these areas produced muck which consisted of dirt, rocks and clay. Slush was soft mud and considered waste. Muck and slush were loaded into ore cars which ran on a narrow rail through the main level which was lighted. This was transferred to ore cages and hoisted to the surface.

Conditions underground were noisy, dusty from the powder blasts, wet from acidic waters which could reach 113 degrees, dark if your light went out, hot, 80 to 100 degrees F. with up to 100 percent humidity. The lower the level mined, the worse the environment encountered. A miner had to be aware of slabs of loose rock, of blasting times, of ore car movements, of bad air and of his footing. As late as 1939 an average of one miner a month was killed in the Butte mines. After a death the men often assembled for a "Boilermaker" at the nearest bar. This mix of beer, ale or brandy was hosted in memory of the departed comrade who now abided in the happy saloons of the heavens.

Miners were a special breed of persons, strong, brave, loyal and hard workers. Many drank to excess, gambled freely and enjoyed the "Red Light District." Their language was spicy, their comradery at the bars a legend. Their story telling held one spellbound either in total belief or jovial disbelief, sometimes a little of both at the same time.

Hoxie's steady work followed a pattern six days a week, eight hours a day. Mass at St. Patrick's or St. Ann's, then leisure with the family took top priority on Sunday, his one day off. Movies were popular. In January at the Rialto Theater he saw "Suwannee River" and "Gulliver's Travels" after waiting one and 3/4 hr. in the cold to get into the later with his family and mother.

He worked on a stope January 9 and finished a cycle study only to start a similar study at another mine, the Mt. Con, the same week. This mine was more than 4,000 feet deep and eventually reached 5293 feet. His partners were Vic Howard and Jim Doran and they worked the 8861-89w.section. On the Thursday night shift Jan.18, he slushed ore which was slow due to timber and boulder blockages. Outside it was forty degrees below zero and down below eighty degrees above. Ice was in a constant demand at these depths. He was a pall bearer for Mrs.Pryor after work. Funerals were always well attended in Butte and to be a pall bearer was a sign of honor.

Next shift he drilled eighteen holes and blasted. Saturday he finished mucking. Sunday he was exhausted. "Didn't go out of house today but read *Imperial City*. Mother and Lee came for dinner." A family tradition began the cold Butte evenings. They read snuggled close together by the spacious glowing fireplace.

A large dump truck had appeared with a load of remnants cut from timber cuttings for the mine tunnels during the previous cold week. "We were instructed to unload this in your backyard!" yelled the men to Tecla. This was the first unusual "gift" to arrive unannounced at their home. Here was enough wood for the winter. Mining officials either looked the other way or sent the load to help allay their guilt about the HDC by a small measure. The hard rock miners and middle management knew Hoxie had been wronged. They knew the true value of the bit and the ventilators. They never begrudged any favors granted Hoxie. He worked hard and was one of them. His family was never taunted or victims of pranks, a common occurrence if unjust words or actions were felt in Butte. He had no need of a bodyguard but did keep "at the ready" a small prospector's hammer pick under the front car seat. All through life this accompanied him but with good fortune it never was utilized for protection.

The rate paid him on January 29 for contract #425 was $5.9104+.75 which equaled $6.6604 per day average for twenty-four days of work. Every penny was stretched as far as possible. Starting the next contract period, he "slushed waste off top of chute, drilled, and hoisted timber." At home Feb.1 he "put on license plate 1-6046 and received both driving permits, city and state." Saturday he came down with a cold and Sunday "stayed in bed all day trying to break up cold."

Up the next day he slushed all week between five and seven large cars per shift plus drilled. Midweek he jotted down, "Cold still hanging on, feel tough as hell." Saturday, Feb.10, his brother Larry's father-in-law died at 12:00 p.m.

Sunday, a fishing trip to Georgetown Lake netted three trout and two gray fish. In the evening "went to Smith's wake with Tec." Feb. 12 "moved into our house year ago today. Finished floors. Attended Mr. Smith's funeral at 2:00 p.m. Hurley instructed Doran to keep lunch time." (Miners worked straight through on occasion to produce more and obtain a higher wage.)Regarding some cable job he wrote, "About 100 ft. of 3/8" cable good but thrown in waste."

Next Sunday:" Tec took Montel and Billy to the Rialto to see Fred Astaire in *Broadway Melody*. Went out to Ski Club and watched the jumps with Buck." He became interested in volunteering with this group of people.

"Started at the St. Lawrence day shift for four days with Mike Milosevich and Sylvan Grollo. Tuesday worked with Al Henrickson and J. Lyman. Cleaned down a stope and began a time study. Friday back at the Mt.Con. Men late getting up shaft. Ride choppy. Took 21 minutes to get out of mine."

This contract period he earned $7.39+.75 for a total of $8.14 a day.

Poker nights were big. Four or five friends usually played all night once a month. Judge Lamb, Bay and Earl Wagner, Pinoche, Buck and Hoxie rotated hosting at their homes. Sat. Feb. 24 he "lost thirty cents at home: A half hour of hard work's pay!" When times were better, they played for a case of beer.

On a bad weather Sunday he worked around the house, "painted end irons and broke one. Started to paint spots nicked in woodwork. Played pinochle with Tec. Won 2 out of 3." He always was a competitor.

During the week he worked raises, rescued men in accidents, commented on his different partners: "R.H. Simmons good mucker and machine man, D.A. Lewis, old and green, tries so hard." Conditions varied, "place has strong copper H2O but ventilation O.K." Saturday after work he discovered a flat tire. Tec was worried when he trudged in at 5:00 a.m. This old car had to go. No phones were in the mine yard to alert her to this situation.

Hoxie worked a grueling schedule. After work one exhausting day he joined some friends at a saloon for a quick one. This turned out to be a little longer than he planned. As he was about to slip away, Hoxie noticed that the bar tender had put out a new punch board. The prize was an Underwood typewriter. If he could win that for Tec, all would be forgiven for his late arrival home. He put up the five cents. His luck held out. He won. The anguished bar tender whispered, "Now Hoxie I've got to be at least sellin' enough to cover its cost. Sure n' wouldn ye be considerin' to leave it here a spell?"

Montel, Lynn and Billy with Judge Lamb and dog, Pal, outside home at 2324 Yale Ave.

Hoxie nodded in agreement. Along with receiving free drinks for his occasional piano playing, now he had another ace up his sleeve. Tecla, the skillful secretary, was delighted. All was well in the home that evening.

In March he saw *Gone With the Wind* with Tec, his mother and brother Lee. A dinner treat at the Rocky Mountain, a renowned Italian Meaderville Café, was a treat. This Butte suburb was named after Meader, an early geologist. who had been hired by Lewisohn, a dealer in copper commodities. The building where the HDC 's former offices were located was named after him. The children relished the bread sticks brought home for an after school treat.

After poker at Bay's where he was taken for $3.10 in March, his assignment changed. He was sent to the office to compile study reports for one week. "Had one afternoon off, hurray, but Montel came down with Scarlet Fever."

Gar left for California the next day. Hoxie went to St. Ann's and made his Easter Duty. The following week a "Quarantine Sign" went up. "Kicked out of my own house. It's hell being locked out of your own house, due to friend A.B." Hoxie moved to his mother's room at the Argyle Hotel.

Tecla told Maurice on the phone the moment had arrived to unwrap her parent's Santa Claus cup and saucer. This special service was only used from this time forward when one of their children became sick. It was always returned empty.

Lucky March 13 his dream car, a '38 Chev, arrived with 19,357 miles on the speedometer. He first drove by his "Quarantined home" where his family longingly waved to him.

On Saturday St. Patrick's Eve, he was given the afternoon off "Yes," he wrote, "The Irish made whoopee but I went to St. Pat's Mass at 6:00 a.m. sober."

Mining was very slow on the hill. The statement made to him at his hiring took on real meaning as he was the only one in the mine yard all week but he had work.

Hoxie was encouraged by his friends to run for the State Legislature. The Hawkesworth name was well known and the work his father accomplished in the Democratic Party gave him good access to key persons. Friday, March 22, Hoxie went in to see J. D. Murphy to give him his mother's address and to discuss the possible campaign.

"Got the go-ahead. Met Dan Kelly who was thrilled. K very pleasant, fine personality and I like him very much."

Montana residents needed legislation shaped by better moral and ethical principles. "All our state's wealth is being exported," Hoxie believed and took for his slogan, "For constructive legislation."

When Montel learned about the upcoming election, she took her father's campaign cards and went around the neighborhood. "Would you like to buy a picture of my Daddy? It cost five cents."

One of his friends responded, "Hoxie, I'll vote for you but damn if I pay five cents for your mug!" Montel's enthusiasm was temporarily squelched but she did have five nickels for the campaign treasury.

On Easter Sunday Hoxie "started to build a double garage with Lee, the real carpenter. Kids got pails, books and toys. Billy in bed."

A lonely husband eagerly moved back March 27. "Home again, Oh Boy, Oh Boy," but in his haste "left the radio on in the car all day." But no more cranking or constant flat tires proved a welcomed relief for the family. Sunday afternoon rides were special though Lynn complained, "My eyesight is getting damaged because I have to sit in the middle and stare at the bar holding the two-piece windshield in place."

Tecla, like her mother, was delighted to have some visual treats other than dingy, dirty Butte. Drives to Helena especially at lilac time, Dillon, Whitehall, Missoula, Georgetown and even the Shalkaho Pass provided these opportunities. This last drive, though beautiful, scared the three wide-eyed children. In the days before seat belts, they would get on the floor, pull a blanket over their heads and not dare to look down the open side, steep, one way dirt road at the 7100' elevation. Fear of another car, though unlikely in this remote wilderness, made an indelible impact on their young minds. They greatly favored going to Silver Star a small swimming resort thirty miles east of Butte where they all learned to swim. Butte had no public swimming pools.

Billy and Montel Fishing with Daddy Maurice near the Big Hole River.

Lynn and Billy Fishing at Bell Creek.

A nervous family including Gar and Lee attended Montel's first piano recital May 19. "The Happy Farmer" piece was a huge success so off they jaunted to Lydia's in Meaderville. As they entered the dining room, Montel played her first slot machine but didn't enjoy losing her precious nickel. That's all it took to diminish her interest in the twirling fruit for the present time. The delightful aroma of Italian spaghetti and meatballs begot a greater appeal.

Spring Sundays Hoxie labored on the garage part of the day followed by an afternoon car ride. When Larry needed help with three loads of black dirt, Maurice leaped at the chance to leave the garage work to come to his aid. Carpentry and plumbing were dreaded chores which he never quite got finished.

Early in April he "pulled a bull buying lumber, didn't need it. $17.20 shot to hell." Daily he listed his partners, their work areas, the challenges, who was fired, problems encountered. Another day was spent in the office working with

Buck on his Leonard mine stope time study. "Got along fine, turned out a dam good shift."

With Buck as his partner, his most challenging time as a contract miner began. They were to work one and a half shifts from 6:45 a.m. until 6:15 p.m. at the Anselmo. "Place hot and gassy. What a headache. Wonder if I'll be able to make it. Sure gassy and hot. Cooler not hooked up. Pretty tough grind. Was glad Sunday came with time to go to the country for a ride."

Next week he endured a 1 and 1/4 night shift for two nights and sighed his relief when assigned to the office. He worked on reports. "Hurray Saturday afternoon off! Bought lumber for garage." Early Sunday a loud noise awoke the family. Two big company dump trucks deposited three loads of sand and six loads of black dirt in the yard! Just what he needed. This "ACM gift" was followed by a week of office work where he wrote out six recommendations for various underground solutions.

1. Two slushers are no good because one is idle all the time. If you had two chutes, then this would work.
2. Better care needs to be used in laying floors. Too many openings at present and the ore slips through.
3. Poor methods are employed in blasting by cutting down on powder.
4. Axles and car couplers are in poor condition in too many occasions.
5. Ingersol Rand slusher is too fast and lacks adequate power.
6. Scatter blasting in block causes bad backs.

"I have the feeling this may be bad for me. Have a hunch by telling office the truth it may get me in bad with the mine bosses. The result will be to move me onto a tougher job. What's a fellow to do? I'm sticking to orders and giving them the truth."

Conscientiously, he made detailed surveys, finished a Jumbo Connection, wrote a valuable report on blasting methods, made intricate sketches, studied drift problems. He proved his mettle. His value to the company other than as a contract miner was about to produce new advancements.

A two-week vacation dawned on Election Day, July 15. "Lee, Larry, Emile, Buck and Putty (O'Donnell) and I checked returns till 6:00 p.m. on Wed. All in today, rested and got car fixed for vacation. Didn't win." His opponent, John O"Brien who was a member of the Fifteenth special session of the state legislative assembly and a member of the present Twenty-fourth, won.

Friday the family started for Yellowstone. "Made Old Faithful. Everything fine. Stayed at Cannon. Went over Cook City Highway. P.S. After getting found, we missed the sights. Staying at Thumb on Yellowstone Lake."

Time came to return to work July 31. Routine tasks ensued until Sat. Oct.19, when he experienced his first accident while conducting tests at the Orphan Girl

Mine. "R-51. Drop on left foot, cracked ankle bone and badly sprained it at 2300." Last entry in his diary.

When this labor intensive year came to an end, he was promoted to Shift Boss and then Assistant Foreman. Officials knew he was a valuable asset who had a pulse on the inner needs of a mine and the miners. He was keen to discover potential sources for mine injuries.

One tidbit of history took place at this time but was not publically announced. The wife of Marcus Daly, Jr. succumbed. Her estate was valued at $14,322,891 but only $163,244 was in Montana holdings. Another item: legalized gambling ended in Butte around this same period.

Music

Hoxie's music kept beat with the times and his work. If mining hadn't been the source of his livelihood, or if the musical miner had emerged in a later generation, he exhibited all the ingredients akin to a professional entertainer. He captivated audiences of any age. "Show Me the Way To Go Home" became his signature piece. Using this song, he composed a narrative to accompany a story about a legendary "Friend's Funeral March," another's "Wedding March," a classical "Piano Recital," "a child's Piano Recital" and a "Dance Party."

For the young he withdrew fleas from their hair and made them dance on paper while holding a hidden but fast moving pencil underneath. A cigarette tossed in the air was caught in his mouth. He created a different antic for each occasion. One greeting produced a chuckle. "Welcome back from the front, it's been a long years since I knows you." A pat on the back followed by one on the front; a pull on the ears, a twitch of the nose, accompanied the words. No matter how anyone felt or ached, his quick humor, sudden distractions stopped the crying or alleviated the pain.

Winter 1941

December seventh arrived. Life changed overnight in Butte. Production at the mines became crucial for the survival of the nation. Wages were frozen. The world was at war. Copper demand became insatiable. Mines worked full shifts. Butte propelled onto the national scene.

Hoxie received a phone call from the owner of a bicycle store in town one frosty 1942 March night around 8:00 p.m. "Hoxie, I know you want to get Montel a bike for her birthday. Come right now and I will open the back door of the store for you. All bike sales are to be frozen at midnight."

The last Schwinn bike sold in the city for the duration of the war was hastily tied to the car in the back alley. Nellie Baker, local school teacher, lived across the street from her favorite neighbors, Tecla and Hoxie. She opened the door gladly that evening and stored the bike until the appropriate day. What a surprise! "My father can do anything," Montel affirmed. Her friends agreed.

Last girl's bike sold in Butte when sales were frozen for the duration of WWII.

Advancements

Hoxie advanced to a safety and ventilation engineer in 1943. The upcoming year he was presented with a new challenge. Property and street cave-ins were occurring near and around the Emma Mine. Complaints had been filed by home owners. Maybe the near surface tunnels which in the past had connected the brothels to the uptown were part of the cause.

While in Canada, Borcherdt knew Hoxie had been shown a "Sand Injection and Filling Method" implemented by the Canadian mines. Maybe he could solve this problem for the ACM if he devised a similar operation. Hoxie delved into this challenge and succeeded.

A six page report to W.R. Russert, Asst. Supt. of Mines on May 20,1944, typed on "Tec's typewriter", detailed the procedures and costs of filling the empty tunnels. A summary follows:

"Steps have been taken to increase the volume of sand handled in the mine. Big Bertha(title given to the machine used to accomplish this feat) has been streamlined. The pipes and valves were changed so that the operator would have fewer moves to make, and now less time is required to put water into it. The chute holding sand was repaired and a good dumping arrangement was installed.

Sand boxes are being installed in the flat vein stopes and are placed so sand goes to the hanging wall, allowing the sand to make its own course to the footwall. It appears that boxes 20" wide are the most suitable.

Various type sprays have been used for mixing the sand with water. A spray consisting of one inch pipe with four 1/4 inch pipe flutes extending from it has been the most successful. It handles a larger volume of sand and the mix of water with sand seems to be of the right consistency.

Difficulty has been encountered with different grades of sand. Sand with lots of clay content does not work as successful as sand without it. When too much clay is encountered in the sand the water does not penetrate it. The water runs off or stays to the top of sand. Sand without a large amount of clay content causes less mess and is much easier to handle.

From May 13 to May 19,1944, 1028 large cars of sand and 508 small cars were dumped. That is, 3212.4 tons of sand were emptied out of 3435.190 actually delivered. The difference of 222.790 tons was in the waste pass.(Hoxie's figures were always accurate.)

Cost for one section that used 418.6 tons at $0.46 per ton was $192.56 with 4 percent tax at $7.70.

Labor costs for 31 shifts @ $6.40 plus $0.29 per shift compensation with four percent tax came to $268.31. With all the costs included, $1.12 was the price per ton of sand run through the pipe line.

Average tons per shift was 38.5.

Average guns per shift was 69.8.

For other sections, similar costs were itemized costing from $0.7321 to $1.333 per ton of sand used during this same week. What a small amount expended to preserve the environment.

To flood a mine was always a known disaster. Electrical pumping worked constantly, day and night, with water removed to precipitation plants. This along with ventilation was a necessary component of every mine. Sand fill-ins helped preclude the possibility of permanent floods and cave-ins.

Family Moments

Nine-year-old Billy quizzed his Dad, "What do you do exactly? The reply was short and to the point. "I am an efficiency expert."

"What does that mean?" his curious son retorted. "Well, I never take three steps doing something that could be done in two!"

"Oh, I'll have to think about that," and Billy went on to another project.

Tea is Served

Children can lighten an otherwise dark, depressing day. Montel's excitement over her latest experience resounded through the house as her dad returned home one evening after a hard day of work. Last week she had been chosen to represent Whittier's Girls Scout troop #20 to serve tea for the wives of mining officials at the most famous home in Butte, the Clark Mansion. This castle like building had eight ample fireplaces, elegant Tiffany styled stain glass windows, parquet floors and even hand painted wallpaper from Chicago's Marshall Field's store. Presidents of several troops were to assemble for the prestigious event. Then suddenly Montel became apprehensive. "I have never served at a tea and I won't know anyone," she moaned.

Gar produced a silver set that had sat dormant since Arthur's death. Tecla brought out a cherished souvenir silver teapot from the Great Northern Railroad and together they practiced with the young first class scout. When the day arrived, Gar whispered, "Don't worry, honey, they will all know who you are."

After a magical afternoon Montel greeted her father, "Daddy," she exclaimed, "When I told the ladies my name they said, 'So you are a young Hawkesworth' and they nodded to one another and were very nice to me. Maybe it was because I won the ski race." A knowing smile passed between her parents as they knew otherwise.

Sports

Skiing became a family event the winter of 1944. "Uncle Buck" O'Donnell was the first president of the newly formed city ski club, "Beef Trail." With his urging Hoxie helped to organize a Ski Patrol and presided over their training. The children began to ski under Buck's tutelage. Montel's Swedish genes came to the forefront helping her win several city championships over the years.

In the summer Lynn and Billy fished at the three-mile long Bell Creek at Butte's Annual Fishing Derby for children. Billy excelled as a sharpshooter at the local shooting range and took boxing lessons as well.

Vacations

Vacations included travel which at an early age broadened the young family's world. One weekend along with Gar they drove to the farm where their Dad had spent so many happy hours. After a full day of horseback riding, barn explorations and animal chases, the children were exhausted much to the adult's delight. Gar and Montel shared a bedroom. In the morning Montel had to use the bathroom and couldn't find one. Her grandmother introduced her to the "Chamber Pot." At that moment Montel decided this was not the life for her no matter how many horses her great-aunt had for them to ride. Fishing, too, she thought was boring. It's more fun to read and she could do that back home.

A trip to Seattle to visit the Wagners, Lenor, Bay, Earl, Fred, Marcia and Montel, was highlighted with a ferry ride to Bremerton. Such excitement as their boat purportedly passed one transporting President F.D. Roosevelt, their hero! They hadn't seen their favorite aunt and uncle since they moved from Butte shortly before the war began and were sad upon departure.

Glacier Park destination was a goal another year. The Royal Mountain Police were so grand but more importantly they went to Calgary and were transfixed with Hudson Bay Store's escalator. Going up and going down as many times as possible was a magnificent experience.

"How do things get names?" inquired an inquisitive Montel. She learned that Latin was the basis for many words including escalator which came from scala or step.

A visit to their imposing uncle, Colonel Thomas Davis and Aunt Frances, at Fort Douglas in Salt Lake, brought them for the first time to a location that was hot. "The temperature rose to over 100 degrees," they informed their wide-eyed friends.

Most of all they loved Yellowstone Park and chattered about the Old Faithful Geyser, and Grizzly bear cubs. As long as the cubs awesome 1500 pound, eight foot long mother stood motionless while the cubs foraged the children were entranced. Looking out the window was close enough for them. One morning as their dad sprinkled the sawdust on the pile of wood he had placed in the cabin's wood burning stove, he impressed his children. "That mother can eat one hundred fish a day. We must never get close to them."

The children decided that it was safer to drop a handkerchief into the fascinating blue "handkerchief pool" and watch it come out clean. The magnificent falls from a lookout point further awed them. With all this wonder to filter into their minds and the promise of a *Cubby in Wonderland* book from Old Faithful Lodge, it was not hard for them to be on their best behavior.

Singing, watching for Burma Shave Signs, and diligently coloring in their new books wiled away the long hours driving. A generation remained content and little realized the future held cell phones, computer games, recorded music and in car movies. The exhausted children were always ready to go home when vacations ended. Butte remained a wonderful place in a child's mind.

Chapter Twenty-Three

Safety First

Safety in the mines remained a high priority for Hoxie as it had for his father Arthur. While World War II raged on, he worked tirelessly on tedious reports with detailed suggestions for safety improvements in the mines. Miners worked at a furious pace to provide the raw materials needed for the planes and ships. School children were given time off to scour the mountain sides for scrap iron and metal of any kind.

Hoxie's innate skills and quick thinking adverted more than one tragedy. Miners followed his leadership willingly. In 1946 a well-earned appointment first as Chief Safety Engineer for five mines, the St. Lawrence Fire Fill, Belmont, High Ore, Tramway and St. Lawrence and then the entire Butte Hill was greeted with approval shortly after the war ceased.

Safety began to improve dramatically due to his relentless efforts. His "miners" experienced many new training programs and safety contests. Fatalities decreased rapidly. When one did occur, Hoxie experienced the heart wrenching moment of informing the nearest survivor. Detailed accounts of these tragedies were sent to John L. Boardman, Chairman of the ACM's Bureau of Safety. Tecla typed his first unpleasant account of a fatality, June 17, 1946.[1]

Fatal Mine Explosion

"The following is a report of the accidental death of John Witthoft, Card No. 78735, age 36, married, and residing at 2512 Elm Street. John Witthoft was fatally injured about 2:40 p.m. on June 10, 1946, while loading a drill hole with explosives at the Leonard Mine.

Raymond Panisko, partner, when interviewed stated that he and Mr. Witthoft were loading a 26-hole burn cut round. They had finished loading the lower part of round(16 holes) and built a staging in order to reach the remaining holes. The staging was about three feet from the sill and consisted of a 7'4" lagging supported by a ladder and empty powder box. Mr. Witthoft was loading the left-hand back hole while Panisko proceeded to load a right-hand breast hole. As they were loading, Mr. Witthoft paused for a moment and said, "Well, I got 12 sticks of powder in but I am going to put in two more," he also mentioned about going fishing on Miner's Union day. Then as he proceeded to tamp the twelfth stick of powder the explosion occurred.

Mr. Panisko also stated the explosion stunned him for a few seconds. He did not lose consciousness. When he regained his bearings, he found Mr. Witthoft had been knocked from the staging and was lying face down in a horizontal position. His face and right arm were covered with blood. There was a half inch of water there so Mr. Panisko put the top of a powder box under Mr. Witthoft's head and started to the station for help. He was met by John Connell and William Wafsted who had heard the blast and had started into the heading to see what had happened. Mr. Connell went into the heading while Mr. Panisko and Mr. Wafsted went to the station to call for help. Mr. Connell stated Mr. Witthoft moaned twice before he died.

Mr. Harry Gibson, Assistant Foreman, Mr. Joseph Harkins, shift boss, and I arrived with the stretcher within fifteen minutes after the call to surface. Upon arriving at the scene of the accident we could not, to the best of our knowledge, detect any signs of life in Mr. Witthoft's body. We removed his cap lamp battery from his belt. The cap lamp was burning although his protective hat had been badly damaged. His body was immediately placed on the stretcher and sent to surface. Upon reaching surface we were met by Dr. L.R. Nesbitt, who, after examination, pronounced Mr. Witthoft dead. The doctor also stated he believed death came almost instantaneously and was caused from concussion, shock and hemorrhage.

Mr. Panisko was sent to the Murray Hospital for a check up, however, he was not hospitalized and returned to work June 15, 1946.

A thorough examination was made of conditions at the working place. Water was dripping from the back and running from a few drill holes. The temperature was 85 degrees dry, 84 degrees wet, the humidity was 96 percent. The lower part of round(16 holes) was loaded and the wires from electric blasting caps were all shunted. The left back hole in which the explosion occurred was slightly sprung and enlarged a little at the collar of the hole. Electric primers were folded and had been placed in the collars of remaining holes to be loaded. The lagging used for staging had been removed, however, the ladder and a powder box used for support were still in place. The only equipment in the working face were the explosives and tamping sticks used in loading round. The tamping stick Mr. Witthoft used was found broken in pieces. One end of stick was mushrooming and splintered. Slide rails were three ½ ft. from a heading. The fan bag extended five sets from a heading and the wire supporting it had been extended two sets further. The pipe lines were 10 sets from the heading. The blasting box was locked and Mr. Panisko had the keys to the blasting box in his pocket. The plug to the blasting reel was disconnected, and the lead wires were four sets back from the heading and looped back for two more sets. The battery motor was standing about 110 feet from the heading, When the control handles of the battery motor were touched an electrical discharge could be felt. The last 100 feet into the heading was very wet. Water was dripping from back and running between the rails.

The remaining electric primers and loose sticks of powder were examined by the Engineering Research Department, and Mr. R. Sherman, the DuPont representative. After their examination no explanation as to the cause of the explosion could be determined. Mr. Sherman is sending several sticks of the loose dynamite found in the working place to the Eastern DuPont Laboratories for further analysis.

The cap lamp Mr. Witthoft was wearing at the times was not damaged. It continued to burn nine hours without showing any signs of dimming. No indication of any possible electrical discharge could be found on the lamp.

The Electrical Department investigated the site and the battery motor to see if it were possible for an electric current to reach the heading by any means other than the blasting lead wires used to set off the blast. After their examination they stated that they did not believe it possible for an electric current to reach the heading, even if an electrical short from motor or electric cable came in contact with the rails, pipe lines, and fan bag wires.

The cause of the explosion is unknown. As yet no evidence has been revealed as to whether the explosion was caused by the electric blasting cap of the Celex #2, 45% dynamite."

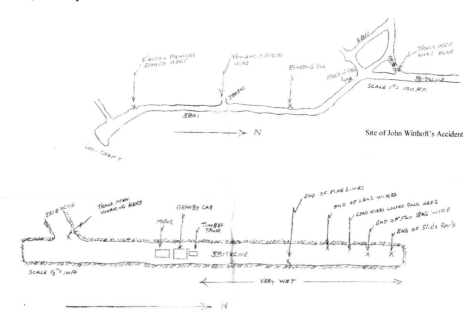

Site of John Witthoft's Accident

Location of John Witthoft's Fatal Accident.

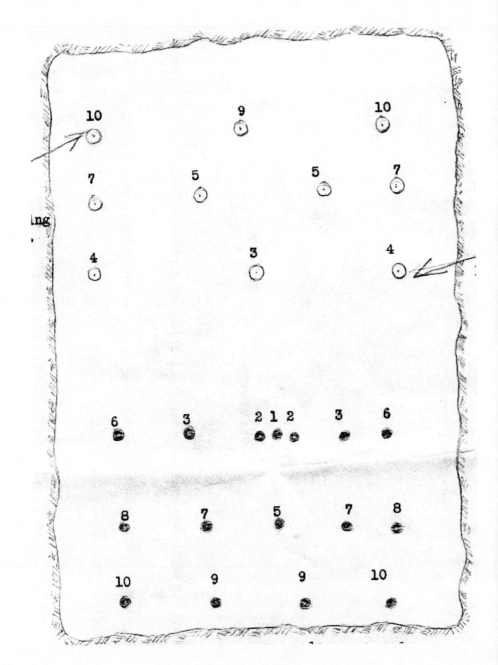

Panisko's Accident

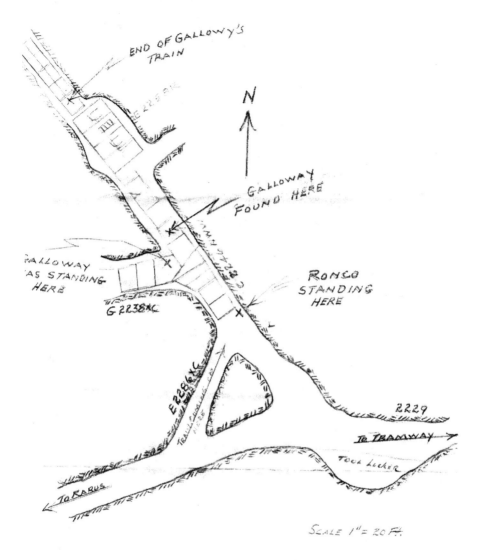

Diagram of Galloway's Accident

Fatal Ore Car Accident

Hoxie sadly sent this recap to John L. Boardman July 2, 1946:

"The following report concerns the accidental death at the Tramway Mine of Frank Galloway, card #11086, age 44, married, having three dependents and residing at 1119 East Galena St. Frank Galloway died at the Murray Hospital on June 24, 1946, about 3:30 p.m.

"Mr. Galloway was employed as a motorman and at the time of injury was performing his duty as a swamper, while his partner, Mr. Nick Fabatz, operated a battery motor.

The last man to talk to Mr. Galloway before he was injured was Mr. Ronco who was acting as a swamper on another motor crew, while his partner, Mr. Joe Darcy, operated a battery motor.

Mr. Ronco stated that he and his partner were going to "Y" four loaded Granby cars and while the cars were being pushed ahead, he stood at the intersection. At this time he met Mr. Galloway who was walking out ahead of his train. Mr. Galloway asked him if they were going to "Y" their cars and he said, "yes." At this time Mr. Galloway blew his whistle and his partner stopped his train. Mr. Darcy hearing the whistle also stopped his train. Mr. Ronco noticed Mr. Galloway standing in the clear at the intersection. Then Mr. Ronco signaled his partner Mr. Darcy by nodding his light, and Mr. Darcy proceeded to move the train. Suddenly they heard Mr. Galloway shout to stop, which Mr. Darcy did immediately. Mr. Ronco saw Mr. Galloway's light and body fall between two cars. Mr. Ronco climbed over a car and found Mr. Galloway lying between the cars. He blocked the car ahead and uncoupled the car while his partner pulled the other three cars back. Mr. Ronco held Mr. Galloway's head in his arms while his partner rushed to the station for help. Mr. Ronco called to Mr. Fabatz about the accident, who was unaware of it.

Mr. James Gregg, shift boss, arrived with the stretcher within a few minutes and rendered first aid, assisted by Mr. Eldred Chazer and the motor crews. Mr. Galloway was bandaged for a broken pelvis injury, placed in a stretcher and sent immediately to the hospital.

Upon questioning Mr. Fabatz he stated they were pushing out three loaded Granby cars and that Mr. Galloway was walking out ahead of the cars. He heard his whistle and stopped immediately, but did not know his partner was hurt until Mr. Ronco called to him.

An inspection was made of the conditions at the place Mr. Galloway was injured. There was ample space for Mr. Galloway to stand. The track was in good condition and the sill was free of any hazards outside of the possibilities of stumbling over the track. The timber north of the intersection was only wide enough to let the Granby cars through, the car clearance to post varying from 3" to 5".

This intersection is used to "Y" cars by four motor crews and a considerable amount of traffic takes place at this spot all during the shift. Mr. Galloway was an experienced motorman and was well acquainted with the method used to "Y" cars.

From the information received it appears that Mr. Galloway suddenly changed his mind, stepped ahead of the train, forgetting the danger involved for the moment and was struck by the front car of the train. He was knocked against a post, pushed between a set of timber and held there until the car passed by and he fell between the couplings.

Dr. Stephen Odgers stated that he believed Mr. Galloway's death was caused from a broken pelvis, punctured bladder, internal injuries and shock."

Just before Christmas on Dec. 19, 1946, Hoxie had a depressing report to finalize.

That morning when he left for work the air was so cold his breath went straight up toward the clear blue sky. Vapors could be seen all over the hill rising straight up into the calm, cold atmosphere. Before he reached the garage, his eyebrows were turning white from his breath. One walked slowly in these conditions. To hurry seared the linings of one's lungs.

"To remain focused in life is difficult," he mused, "from approaching cold weather being properly attired to preparing for the popular boxing events in town, from surviving the just finished war to driving in furious blizzards. Even family situations can take a toll on a person for a moment's lack of concentration. He remembered what Montel had told her mom the night before about the brothel."

Sex was not a subject discussed at any length between a fourteen year old and one's parents in the 40s. Montel and some friends discovered an interesting, high green fence two ½ blocks from Butte High. A curious sign proclaimed, "Men under 21 Keep Out." Now why they reasoned weren't the girls forbidden? They giggled when someone told them an outstanding statistic. A woman could pay $2.50 a day and enter and maybe make $100 a week when the mines were working. "Once we learned what a crib was and what services were rendered, we avoided the area," she had confided in her mom.

These thoughts momentarily distracted him from the task before him. Later that day, just one week before Christmas, he reluctantly wrote with a heavy heart to Boardman.

Air Compressor Accident

The following is a report of the accidental death of Joseph Sullivan, age 46, married, having seven dependents. He resided at 27 East LaPlatte Street. Joseph Sullivan has been employed as a machinist in this compressor plant since Oct. 2, 1943. Mr. Sullivan was instantly killed while changing the valves on No. 1 compressor at the Butte Hoist Compressor Plant on Dec. 14, 1946 at 8:55 a.m.

Knut Wikingstad employed as an iron worker in this plant since Jan. 14, 1946, was the working partner of Sullivan. Wikingstad was hospitalized for minor injuries of the head and left arm. When questioned Wikingstad stated that Harold Nevin, foreman of the plant, had reminded them to turn off the air valves and bleed the compressor before attempting to change the valves.

Sullivan went to get his coat and turn off the valves which were located outside the building. He returned within a few minutes with a set of socket wrenches and they removed two valve caps, not realizing that they had failed to turn off the air and bleed the cylinder. Sullivan placed the wrench on the nut to valve packing on his side. Sullivan held the socket wrench while Wikingstad stooped over to pick up the wrench bar, when both the valve assemblies flew out and one struck Sullivan. The air blast knocked Wikingstad down and stunned him for a few seconds. He then recalls crawling toward the north wall and realizing what had happened he started for the basement exit where he met Harold Nevin, John McGarry and Edward Kelly. These men had already turned off the air. Wikingstad was taken to the wash room where he received first aid treatment and was then sent to the hospital.

Lawrence Fellows, a compressor man, was about 50 feet from compressor No. 1 at the time of the accident. When the air was turned off, he noticed Sullivan was badly injured and immediately went to the phone and placed a call for the ambulance and a doctor.

Harold Nevin, machinist foreman of the plant, stated that he had lined up Sullivan and Wikingstad to remove the exhaust valves on the high pressure side of compressor No. 1. He called their attention to the importance of turning off air valves, and bleeding the residual pressure remaining in cylinders of the compressor before starting to remove the valves. Sullivan then walked to the basement with Nevin to get his coat before going outside to turn off the valves leading to the compressor while Nevin remained in the basement tool room. Within seven or eight minutes he heard a terrific air blast and immediately went upstairs to investigate. He found it impossible to get near compressor No. 1 because of the discharging air. The discharging air also blocked the exit to the door near compressor so he started for the basement exit where he met John McGarry and Edward Kelly, and motioned for them to follow him. They helped him to turn off the valves leading to the compressor which they found wide open. At this time they met Wikingstad who was on his way to turn off the valves. Wikingstad's face was bleeding so they sent him to the locker room where he was given first aid treatment and sent to the hospital. Returning inside the plant, they found Sullivan lying on his left side about 12 feet away from the high pressure cylinder of the compressor. Sullivan's head and chest were badly cut and they could not detect any signs of life in his body.

Dr. John B. Frisbee, after examining Sullivan, stated he believed his death came instantaneously, and was caused from a severe blow in his upper chest and internal bleeding.

Examination of conditions at the scene of the accident showed that the valve assembly, which weighs 55 pounds, after striking Sullivan was deflected and struck part of the compressor and bounced toward the north wall. The other valve struck the west wall of the plant and must have blown out while Wikingstad was stooping over, otherwise it would have struck him.

The recording pressure charts show the accident took place at 8:55 a.m. The air pressure at this time was 88 pounds per sq. in. The charts also show the air was turned off within three to four minutes after the accident. No. 1 compressor is a Nordberg High Efficiency two stage compressor, having an air intake of 7500 cu. ft. per minute. This compressor is located at the north entrance to the plant, which has seven other compressors.

Conditions in this plant are excellent. It is neat, clean and operated very efficiently.

The cause of this accident no doubt was forgetfulness on the part of Sullivan and Wikingstad. It may be advisable to have a large sign placed on any compressor needing repair work which would warn men to turn the air off and bleed off residual pressure."

Deathly Powder Explosion

Four months later death struck again as his report to Boardman relates.

"The following report concerns the accidental death of Percy Harris, age 45, single, having one dependent and residing at 3103 Carter Avenue. Percy Harris was instantly killed by an explosion of powder about 1:45 p.m. on April 14, 1947, while blasting a boulder in a Square Set Stope of the Tramway Mine.

Percy Harris was an experienced miner and was considered by his shift boss and fellow workers to be a safe and competent worker. He and his brother, Jim Harris, were working partners. They were cleaning down the broken rock in the stope at the time of the accident.

Jim Harris states he was operating a slusher while his brother was picking down the ore in the stope. Percy called to Jim and told him to get the slusher cable out of the way and get in the clear, because he was going to blast a boulder. Jim moved the slusher cables out of the way and went over to guard the manway and wait until his brother blasted the boulder. While waiting, he smoked a cigarette. After he heard the blast, he waited a reasonable length of time and started back in the Intermediate to put the slusher cables in position. He then found his brother lying dead in the Intermediate and immediately went for help. He met James Gregg, his shift boss, and John Riley on the 1700 Tramway Station. A call was placed to have the stretcher sent down and they went back to the working place. After examining the body Gregg sent Jim Harris to surface.

Jim Harris was asked what method was used when blasting boulders and he stated: Sometimes they would lay a stick of powder on a boulder while other times they would remove the wrapping from the powder and make a paster, leaving the fuse and primer in the center of the paster. They always used a full length fuse and after the charge was placed they would cut off all but about two feet of fuse before lighting it. One or two sticks of powder were used when blasting a boulder. He never saw his brother smoke while handling explosives. On the morning of April 14, 1947, Percy blasted boulders twice in the stope and he (Jim) blasted a large boulder in the Intermediate at 11:45 a.m. There was only the one blast made in the afternoon.

Due to the air current exhausting down the Raise, Jim Harris stated he was unable to see fuse or powder smoke when boulders were blasted in the stope.

When I reached the scene of the accident, the body was found lying face down in a humped position and the abdominal and chest organs were protruding. The right hand was pitted and bruised, and his clothes with the exception of his mine boots were blown off. The body was removed from the working place with the aid of shift bosses James Gregg, John Riley and Paul Wells.

The State Mine Inspectors Dennis Murphy and Alfred Giecek, chairman of the Tramway Mine grievance committee, were notified and taken to the scene of the accident.

Upon investigating the accident, it was found that the explosion took place on the third floor of stope in a hanging wall set. Blood, skin and parts of clothing were found in this location. The explosion had thrown Harris's body to an open set and his body fell two floors to the Intermediate. An eleven ½ foot long unlighted fuse was found near the scene of the explosion. The unpainted end of fuse was frayed which indicated the primer had been set off by a blow of some kind. Pieces of a can of Velvet tobacco were found scattered around. A metal cigarette case containing Camel cigarettes and matches were found in set next to site of the explosion. The case was closed and had several dents and small holes in it. A closed pocket knife was found at the base of a stope post close to the cigarette case. One wrapping from a stick of powder was also found. The stope was in good condition. The mining floor was covered and back lagged. No primers or sticks of powder were found in the working place. The muck pile on the third floor was tight and the boulder which had been blasted was in a hanging wall set, about 3 feet above the floor where Percy Harris had been standing. Only about one half a small mine car of rock had fallen to the Intermediate after the blast.

From the evidence obtained from the explosion, it is my belief the accident occurred when Percy Harris unwrapped a stick of powder, placed a fused primer in the powder and patted it down on top of the boulder to be blasted. After the charge was placed, it appears he was placing a rock over the charge to hold it in place. While doing so he either let the rock slip out of his hand, or set it down too hard on the primer, causing the primer to explode."

Carbon copies of this report were sent to A.C. Bigley, T.C. Wise and Company File.

Mandatory first aid training classes for the miners were his next accomplishment. Contests were scheduled and cartoon posters were visible at the entrance of each mine shaft. J. L. Burns drew a monthly poster. One featured St. Patrick wielding a shank with bit attached for a staff. He was chasing a snake named "Time Lost Accidents." The Tramway logged 7029 shifts with no time lost accidents while the Mt. View logged 8433 safe shifts. John Power's cartoon of a miner with a cigar whose smoke spelled out the numbers of safe shifts was an eye catcher.

8433 Shifts without an accident—Maurice Hawkesworth, Head Safety Engineer
l. to r.

1st row.-P. Scanlon, F. Schloss, A. Schoenberger, R.Bennett, M. Hawkesworth, R. Barich.

2nd row-A. Bjorckabacka, J. Sullivan, R. McKinney, R. Tait, F. Skubitz, L. Bogatz, G. Pascal.

3rd row-K. Williams, E. Best, V. Leonardi, L. Mitchell, E. Sullivan, G. Connors, J.W., G. Miller

4th row-W. Creber, T. Bennnett, P.O'Neil, J. Ferko, A. Thomas, T. Pardon, D. Martin, Campbell, R. Penzenik.

Each accident of the past year was analyzed and explained to the men. John Hara was instantly killed when his head was caught between the cage bar and a wallplate in the Diamond Shaft. Sherwood Lynn died in Murray Hospital after a fall at the Anselmo Mine. William Panion died of a ruptured liver eight days after he was injured when he fell through a hole on the first floor and landed on a timber truck stake at the Leonard Mine.

Other Fatalities

A fall of ground in a crosscut at the Mountain Con Mine instantly killed Sylvester Thompson on May 16. The same day Andrew Lindgren received fatal injuries after being stuck by an ore train at the Anselmo. He died the next day at the Murray Hospital. This same week Thomas H. Brown was injured when he was

171

struck on the left leg by a priming port cap which he was removing from a pump on the 1200 station of the High Ore Mine. The report from St. James Hospital where he died May 27 stated that he had a weak heart and that the mine injury brought on conditions which resulted in his death.

The classes proved effective. Injuries and death did occur but at a much slower rate.

A Family Awakens

At 1:30 a.m. on a cold spring morning the family was awakened from a blast that sounded as if a keg of powder had exploded. Two cars met headlong at the intersection of their corner home at Yale and Farragut. One was propelled onto their front porch. Within moments, Hoxie had four patients lying on the floor of their living room. Tecla phoned for an ambulance which was twenty minutes away. By its arrival Hoxie had an arm splinted, a neck stabilized, all adults covered with blankets and all bleeding under control. His children knew he stopped for any road side accident they encountered. A well-stocked trusty first aid kit was as close to him as a teenager's cell phone is to one of them in today's world. But this was a bit dramatic to three wide-eyed but very silent children.

The "Good Samaritan Rule" was highly regarded both for roadside or ski accidents. Qualified persons could provide medical aid with no fear of being held liable or sued.

Accidents never took a vacation. During the summer Patrick Deasy died of injuries received when he attempted to free a chute of a skip pocket at the Emma Mine. A fatal injury by a fall of ground in a stope of the ACM'S Phospate Mine at Conda, Idaho took the life of Elden Skinner, Sept. 8. Another fall of ground Nov.17 fatally injured J. W. McCloskey in a raise at the Emma Mine.

A total of 1,109,423.00 shifts were worked in the Butte Mines during 1947. This included 32,307.50 from the ACM's Phosphate Mine in Idaho. An additional 174,782.25 shifts were put in by the above ground shops. In the Butte mines a total of ten fatalities occurred in 1947 with only one of these in the five mines for which Hoxie was totally responsible. Each one was a grievous tragedy for the family involved. On the brighter side, this was a huge decrease from years ago when an average of one person a day met his demise.

As a matter of interest, the Hawkesworth Drill Shop had retained its name. This same year 8,328.25 shifts operated there. They had zero fatalities and zero accidents.

Statistics were kept for various categories which included fatal, serious, slight, lost time and no lost time injuries per 10,000 shifts for the six years he worked in the safety department. Hoxie kept meticulous records since his father had supervised his first diary. No calculators or laptops were invented yet but he relied on his trusty slide rule.

Total number of shifts worked in all ACM departments decreased yearly from the high in 1942 at the start of the war, 2,417, 790, to Hoxie's last full year, 1947, when the shifts totaled 1,284,205.25. Accident statistics also decreased.

On Feb. 19, 1948,unbeknown to him, Hoxie wrote up his last fatality report.

This report concerns the accidental death of George Shovlin, age 38, single, having no dependents and residing at the Gagnon House, 10 East Gagnon Street, Butte, Montana. George Shovlin died at the St. James Hospital on Feb. 14,1948. His death came as the result of injuries suffered on Feb. 13, 1948, about 11:30 a.m. at the Belmont Mine.

Timber Slide Accident

"George Shovlin, an experienced miner from Nevada, started to work for the ACM Jan. 24, 1948, at the Leonard Mine. He quit there Jan. 28 and started at the Belmont Mine on Feb. 3.

Investigation revealed the following circumstances regarding the accident:

On Feb. 13, Curtis Stanius, the shift boss, sent Shovlin to work with Charles J. Schons in J3044 Raise because Schon's regular partner was off. This was the first time they had ever worked together.

Schons said a blast had been made in the raise, and after they had barred down and were ready to timber, Shovlin went to the sill to hoist up the timber. While he was waiting for the timber, two saws were hoisted up with a note attached, asking him to send down his dull tools. Schons attached some tools to the hoisting cable and signaled his partner to lower the dull ones.

When the tools were being lowered, he noticed that the hoisting cable would not go down, so he climbed down six sets and found the counter weights jammed in the timber slide and held there by one 3" lagging. While he was freeing the counter weights, the 3" lagging fell down the timber slide. After the hoisting cable was freed, he went back up the raise. About 11:50 a.m. nothing had been hoisted, so he blasted a missed hole. Coming down the manway, he found another 3" lagging on the second floor and dropped it to the sill. Upon reaching the sill, he learned that his partner had been injured and sent to surface.

Fred Boeder, a repair miner, stated when Shovlin came down the raise, he asked him to run the timber hoist for him. Shovlin placed three 3" laggings on the timber chain of hoisting cable. Bruno Celli, the nipper, tied two saws and a note on the ring of the timber chain. When he started to hoist the lagging and saws, he noticed Shovlin standing at the bottom of the manway and told him not to stand there. Celli also told Shovlin to get away from the manway because something might fall. At this time, one 3" lagging fell down the timber slide. It only missed Shovlin by inches. Again Shovlin was told to move away from the manway. This time Shovlin moved across the drift directly in front of the manway. In about two or three minutes another 3" lagging fell. It struck Shovlin on the right side of his stomach. Celli and Boeder went to assist Shovlin. Upon examing him, they found no cuts but a large bruise on the right side of his abdomen. They placed him on a timber truck, covered him with their coats and took him to the station. At this time, Shovlin asked them what hit him, however, he was in a semiconscious condition. Surface was called and Shovlin was given first aid treatment, placed in a stretcher and sent to the hospital.

Examination of J3044 Raise was made with Dennis Murphy, State Mine Inspector, Frank Moore, Chairman of the Belmont Mine Grievance Committee and H. D. Gillis, Foreman. The raise was up a distance of 165 feet at an incline of 50 degrees. The timber slide and hoisting facilities were found to be in excellent condition.

The cause of the accident was the failure of Shovlin to stand in the clear of the manway especially when he had been forewarned. Furthermore, it seems that the lagging had not been fastened properly to the timber chain. Dr. Rotar of the St. James Hospital stated that Shovlin's death was the result of a ruptured kidney, liver, lower intestines and shock.

Hoxie's Accident

Next month Hoxie became a victim. A large boulder hit and broke his leg in two places. Hoxie relished showing family and friends his X-rays which vividly captured the images of the screws implanted in him by Dr. Pat Kane. His best friend, Buck, the acknowledged Butte cartoonist, provided an appropriate card.

Hoxie's recuperation was coming to an end. A strike was looming on the hill. Discontent with pay rates rose to the surface. Wages had been frozen during World War II. ACM's average gross income was $437,000.000, double its prewar levels. Copper had been in great demand throughout the war. Presently, automobiles were popular. An average car contained forty-five pounds of copper, the bulk in the radiator core. (Fifty years hence an average 2,200 sq. ft. home would contain 450 pounds of copper.) ACM had paid off its enormous debt. Their workers had been and were being exploited. A conflagration was about to erupt which would change Hoxie's life and that of his family forever.

Buck O'Donnell's get well card for Maurice in 1967.

Chapter Twenty-Four

Butte on Strike

The Miner's Union scheduled a strike for April 9. Hoxie received a phone call with instructions to arrive at a designated street corner at six a.m. promptly the morning of April 8 before the picket lines formed. An armored car would pick him up and transport him onto ACM property. Non-union men were expected to work. They would live in Pullman cars which were brought into the various mine yards.

Each of these men had to decide whether to work in order to maintain his job or to stay home in support of the miners. Several friends gathered around Hoxie's large dining room table two nights before the ominous moment. Montel sensed the tension, lay on her bedroom floor, watched and listened to the subdued conversation through a small opening in the door.

The stressed men discussed their options and the challenges that confronted them. At the conclusion of their conversations, they clasped sturdy hands in the center of the table and soberly vowed they would remain friends no matter what each one's conscience dictated.

Hoxie stayed home. The next day his three children were told not to answer the phone at any time and to come directly home from school. His tone put fear in their hearts.

The short wave radio, the family had tuned to hear Big Ben chimes in London while the World War II raged and the bombs dropped, was tuned now to the police reports of Butte. Before they had responded in unison, "London still stands!" Now it was, "Daddy, you're not a miner. Will we be safe?"

Every ACM worker was called or personally contacted. When the caller verified the man was home, he hung up. Those homes with no man to answer became targets. In school students formed alliances based on working and non working fathers. The lethal, brutal strike had started.

Union men snaked through the city streets in long lines of honking cars. When the targeted home was found, everyone jumped out, completely ransacked the home and painted a large yellow SCAB on the premise. Workers who were home owners watched from the gallows frames with binoculars to see if their property was a target.

A neighbor called Hoxie and said, "My wife and children boarded a bus to Idaho in the middle of last night. Would you please go into our house and take her cedar chest over to your home? We are prepared to lose everything else."

Under cover of darkness, Hoxie and a friend dug under the fence, furtively snatched the small chest and stored it in the attic unbeknown to his children. That house was not razed but the frightened family were forever grateful to Hoxie.

As the terrifying strike continued, a young teenage boy who sat next to Montel in Geometry class lost his eye in the family driveway, a random gun shot victim as he returned from school. A member of St. Ann's parish, Mrs. McNally, called the pastor and announced, "My boys and I have shotguns and we will shoot whoever comes into our yard. I hope God fogives us." Their house was spared.

When the short, divisive strike ceased on April 19, Hoxie got his job back on a "sick time" technicality. But a big decision had been made. No longer would he work for such a company. Recently friends made in Canada years before had been in contact with Hoxie. They had asked him to join their new bit company. The time was ripe now to respond in the affirmative. He was directed to the Western Rock Bit Manufacturing Company in Salt Lake which was presently in the planning stages.

Seven years ago Hoxie had entered the intimidating ACM head office to demand work. Today he started with a different approach, "I would like to request a leave of absence."

Bigley, head ACM official in Butte at the time, was not one to be caught off guard. He cagely responded, "Hoxie, you leave, you're gone."

Hoxie's heart dropped to the bottom of his stomach once again. Bigley continued, "I know what you plan to do, whom you have been in correspondence with and where you plan to go."

After a short pause he ended, "If your new employment doesn't work out, you can come back here and there will be a job for you." His next remark startled Hoxie but he kept a calm demeanor. "We've spent a lot of money on your training so make good use of it."

Hoxie left relieved, perplexed and wondered how much this man knew about the Hawkesworth Drill Company's contribution to ACM's financial success. Years later he would learn the answer.

Montel was disconsolate. She had just won the Senior Women's Ski Championship in her Sophomore year at Butte High School. The trophy had to be won three times to retain its ownership. After much thought and a few prayers, her parents came up with a solution to this problem.

Early one crisp May morning their new sixteen year old young lady went with her father to the St. Lawrence Mine yard. The steel head frame, hoist house, change house, large steel ore bins and ventilation building engulfed her presence. Donned with a yellow slicker, a tight fitting electric-lighted, heavy hard hat and ugly black rubber boots, Montel stepped into one of the four-decked crowded mine cages. Her instructions were clear. Don't look up, don't look down the narrow dirty mine shaft. A mine bell resounded, loud and clear. Grit was pouring on her hard hat from the scrapping feet on the open floor slats from above her.

Drop she did—several thousand feet free fall, long before the days of bungee jumping. After an abrupt halt she stepped from the crammed cage. Hoxie's friends were forewarned, "A young woman was coming so be on your best behavior." A sober no longer complaining Montel experienced the reality of a mine, the heat, the confinement, some terror, a new appreciation of life and open space.

That night her parents said all that was needed. "Your dad has put in his time underground. There is no longer a future here for us. Your grandfather never intended this to be his legacy. Sacrifices will be required from each of us. We have just finished the last mortgage payment on this house and we will have to start all over because our new home will cost more. Bill will have to forgo his next year's eighth grade graduation parties with his friends. Lynn will be going to a school alone without a brother or sister to walk with as Salt Lake has a middle school program."

Tecla went on, "Your dad is taking a considerable cut in pay at the start. I have to leave my lifetime friends. We will all be brave and go on to a new life."

Their cherished six room home with three bedrooms on a 90x100 foot lot with Uncle Lee's garage sold for $7800. The apprehensive family cried as they took a long last look and drove away.

Chapter Twenty-Five

A Bright New Beginning

Cultural shock confronted the three pilgrim children in Salt Lake City June 1948. None of them dared mentioned to Butte friends that they were about to live in a brick house! Only the poorest had brick homes in Butte's Dublin Gulch area. As they pulled into the concrete driveway to discover a beautifully manicured lawn and modern home, they gasped. Neighbors appeared as the awed family stepped from the 1938 Chevrolet car. "Hello," greeted one teenager, "What ward are you going to attend?"

Hawkesworth Home at 1661 Downington, Salt Lake City, 1948-1987.

Montel replied with some sophistication, "I'm not old enough to vote yet!" Mormons were to Salt Lake what Catholics were to Butte, the majority religion. They went to wards. She went to church. But the positive Hawkesworth spirit prevailed and the new residents leaped forward to a new beginning.

Hoxie began on his quest to become a brilliant mine engineer. Twenty-five years after Arthur's invention, Percival Liddicoat of Thompson Products, Canada, designed an improved detachable bit. Several million dollars in research aided him in this accomplishment. A successful heat and tempering process for the selected steel as well as the machinery needed to make them was the result. An innovative shipping feature included heavy gauge five-gallon cans that had stenciled on the exterior the essential content data. No more canvas bags were to be used for shipments.

Their first United States production and distribution center materialized in Salt Lake City. Hoxie accepted the position of field engineer along with Horace Siegel as Manager and Frank Gordon, production foreman. Hoxie demonstrated and sold the Liddicoat Bit.

In a short time a design of Hoxie's was added to their bit selections. Ironically, in *The National Geographic*, June 1950, the article about Butte featured a picture of an unnamed miner. It was Hoxie drilling with his father's bit!

At the "American Mining Congress" in Denver Sept.22, 1952, four years after his departure from Butte, Hoxie delivered an address, Excerpts from this filtered through the mining world.

Progress in the Development of the Rock Drill Bit

"The history of rock drilling has been a most interesting one. First, rock drilling was accomplished by hand, then pneumatic rock drills were used until the detachable drill bit invented by my father between 1918 and 1922 revolutionized drilling. This bit was improved by the threaded type bit which reduced fabrication costs. Progress on this was made because of slip—on connections. The one-bit used to destruction practice gradually replaced the threaded multiple use steel bit.

Since the introduction of detachable bits for use to destruction, the potential bit user today has a selection of bit connections and bit designs from which to choose. Experience has taught us that no one type of bit is suitable for every drilling condition. The reasons are the variations in rock formation and drilling practices.

There are bits designed with pilot construction for fast drilling. There are bits with under-cut wing design that offer maximum gauge wear when highly abrasive rock formations are drilled. The tungsten carbide bit has its place. Today manufacturers of rock drilling equipment continue to make improvements to increase the efficiency of the desired drill method. The choice of proper drilling equipment is most important."

Hoxie had input on the type of bit to be used in construction of the Glen Canyon Dam. When the first cable walkway, the width of a sidewalk, spanned the Colorado for this enterprise, Hoxie brought Tecla over to examine it. The searing temperature was 104 degrees with no shelter available on the Utah side. Tecla had to choose to "stay put or venture across." Hoxie cautioned, "Don't look down. It's 700 feet to the bottom!"

"The scariest moment of my whole life was this experience," Tecla confessed. "I could never do it again. My knees shook so badly it took days for them to quiet down."

The Feather River Dam at Orville, California, the tallest in the U.S. at 754' and "Hoxie's Highway," better known in Nevada as Glenbrook stretch on Spooner's Summit on Highway 50 were other projects on which he made an impact. Western mines, especially those in Colorado, and eastern coal fields used the bits he recommended.

Hoxie Indicates Site of Future Glen Canyon Dam.

Tecla walks over first span laid for the Glen Canyon Dam, 700' above the Colorado.

Best of friends: Maurice, Buck o'Donnell and Bill Moore.

Buck and Putty O'Donnell at Hawkesworth home.

Horace Siegel became a trusted friend as well as a business partner. Hoxie treasured his friends and was a good judge of character as well. The blue-eyed, friendly engineer could size up a situation quickly. Many volatile moments continued to be diffused with his quick wit and Irish humor.

Four of Tecla and Hoxie's best friends, Buck and Putty O'Donnell, Bill and Mary Moore, relocated to Salt Lake from Butte. All expressed disgust with Anaconda's exploitations and unethical practices. The depression and World War II had kept them marooned in Butte, the same as Hoxie and Tecla, but those days were in the past. What a relief to be free to explore other sites and bring their skills and experience with them.

New life time friends, Ben and Bev Andrus, Earl and Pearl Donnan and Mary Jeanne and Norbert Neumann enriched their leisure times as did others from the *Forty-Niners Club* at St. Ambrose Parish.

Together they shared many evenings around the beloved piano. One hundred and six well preserved sheet music copies dating from 1899 remained by the piano. Hoxie's story telling, love of singing and playing, surpassed his father's expectations. Straight-faced Bill Moore often recalled, "When Christmas holidays came around, Midnight Mass in Butte was packed just to hear Hoxie sing a solo. Buck and I had to push a wheelbarrow down the aisles for the collection. The church reaped more," he quipped, "than the former days when

183

a cup, no basket, was passed in church and gold dust was deposited for the contribution."

A pact was made by these former Butte mine workers that whoever died first, the others would water the grave to alleviate his thirst in the nether world. After the other two had passed, Hoxie exclaimed, "I'll only give them recycled Scotch as there is a shortage of the good stuff in dry Utah." In later years Hoxie never missed a Memorial Day at the cemetery.

Montel agreed with this decision as she recalled a difference in the drinking habits of the two cities. After she and two of her friends had walked the length of Main Street in Butte one day, the weary girls reported their tally: one hundred swinging door saloons and equally as many cuspidors. She knew Butte's reputation for drink. She told her wide-eyed Mormon friends that during Prohibition Butte had more illicit alcohol available per person than Chicago. Thirty-three pending Federal charges against Butte locals were dropped by the Supreme Court when prohibition ended Feb. 6 when she was one year old. Utah remained a dry state.

Chapter Twenty-Six

Butte and Beyond

Seven years after the Hawkesworth family departed, Butte mines progressively produced a lower grade of ore the deeper they descended. Excavation, ventilation and pumping became more of a challenge and less cost effective. Con Kelley and top officials decided to dig an open pit mine which they designated the *Berkeley Pit.* Displaced families scurried to find housing. The favorite restaurant town of Meaderville was about to be swallowed. Much to the dismay and sadness, the anger and protests of the population, the Columbia Gardens was obliterated but not until a mysterious fire had consumed its landmarks including the beloved roller coaster, merry go round, bi-planes, arcade and dance pavilion. Butte's most beautiful place, donated by the Copper King Clark, vanished even though it never did become part of the pit.

Hoxie shared these facts with his family after a business trip to Butte. He continued, "The Pit will eliminate a dozen mine yards including the St. Lawrence which Montel had descended. The forlorn hill is being denuded daily of 17,000 tons of ore. The Company offered only $1500 for the houses in Meaderville. Occupants had no choice as the homes were built on land leased from the Company."

Lee Hawkesworth at their home at 2021 Florida Christmas Day, 1955.

Last Copper King Expires

After fifty-five years with Anaconda, Con Kelley, the last of the Copper Kings, retired. Two years later the ruthless man expired. It was 1957.

Mining Convention

The "National Western Mining Conference" was held in Denver, Colorado February 7, 1957. Hoxie gave an informative address to the assembled mining officials, *Advantages of Single Use of Carbide Bits*. Sections of this speech would have intrigued his father. A short synopsis follows.

"The Liddicoat steel bit was the first bit made without threads. It was used to destruction without the necessity of re-sharpening. Several million have been sold each year. Over eighteen months ago work began on an entirely different approach to design and we now have the newly patented Liddicoat one-use Tee Cee bit. This six-ounce tungsten carbide insert bit is completely forged from a high nickel alloy steel. It is made with a taper socket in which there is inserted a brass shim.

Miners have experienced tremendous footage before failure, varying from double to several times the footage obtained with straight carbon and other alloy drill steels. The advantages of the Tee Cee used to destruction Liddicoat bits are:

> Low cost per bit.
> Increased drilling speed.
> No re-sharpening costs.
> Less handling of steel and bits.
> Increased production.

Hoxie cited examples of its efficacy. One of which was the following.

"Bits were tested in development drifts where conditions could be considered quite rugged. The integral steel, presently being used, drilled twenty-four feet before sharpening or a total of 124 feet per rod. In this ground the Tee Cee bit averaged sixty feet. The drilling speed increased fifteen to twenty percent. The over-all mine average at this property is about 115 feet for the Tee Cee bit."

The bit was successfully used by uranium companies. The footage drilled in the sandstone formation varied from 400 to over 1000 feet. Underground missile sites in the west adopted the bit for construction purposes as did the LDS church for caves in which to house their records. Hoxie experienced history at rock bottom.

Homebound Tecla

While Maurice traversed the world, Tecla kept their home his true haven. Each time he returned either to a newly painted room, a colorful crocheted afghan or a fashionably knitted pair of ski gloves. Once he received a shock. She had completed a "canning" project and had a homemade loaf of bread waiting for him. "What brought about this audacious talent?" he pursued.

Tecla countered simply, "Because all the neighbors do it!"

Her only unsuccessful project, wallpapering, brought about a few good laughs. Bill couldn't sleep one night because the paper kept cracking and falling in his newly decorated room!

Over the years she accrued travel miles as a chauffeur for the Sisters of the Holy Cross from the hospital or St. Mary of the Wasatch.

1960 to 1964

From St. James Hospital in Butte, Gar phoned her granddaughter, Montel, now known as Sister Claire Maurice, a first grade Sister of the Holy Cross teacher at St. Pius School in Redwood City, California. It was eight in the morning March 21, 1960. She calmly stated, "Honey, I am going to die today and I want you to know because you will not be allowed to come to the funeral. I don't want you to worry about that. I love you so much."

At noon Hoxie phoned and before he could say anything, Montel said, "I know, Gar has died and it was her 84th birthday."

Were Arthur and Gar remembered by the people in Butte? Besides her family 224 people attended her wake and/or funeral, fifty-four Masses were offered, two priests were in attendance and thirteen floral arrangements surrounded the altar. This was thirty-five years after Arthur's death.

Gar became entitled to Parent's Insurance Benefits under Title II of the Social Security Act three years before her death with a benefit of $72.70 monthly retroactive to July 1956. Her first check was for $945.10. At her death she owed the State Department of Public Welfare $1465.00 along with other bills and taxes accrued during her illness. These were covered from the sale of her property. The white, enclosed home with a sun porch at 2021 Florida sold for $3,000. As fate would have it, this was the price Arthur paid for their Argyle Street home in 1916.

A Visit With Gar. l.to r. Maurice, Milt Brown in back with
Sr. Claire Maurice, Sr. Agnes Loretto, Tecla and Gwenie Brown.

Hoxie's territory grew to include North and South America, Panama, Mexico, Hong Kong and the Philippines. To travel became a natural occurrence for him. He was at the forefront of a growing international business generation. A million-mile flyer ID metal card from United was awarded him in case "he would ever go down!" That card stood him in a good stead for a Chevas Regal on any United Airline trip he took even after retirement.

Western Rock Bit merged with Kennametal. Hoxie became the vice-president of what now would be termed the Pacific Rim Division with Horace Siegel, as president.

Tables turned. Hoxie received a request from ACM's Chuquicamata Mine officials in Chile to bring them up to date on new bits in November of 1963. At the airport in Santiago, some former friends brought him first to the Hotel Carrera and then to the expansive mining site. Hoxie encountered a pleasant surprise, Joe Novak, the mine's foreman.

"Isn't life strange," he informed Tecla during a phone call. Joe had grown up next door to Tecla on Second Street in Butte and their families were very close. Hoxie continued, "I've met several old Butte friends who have extended great hospitality to me. Sales are excellent."

Everywhere Hoxie traveled, be it in Cuzco or Lima, Peru; Arizona, California or the coal fields of Pennsylvania, he met mining people who had once worked with Anaconda. They all were familiar with the Hawkesworth Bit and its usurpations by Anaconda. They respected Hoxie and he, in turn, always gave them a fair deal and when abroad a piano rendition of the latest tunes back in the states. Hoxie once encountered former Senator Mike Mansfield who attended the School of Mines with him. He, too, knew all about the Hawkesworth Bit as did former President Hoover.

Jaunt to Mexico

In the spring of 1964 Tecla accompanied Hoxie to Mexico. At the last minute he needed to get twenty-five "jack bits" each weighing one and one half pounds across the border. He implicated Tecla and later told his children, "Your mother could always pack a purse and I promised her I would bring her the finest flowers if she were put in jail."

His humor continued, "It is so good to have Mother with me and take advantage of her vast knowledge of Spanish, if you know what I mean."(Tecla had two years of Spanish in college.)

Hoxie received an invitation while in Mexico from his old boss Bigley who presently was employed in Mexico City. Together the two couples toured the city's main attractions, including the University, and drove by several beautiful homes.

"It was a lovely day but I had trouble eating at the right times and was always glad for orange juice. People eat at different hours here," diabetic Tecla shared.

Bigley jokingly asked, "Hoxie does that fence still stand around your old home in Butte?" At that moment Hoxie knew the source of the sudden arrival of "products" at their former Butte home. When he drew up plans to build a fence, enough strong seven by nine-inch, eight and one-half foot long trolley ties for the fence posts had arrived along with two ten-foot poles. The city was discarding the trolley tracks in favor of buses.

"Yes," he nodded. "The fence remains as well as the house." Remembering the sturdy mine rope that accompanied the posts during a dark night, Hoxie laughed, "So does the swing."

"Your father was a great man and you're not so bad yourself," Bigley concluded as they departed his elegant home.

Reunion with Borcherdt

By the winter of the same year the Borcherdt's had moved to Salt Lake. Ed contacted Hoxie and invited the couple to dinner. Tecla wrote to Montel November 11. "Martha Borcherdt has cancer of the throat and is in bad shape. She is only sixty-one. I don't know how much they can do for that. We were there for dinner about a month ago. Ed has become a fine cook."

Two years later Tecla wrote after a dinner prepared by Eddie, "Martha is able to speak now. Last year she could just whisper. The cobalt treatments she took for cancer of the tongue and throat were very severe. She can't eat solid food as yet but she's holding her own. In six more years she will know if she is cured."

Hoxie came to realize that the middle management had no part of the stock manipulation or the demise of the HDC. These men appreciated the brilliance of Arthur. Try as they might they could not replicate or improve on his invention. Con Kelley, the daily Mass attendee, had called the shots. No one dared challenge this strong willed man concerning the Hawkesworth Drill Bits and Grinding Machines. He amassed them for his empire.

1965

Hoxie's second trip to the Chuquicamata Mine in Chile and other sections of South America started out by rail from Salt Lake via St. Louis and New York City Sunday, January 12. As he departed Indianapolis, three cars were added going to Washington, D.C. The weather turned bad. The train ran out of food but finally stopped to get more along the way. One car had a "hot box." To compound matters there was no heat on the train. Hoxie wrapped in a blanket. The train was hours late; Hoxie missed a dinner engagement but he was safe. Had he been flying, he would have been grounded. He had to wait until Jan.19 when the next flight left at 9:00 p.m. There was just one jet flight a week from New York to South America. As Mark Twain once expounded, "To travel is to experience the unexpected."

At the airport he met his old neighbor, Herbie Wendell, who was scheduled for the same flight. Herbie was present head of Anaconda's Safety Bureau. The long trip passed pleasantly. Herb recalled Hoxie's escapade of the furtive rescue of his family's chest during the strike. Hoxie learned about the latest conditions of the Anaconda Company. Herb in the past had invited Hoxie to judge the First Aid Contests held yearly at the Columbia Gardens.

Butte would always be a part of the Hawkesworth family, one way or the other. Hoxie's old friends made for an enriched, five week business trip.

On his return flight to the U.S., Hoxie had time to meditate and be thankful that he left the ACM when he did. It had been a big risk but the outcome many times superceded the initial pay cut he took. His work environment changed dramatically and his wages soon doubled his former salary from ACM. While his son attended Notre Dame University, a bonus check arrived every time a tuition bill did. Company bonuses ended when Bill graduated. Uncanny coincidences occurred all his life. Moments such as these fortified his belief that he had made the right choice and maintained the right attitude in the handling of his father's company. Grudges, thoughts, of what could or should have been done, did not produce happiness nor peace of mind. Hoxie always slept well, even on planes or cold trains.

Retirement

Over the years Hoxie attributed his success to the love he received from his high school sweetheart and to the guidance of the Holy Spirit. On his sixty-fifth birthday in 1972 he retired in good health and at peace. Another promise was fulfilled. "The day I retire I'm going to drink a bottle of Chevas Regal" and he did!

Maurice, the Pastie Maker.
Picture courtesy of the *Salt Lake City Tribune*,
March 3, 1983 with photo by Al Hartman.

After his retirement, Hoxie discovered a new talent. He became the daily breakfast and lunch cook in addition to mastering the art of making pasties. He beamed, his blue Irish eyes twinkled when pictures of this enterprise appeared on the front page of the Salt Lake City Tribune's food section.

The ACM was in financial distress by 1977. They had not kept up with the times and their lucrative Chuquicamata Mine in Chile was expropriated by Salvadore Allende. This largest mining camp in the world was supplying 2/3 to 3/4 of the ACM's profits at the time. The world market in copper was shrinking. Foreign competition with large ore reserves and lower labor costs ate into their profits. The corporate leaders decided to sell. Ironically, the ACM financed originally in large part by Standard Oil money was bought out by ARCO.

Berkeley Pit

For the next five years mining continued, then work ceased. A disastrous decision was made. The pumps in the mines were stopped. Toxic water began to weave its way through a minimum 2700 miles of tunnels and forty-two miles of vertical shafts. It searched for an opening like cars wending their way through a grid-locked interchange and entered into the vacated pit by 1983. A gruesome site, one and a half miles long, one mile wide and one-third mile deep, had been gorged out of the "Richest Hill on Earth." The city hurt, the people hurt, the wildlife hurt.

Twenty-five years after Kelley's death the city reeled from his decisions. The cavernous Berkeley Pit received six million gallons of contaminated toxic water a day. It had become the nation's largest Superfund Site. Some pertinent facts put this latest tragedy in perspective in 2005.

1. Butte's ground water level is above the present water depth of the pit.
2. The pit will never be completely emptied.
3. BP/Atlantic Richfield and Montana Resources, present owners, are responsible in perpetuity not to let the water rise above the 5410' elevation or steep fines will be imposed.
4. The water level was at the 5,255' elevation in the fall of 2005. The water depth is over 900' feet.
5. The water in the pit rises approximately one foot per month depending on weather conditions.

What is being done to alleviate a pending disaster?

1. A treatment plant called Horseshoe Bend Precipitation Plant is in operation. Water is pumped upward from the pit. A simple process of copper recovery is employed whereby water flows through piles of scrap iron which contains chemicals that cause the copper to deposit. Iron water, in turn, is carried back

to the pit by means of a waterfall. The copper is subsequently smelted and the iron water decreases the toxicity of the pit water. In the fall of 2005 two million gallons a day was pumped from the pit through the plant. The goal was to retrieve 400,000 pounds of copper a month from this process.

2. To protect wild life, especially migratory birds, natural predatory sounds are used. A houseboat patrols the waters with the crew rescuing distressed birds. Experts state a bird can sustain life up to four hours on the water before permanent damage is done. Water and wild life are being monitored as are earthquake potentials.[1]

Water and wild life are being addressed. What about the third "W," the retired, the laid off and injured workers of this vast enterprise that began over a century ago as the Anaconda Mining Company? A question few dare or want to discuss.

Life, memories, hope continued to be drowned. A generation slowly disappeared in Butte.

The Vast Beyond

Hoxie ended his vibrant life at his daughter Lynn's home in Reno June 9,1985. In contrast to Kelley, he left a legacy of honesty, perseverance, cheerfulness and hard work. At an intimate family funeral at Our Lady of Snows, Montel shared some highlights of his life.

"Hoxie loved his wife and family. They were number one in his life. "The Little Giant", as he was often called, took great interest in their activities and accomplishments. He loved to hear from and about them.

For each person in his life he had a song. He could play any tune one could hum. He composed the music and wrote "Heaven on Earth" for mom. Bravely, but with a slight quiver, he sang it a cappella to her during their fiftieth wedding anniversary Mass.

As a favorite story teller, he had an anecdote for every occasion from Hong Kong to San Francisco, his favorite city.

A romantic at heart, he remembered every anniversary with a celebration and had a fresh rose for Mom every day on the table after his retirement.

He loved life, lived it to its fullest. He always did his best and would say, "If you do your best that's all that matters." Those words in regard to a sub par grade received at school remedied that situation for his children.

For his lucky number of grandchildren, thirteen, Grandpa dear had a unique song. He often quipped, "I've got two joys in my life, joys when they come and joys when they go."

A deep love of Montana, especially Butte, was always evident. He was a mining man—even to his language—which at times could be sprinkled with a few, "Well, I'll be a son of a b . . .."

Dad loved his Catholic faith. He lived to bring us life and he showed us *The Way to Go Home*. He will greet us when we arrive in the land of milk and honey."

All his life he defused poignant situations with his humor. At the Gate of Heaven Cemetery in Los Altos, Ca a deluge engulfed the funeral party as the cremains were about to be placed in the flower box surrounding the Virgin Mary's Shrine. An embarrassed employee hurried to bail some water out. Montel assured him, "Don't worry, my dad was a hard rock miner and he can deal with this environment." Hoxie provided his last gift of humor to us.

Tecla continued to keep in touch with her family. She moved from Salt Lake after thirty-eight years as a resident to Palo Alto, California, to live with Montel and Al in 1986. With her came the piano. For its one hundredth birthday a surprise party was thrown in its honor. A digital image was transcribed onto a cake's frosting while Hoxie's original copies of hit songs popular over its lifetime were framed and on display.

Tecla's bright smile and shiny eyes greeted all who came in contact with her for the next eight years. After three hip surgeries and a broken leg, her health deteriorated. Her final two months were in a nursing home where her pain could be better alleviated.

At five p.m. twelve hours before her death she weakly said, "I hurt." A pact had been made when she came to live in Palo Alto. She would be told if death were imminent. Montel produced a mini Chevas Regal and said, "Mom, it's cocktail time and if I send you off to Dad without your drink, I'll be in deep trouble. Here's thanks from all of us for such a wonderful life. Please tell Dad the same. Now you will never hurt again."

The nurse administered the morphine. Tecla managed ever so slight a smile but a look of deep love radiated from her tear-filled eyes. The next morning Tecla had a serene and beautiful countenance. It was Dec.28, 1994. Her eighty-six years were now a legend. For her funeralHoxie's song, "Heaven on Earth" was sung.

God gave me you
God gave you me
For better or for worse.
He gave to you
He gave to me
A Heaven here on earth.
We've had our ups
We've had our downs.
We've had teardrops in our eyes.
We've had our laughs
We've had our smiles

As years go rolling by.
Most of our plans
Most of our dreams
It seems have all come true.
Because God made a Heaven here
On earth for me and you.

How touched the couple would have been to know this song was to become part of many weddings of their grandchildren. Bill wrote a fitting tribute to a most wonderful wife and mother.

"One of the ancient Greek philosophers wrote that what a person does speaks so loudly that you cannot hear what they say. This philosophy reflected our mother's life in many ways.

She and our father were splendid teachers while my sisters and I were growing up. We learned the virtues of honesty, integrity and respect—not from what they said—but what they did—through their examples. Educators talk of the importance of learning the basic skills of reading, writing and mathematics. But equally important, they stress, is the building of confidence and self esteem.

Along with the basic skills, we were taught to be self confident, so much so that whether we were that capable or not, it didn't matter. We thought we were and it became self fulfilling. We were raised on comments like 'you can do it, try harder, don't give up, self pity stinks, self praise stinks.' We learned to rely on our own abilities and to keep trying.

Most of mom's comments were positive and supportive. I can't remember her using a vulgarity, not so with Hoxie. Mom was always trying to clean up his act. But there was one word I do remember, that was being called, "Chump." It means a fool. That was my punishment for disobedience.

Mom gave a wonderful example of self discipline. As a diabetic for more than forty years, she had to be extremely careful of her diet. I remember seeing her measuring and weighing her food in the early years of her illness. This discipline was directly responsible for her living many more years than would be expected.

Even though she demonstrated strong self control, she never tried to control others. Rather she was positive and supportive of us all no matter what adventure we undertook. A good example was her support of Montel when she entered the convent. Her only comment was, 'If you are not happy, you come home.'

On the other hand, when I was so lucky to go away to Notre Dame, she said, 'I hope they don't send you home.' In the past few years after mom had two or three strokes, she had difficulty speaking, but here she was positive, too. 'Very good' became a part of her vocabulary.It wasn't 'I can't' or 'don't'. What she said most often was 'very good.'

As her condition worsened, our mother accepted life on its own terms. She had to rely on strangers for many of her basic necessities her last two months of life when it became impossible to care for her adequately at home. She never once complained and instead said, 'You have to adjust in life.' She did it with grace and good spirit. She was still teaching us about life. But now there was a new lesson, one that we all have to face—death. She met it with courage and acceptance."

Tecla and Hoxie had a special affection for the Notre Dame Football team. By chance, Tecla was featured on the front page of the *Honolulu Star Bulletin* with Lou Holtz as he arrived in Hawaii to coach the All Star Game after N.D.'s national championship. Her niece and her husband, Nancy and Paul Giel, had hired Lou as coach of the Minnesota football team and let him have a release clause "if Notre Dame came calling." Lou did not know Tecla until the Giel's sent him a picture and identified her. So for Tecla's funeral recessional, the Notre Dame Victory March boomed out. After a second of surprise, the full church burst out in applause and said, "Now that's the way to go home." Tecla was a winner.

Chapter Twenty-Seven

Reflections

1900 to 2000 has now elapsed.

During this span of time Montana Territory became the fourth largest state in the Union.

Butte continued to be exploited.

ACM became defunct.

Arthur became forgotten.

2000 onward: A new century progresses forward.

Montana is a tourist haven where the millionaires return now to enjoy its natural beauty.

Butte struggles with the Berkeley Pit which has become a tourist attraction with admission fees.

Arthur's ancestors contribute globally.

New discoveries of copper, coal and natural gas provide energy resources once again for the nation. Resurgence in mining is at a high for modern times.

In the fall of 2005 Montana Governor Schweitzer announced to the nation that the "Treasure State" or "Big Sky Country" as it came to be called should become a leader in energy in today's economy. It possesses 30 percent of the nation's coal and 9 percent of the world's supply. There is adequate coal to provide diesel and aviation fuel for the United States for forty years. With this the country as a whole has enough fuel resources for the next 150 years.

If production becomes a reality, hopefully the environmental issues associated with mining will be addressed. Current issues of saline and sodic water (CBM water or coal bed methane) can be overcome.[1]

OT Mining Corporation is revitalizing mining. "By following a distinctly modern geological approach, using the latest cutting edge technology . . . OT Mining has identified features . . . of an undiscovered ore body. They estimate a geological reserve of immense proportions still exists, possibly several billion tons in the Butte district."[2]

Montana Resources production for 2004 was estimated at 65 million pounds of copper, 580,000 ounces of silver and 6 million pounds of molybdenum. Montana Tech, formerly named Montana School of Mines when Tecla and Maurice attended there, graduated their first class in the new century of "Underground Miners" in the spring of 2004. Instructor Al Elge shared, "They learn the biggest thing to underground miner training is safety and proper work area inspection and pre-shift gear inspection."[3]

Hoxie and Arthur would approve. The nation as a whole realizes this after the mine disasters of 2006.

Butte and Montana can learn from their past. New bits and drills can bore into virgin fields. Hopefully, progress can be made without excessive corruption and exploitation. The future looms brightly once again in Montana.

A Question Remains and an Answer is Postulated

Who won and who lost during the saga of the Anaconda Copper Mining Company and the Hawkesworth Drill Company?

Losers:

1. Anaconda Copper Mining Company: a greedy company, a cunning company, a now defunct company.
2. A Copper King whose legacy included the destruction of the Columbia Gardens, the polluted Berkeley Pit, the struggling, raped city and its exploited workers.
3. Corrupt politicians.
4. The persons responsible for the flooded mines and the Milford Dam.[4]

A microcosm had been set in motion in the wilderness of America. A state, a city, an individual had been exploited and terrorized by an unethical company.

Today an Enron, a Worldcom, religious extremists, corrupt politicians and lobbyists, terrorists such as Al Q'aida exploit or terrorize on a larger scale. Money, greed, power, fame remain the magnetic elixirs for them.

Winners:

1. Mike Mansfield, a wise and honest Montana politician who began in 1943 as a member of Congress and then leader of the US Senate. He obtained approximately 22 million in Federal Funds for Butte's Urban Renewal and Model Cities programs which commenced in 1969. This was followed by his ambassador post to Japan. He ended his years of service in 1988.[5]

2. The Butte City Council Members who kept the uptown district as a Historical Site with the help of the Montana Power Company rather than have ACM amass the area for its open pit mine.

3. The Butte people who erected a monument to its mothers, "Our Lady of the Rockies",located on the eastern mountain top at a popular site known as Saddle Rock. This 100' statue is illuminated at night. In the day time it overlooks the beauty of Montana to the East and the devastation of the once "Richest Hill on Earth" to the West. Three deceased Hawkesworth mothers have their names engraved at this memorial.

4. The Butte artists who plan to contribute a magnificent hand-carved replica of Columbia Garden's merry-go-round in memory of the original one. A section of this features a carving of the Hawkesworth bit designed by his grandson, Bill.

5. The historians and technicians, Terry Lonner and Fritz Apostle. They produced a PBS Documentary about Butte's former ski club, "The Beef Trail."[6] Three Hawkesworth children contributed to the filming of this production.

6. The Butte natives who moved onto other sites in the world but who brought warmth, dedication to hard work and a spirit of friendliness nurtured in them by living in Butte.

7. The "ordinary" people of Butte, the miners and their families who over the years despite unsurmountable hardships hold this city of 34,000 residents together and who hope for a new tomorrow.

8. Arthur and his son, Maurice, who were great men, honest men, beloved men. They among other forgotten heros made possible a better environment for miners and construction workers wherever they journeyed.

Along with these winners the world has produced the Jimmy Carters, Bob Hopes, Mother Teresas and Pope Johns. Service, humor, wisdom, compassion were their goals.

Pope John Paul II issued a "World of Peace" statement Jan.1, 1990, "The earth is ultimately a common heritage, the fruits of which are for the benefit of all . . . It is manifestly unjust that a privileged few should continue to accumulate excess goods, squandering available resources, while masses of people are living in conditions of misery."[7]

In the past as in today our world has the truly wealthy and the devastating poor; the well fed and the starving; the honest politicians, the corrupt exploiters; the far right conservatives, the far left liberals. To find one's path through the maze is a monumental challenge but it can and has been done. A truly human genius whether a humorist, musician, politician, business or religious person can stand in the middle and touch and serve both extremes in life. Arthur and Maurice were two who accomplished this feat.

Epilogue

Arthur and Gar Hawkesworth's Descendants

Maurice and Tecla's Children

Montel became a Sister of the Holy Cross for twenty-one years. During four of her active work years she taught in the Watt's District of Los Angeles. She was in the curfew zone during the riots. "Sisters, just stay inside. We will protect you." Not a mark was put on their school and two weeks later when school started the nuns could have quadrupled the enrollment if there had been room. Teaching was in the family genes.

After leaving the convent in 1971, Montel became an "instant mother" to four children when she married Al Menting, a widower, Sept. 2, 1972. Montel once said, "I rode across the Missouri with my Uncle Reese, a railroad engineer, in the cab of a Great Northern steam engine, went deep underground with my mining engineer father and rode in the cockpit of a 747 for a few minutes with my pilot engineer husband across the Pacific. This last in the good 'old days of flying'. I've been almost a mile deep, over a mile high and a mile on an even grade across the Missouri River."

Montel, as a director of religious education in San Jose, California, organized a "Theology of Leisure" program and chartered a United DC8 for parishioners in 1973. Four nights in Honolulu and three on the Big Island for $ 343 per person included airfare, hotels and land transportation. Twenty years later Al volunteered at Stanford Hospital in the Chaplaincy Program. He entered a room of a dying patient. The wife exclaimed, "We just shared the happiest moments of our long life and we both agreed that the St. Martin's Parish Hawaiian Trip was our best vacation and in you walked!" Montel always believed leisure was as important as work, a trait her parent's exemplified.

When President for a two-year term and long time board member of Palo Alto's Sister City, Neighbors Abroad, she participated in programs with Oaxaca, Mexico and Palo, Leyte, Philippines. The birth city of her grandmother Davis, Linkoping, Sweden, was part of this international group as was Enschede, Holland and Albi, France. She obtained a world wide vision.

Her step children live in three different states. Tina and her son, Joe, enjoy many things including computer projects, fishing and ceramics. Tony is an interstate truck driver and his son, Cody, and Mary, the love of his life, always are happy to see him home. Terri operates a home care program for three infants. Her husband, Brian Setnick, is a Senior Vice-President and cash management expert in the banking world but most of all they comprise a loving family with two delightful young children, Erica and Sean. Ted, a graphic artist, has three sons, Kevin a U.S. Marine and T. J., from a first marriage and McLane with Sheri whom he married in Michigan.

Montel revisits a mine cage at the Mining Museum in Butte.

Summer Sunday afternoons for the family at St. Mary of the Wasatch in Salt Lake.

Montel and Al Menting's Wedding with her uncle Larry far right and
Aunt Etta, far left in Palo Alto,CA.

Bill Hawkesworth and Family

Bill, with his Communication Degree from Notre Dame, served in the Marines. Then he began work with Joe Boland at WSBT in South Bend, Indiana, and on to the UPI in Salt Lake. He followed in his father and grandfather's political footsteps when he managed a gubernatorial campaign for a candidate running for Utah's governor.

For twenty-five years he was Director of Community Relations for Hercules in Delaware. Bill's creative and artistic mind contributed to the award winning ecology film, *Hercules at Hattiesburg*. He spent many hours as a volunteer for the local Red Cross, as had his Ryerson ancestor, receiving the highest honor the Delaware Chapter of the American Red Cross bestows. Bill and Montel gave many gallons of blood while Lynn holds the family record of more than one hundred donations.

Bill and his wife, Martha Beikes, brought five creative children into the world. After the children left home, Bill and Martha journeyed back to Salt Lake where Bill helped with environmental projects for Hercules and subsequently became owner of the Sylvan Learning Center.

Bill's Offspring

Upon Martha's sudden death, Bill, Jr., their oldest son, became director of the center. He. continued to provide encouragement and tools for success for students. Also as a teacher for his parish's Confirmation classes, he helped his pupils to witness their Catholic faith in Utah. When told of his father's confirmation experience in Butte, he laughed. "Jim McCracken, the owner of Butte's junkyard appeared at practice attired in dirty work clothes! His father had a nightmare before the event and didn't want to be confirmed. What relief it was to him to see Jim dressed in a suit. That's all my father remembered about his confirmation." (Bill, Sr. became sponsor for his granddaughter Ashley in 2006 and came to practice in a suit!)

Bill, Jr's two daughters bring vitality and hope to the family. Laura, a University of Loyola student previously helped manage and taught three years in a Time Warner compound in Shanghai. Fluent now in Chinese another Hawkesworth has contributed internationally. Christie prepared for her future as a teacher graduating from the University of Utah in Education and Business in 2006. Debbie, his energetic wife, is a leader in the Phoenix Department of Agriculture.

M. Maurice, their second son, inherited the Hawkesworth love for music and art. He and his two student sons, Ian and Niclas, live in Denmark. Maurice discovered and mixed the music for the group "Ace of Base." The original album *Happy Nation* sold seven million copies, repackaged as the *Sign*, it sold another 20 million. He helped place more than thirty videos on MTV and was the founder of the label *Iwaves Records* in 1999.

His *Hole in the Wall* poster depicts the first crack in the Berlin Wall and was exhibited in Amsterdam. Along with this another poster, *Berlin 1990,* is among the Hoover Institution Archives Poster Collection in Stanford, California.

Joe married Kenni Ann, the joy of his life along with their daughter, Skylar. Joe is an independent construction engineer and former project manager of many commercial sites in and around Jupiter, Florida. His family enjoys their boat on the Florida inland waterways.

Mary Delores Fasick is an energetic, only daughter, whose personality and sense of family keep everyone together in spirit. She, too, is a VIP donor with the Red Cross. Jessica Gispert and D.J., her delightful children, are at an age where they, too, can help make the world a better place. D.J., a new teenager in 2005, visited a nursing home monthly. He and his cousin, Ashley, conducted Bingo sessions. Jessica obtained her AA from Holy Cross College at Notre Dame and finished her education graduating with honors from the University of Pittsburgh. She helps manage the family's daycare, "Bright Beginnings" in Oxford, Penn.

Mary guided her nephew, Niclas, for a year to give him an opportunity to study in America. She helped with her brother Tom's children, Ashley, Dylan and Meghan. Her love of family and her heritage as well as decorating and golf keep her mind and body challenged. Once she was a successful bone marrow donor, a winner with a warm and loving heart.

Tom resides in Deleware. His magnetic personality and generosity are traits which enabled him to become an expert salesperson.

Lynn Heydon

Lynn married Tim Heydon before graduating from the University of Utah in Speech and Speech Pathology. For several years she was a substitute teacher at Lake Tahoe and was an office nurse for twenty-two years in Reno. Her main interests include her family, travel, and sports. With Tim, a University of Utah business graduate, a professional ski instructor and a journeyman carpenter, they lived in many Western ski resorts and now reside in Reno. They have led innumerable world wide trips.

Each of their four children, all graduates of the University of Nevada, Reno, is involved with service oriented work in the area. Together the family has hiked the rim to rim to rim of the Grand Canyon, biked around Lake Tahoe and skied throughout the west.

Cathy, their oldest child, obtained her Masters in Nursing, has assisted in heart surgeries, and is a member of the Association of Operating Room Nurses. She ran the Boston Marathon and did a triathalon with her brother and sister. Her husband, Ken Retterath, has a Master's Degree in Social Work and is involved with the Seniors in the county. Both Cathy and Ken are clinical and adjunct faculty members for the University of Nevada, Reno. Alex Harper, her son, is a student and active in sports, especially baseball, track and skiing. All are avid sports fans.

Maureen Montel graduated in Education and worked for the Bureau of Land Management fighting and dispatching forest fires for many years. Presently, she is a substitute teacher, accomplished artist, President of the PTA and a Girl Scout leader. Her husband, Andy Koski, is a Captain with the Sparks Fire Department and has a degree in Fire Science. Their outdoor activities include hunting, camping and fishing. Their two daughters, Michelle and Christine, are students and active in Girl Scouts, Martial Arts, athletics, and are Young Chautauquans.

Tim, Jr. has a finance degree and was vice-president of Clark Sullivan Constructors for Northern Nevada before retiring. He has run marathons and is a skier and a bike rider. He and his dad also have a small construction company. They remodel old homes and apartments. His wife, Marie Drakulich, has a Masters in Social Work. For nearly twenty years she worked at a local hospital, the majority of this time in the capacity of a medical social worker. She is involved in their four children's activities and is a CRE teacher along with part time social work with the elderly. Madison, AnnaMarie, Catherine and Michael are active in sports, music and scouts.

Kelley Ann has her degree in Criminal Justice. Her husband, Don Depoali, has a Criminal Science degree. Together they serve the community in law enforcement. Both work in an undercover capacity. They are sports enthusiasts and active hunters.

Larry Hawkesworth

When the Hawkesworth Drill Company was dissolved, Larry Hawkesworth left Butte. He located near the shipyards in Richmond, California near San Francisco Bay just prior to World War II. His mechanical skills were put to good use throughout his life. He met Etta Patton when he stopped to help two women with a stalled car on the freeway. This led to many years of married life and three new Hawkesworth sons. (Prior to this marriage Larry and his first wife, Virginia Smith, had adopted a daughter named Joan.)

Roger Hawkesworth

Roger Lee was born October14, 1951 in Oakland, California. He met Su Chen in Taiwan while he served in the Air Force. They have two children, Wendy Mae and David. Roger was imbued with his grandfather's mechanical skills. After graduation from Spartan School of Aeronautics in Tulsa, he became Production Supervisor of Aircraft Maintenance at American Airlines. In 2004 his task was to oversee 116 mechanics who work on the Boeing 757 aircraft.

He explained, "We call it the heavy check. The aircraft is in the hanger for fifteen work days. When the aircraft comes into the hangar, we spend two days opening it up and off loading all the cabin stuff. Seats, lavs, galleys, sidewalls and ceiling panels go to a sub shop for overhaul. The floor in the cabin is opened up as well. Out on the wings and engines we open up the fuel tanks after a leak check has been accomplished. The engines are all opened up and a borescope of the inside of the engine is accomplished. Inspectors then spend three days doing a thorough check everywhere. The next several days are used to fix and repair any deficiencies.

We also accomplish mods and airworthiness directives as well. Once all repairs are finished, we put everything back on and close things up. Everything is documented in writing. Once it's all together, we do an engine run and jack the aircraft and swing the gear. Then I release the aircraft to the flight crew and they fly the aircraft and do ground checks for about a half day. We will correct any of their finds as well. After the crew releases the aircraft back to me and all the items are done, I sign the log book oking the aircraft for service and its OK to put passengers on board now."

The Hawkesworth's contribution to safe environments over the years has extended from a mile under the earth to many miles above the earth.

Roger's championship avocations include billiards and bowling tournament championships as an adult and several roller skating awards during his teens. He enjoys camping with a fifth wheeler and being a new grandfather to daughter Wendy and Scott's first child, Conner Lin Matson. In 2006 he became the proud grandfather of their twins, Haley Mae and Andrew Scott born January 2, 2006. Both their parents are college graduates and are very active in church affairs.

His son David has an A & P license and works in the AA maintenance plant with him. He and his wife Amalain "Amy" live in Oklahoma.

Roger Hawkesworth with Wendy and children, David and Wendy Matson.

Michael and Gary

Larry's second son, Michael, and his wife, Debbie, live in Kansas. His skills are utilized at the nearby nuclear power plant.

Larry's third son, Gary, lives in Richmond, California. His daughter, Shanon Mae is a college graduate whose passion is to help other people. She works for the Salvation Army.

His son, Alexander Lynn has a son Giovanni Alexander Hawkesworth.

The Wedgwood, Darwin, Ryerson and Hawkesworth descendants contribute positively to our world today. They have soared into orbits around a planet of noble examples and they emanate a beam that continues to glow in this uneasy universe.

One orbit provides health care workers, housing contractors, inspirational teachers, humane law enforcement personnel, exacting mechanical experts and dedicated carpenters. The outer orbit cloaks their activities with wholesome leisure time activities that are engulfed in brilliant artistic works and meaningful music celebrations. Shared religious beliefs, family values, environmental concerns and educational insights continue to flow within the bounds of God's creation.

Glossary

Annealing furnace—an oven that heats and then gradually cools at a controlled temperature. This prevents cracking and warping of a metal.

Carrier—metal containers loaded with the bits the miners carry to their jobs.

Cast iron—a less malleable metal than most steel.

Chautauquans-programs where individuals assume a character they wish to portray. They dress like their personage, give a dramatic monologue and answer questions from an audience. The young Chautauquan program began in Reno, Nevada. See: youngchautauqua@hdpl.org.

Contract Miner—a non-union miner who is paid minimum wage plus extra for additional work

Crucible steel—"hard cast steel used for dies and cutting tools. Made in pots that are lifted from the furnace before the metal is poured into molds.

Draw the temper—term used in reference to shanks. It is a process that softens them by reheating them at a temperature well below that from which they were originally quenched

Draw press—a machine used to form the hollow part of some bits

Dressing of steel—shape metal by grinding.

Eccentric Press—a gyrating mechanical devise.

Flash dies—machines where bits are given a brief exposure to extreme hot or cold temperatures.

Gallows Frame—mechanism used to operate the cables which lower cages into the mine shafts.

Jig—a device used to maintain the steel in a correct position while a bit is being forged.

Knock out or off block—a mechanism for cutting off pieces of iron.

Level—a hard rock mine usually has 100' between descending levels.

Lode—A mineral deposit in solid rock.

Milling shanks—to shape by means of a rotary cutter.

Nipper—person accountable for the distribution of mine equipment underground and for its proper return.

Open hearth steel—that which is made in an open hearth furnace usually from pig iron which is mixed with scrap or iron ore

PH—a symbol for the degree of acidity or alkalinity of a solution. Ph values 0-6 indicates acidity;8-4 indicates alkalinity; 7 is neutral.

S.A.E. 6150—Society Automobile #6150 standard which consists of 50 percent carbon, 1.00 percent chromin, 15 percent vanadium.

Screw Press—a machine that has a ram that is forced downward by the turning of a spindle.

Shaft—a vertical pit similar to those used for elevators. Some mines have a ladder affixed to the sides of the shaft which can be used as an emergency exit.

Slag Pile—residue remaining from ore refining—highly toxic ground.

Slugs—sections cut from a circular steel rod into various bit sizes. These in turn are tumbled, heated and made ready for forging.

Tailings—The refuse water resulting from the treatment of ore. A tailings pond is a water deposit.

Traprock quarry.—various dark fine-ground igneous rocks used in road making.

Tempering shanks—to harden and then reheat in oil at a temperature well below that used for the usual quenching in order to soften steel.

Upsetting shanks—an operation performed by a forging press operator that can "increase the breadth of a piece of metal" through a heating process. (*Dict.* p.2519.)

Endnotes

Introduction

1   C. B. Glasscock, *The War of the Copper Kings* (New York: Bobbs-Merrill, 1935). Detailed account of early Butte history. Courts were too corrupt to tackle corporate crime.

2   Writers Project of Montana, *Copper Camp* (Helena, Montana: Riverbend, 2002) 300.

3   Writer's Project of Montana, 38.

4   George Everett, "Mark Twain's Trip to Butte", Sept. 2,2004 <butteamerica.com>.

5   K. Ross Toole, *Montana An Uncommon Land* (Norman: U of Oklahoma,1959) 165-166.

6   Toole, 209 states $10 million and gives complete story of this development. Montana's Dept. of Environmental Quality states $12 million p. 6 of their internet account. Various other sources mentioned in the bibliography range from $10.5 million to $12 million.

7   Writers Project of Montana, 301.

8   Writers Project of Montana, 303.

9   Montana Department of Environmental Quality. Search:" Butte Mining District", April 21,2006.

10 John Stucke, "Dan Ryan", Search, 100 Montana's, July 10,2004. This list includes additional information about many persons mentioned in this work along with the rankings assigned to them. 1 Mansfield, 5 Rankin, 6 Copper Kings, 9 John Ryan, 16 Toole, 29 C.Kelley, 32 Butte Miners, 65 Mike Malone, 69 Mayor Hauswirth, 80 Craney. No mention is made of Arthur Hawkesworth.

11 Jeffrey St. Clair, Search: "Something About Butte", April 21,2006. Marcosson, Issac, *Anaconda* (New York: Dodd, Mead and Co.,1957) 9. Everett, George, "When Toil Meant Trouble: Butte's Labor Heritage" <butteamerica.com > August 5,2005. Butte was recognized as the birthplace of American Labor.

12 "History of Butte" <hometown.com > or search "History of Butte", second listing, September 17, 2005.

Chapter One

1 Tom Stout, ed., *Montana: Its Story and Biography*, "Arthur L. Hawkesworth" (NewYork: American Historical Society, 1921) 1173.
2 Hawkesworth, Julia Clark, letter to Mamie Hawkesworth, June 9,1927, private collection.
3 Irving Stone, *The Origin* (New York: Doubleday, 1980) 69-70.
4 "Our Yesteryears", *Toronto Star* (1970s date partially obliterated-caption was written under a photograph of the horse drawn hearse), private collection.
5 Donald Jones, "Historical Toronto: Doctor Proudly Raised First Red Cross Banner", *Toronto Star*, 1985.
6 *United States Census*, July 5, 1870 (LDS Genealogy Library: Salt Lake City, Utah, Microfiche Film 947219) Accessed 1976.
7 Charles Eggleston, "Helena's Social Supremacy", *Anaconda Standard* 1894,pamphlet located in Montana Historical Society Library, also cited by Laurie Mercier, *Anaconda* as found in *http://www.press.uillinois.edu/epub/books/mercier/ch1.html.* Nov.15,2004.
8 "Jefferson County" Feb.13,2005, *<http://www.co.jefferson.mt.us/communities/county.shtml >.*
9 "Michael Lynch", *Helena Evening Herald*, Dec. 16, 1902.
10 Menting, Montel, *Generations Have Trod Have Trod* (published privately, 1978) 29.
11 C. A Caird, letter to Hon. J. K. Toole, Governor of the State of Montana, Dec. 27, 1904, private collection.

Chapter Two

1 Hawkesworth, Maurice, "My Friend Shorty", tape recorded conversation, July,1982.
2 Pat Williams. "Jeanette Rankin",Sept. 26,2004,100 Montana's.
3 Stout, p. 1174.

Chapter Three

1 "Butte Man's Invention to Revolutionize Important Feature of Mining", *Anaconda Standard,* May 14, 1922.
2 *Anaconda Standard*, May 14, 1922.
3 "Pioneer of Old West Summoned", *The Montana Standard*, Dec. 28,1942,1.

Chapter Four

1 Hawkesworth, Maurice, "Diary", 1920, private collection.
2 "Collected Letters of Arthur L. Hawkesworth-1904-1924", private collection.

3   Stout, 1174.
4   Original copy of the agreement was signed by A. L. Hawkesworth, Roy S. Alley, J.D. Murphy and John J. Riley on January 12, 1922 in Butte, Montana.
5   A three page agreement was drawn up April 16, 1920 signed by the same persons as cited above with the addition of Mary W. Hawkesworth.

Chapter Five

1   "Mine Experts See New Drill Sink in Rock," *Butte Miner*, May 13, 1922.1.
2.   *Anaconda Standard*, May 14, 1922.
3.   "Four Ounces of Steel: A Revolution in the Mining World"(Butte, Montana: McKee Printing Company, 1922).

Chapter Six

1   Shovers, Flege, Martin and Quivik,ed., *Butte and Anaconda Revisited*, "Tuttle Foundry", Sept. 19,2005. Search :Tuttle Foundry or *<http://www.affcomfg.com/History_Main.html* >* Foundry was closed in 1980 but reopened as AFFCO and was the state's largest foundry in 2005.
2.   "Radio". *Encyclopedia Britannica Deluxe*, 2001CD.First commercial radio broadcast was by KDKA in Pittsburg on Nov. 10, 1921 announcing President Harding's election.
3.   Brecher, Lombardi, Stackhouse, ed.,*Brass Valley*, 1982, 5. States story is a myth. Marcosson, *Anaconda*,1957, 169-170 states this as factual.
4.   *Butte Miner*, 1.
5.   "Guggenheim", *Encyclopedia Britannica Deluxe*, 2001CD.
6.   Felix Wormer, "The Hawkesworth Detachable Drill Bit," *Engineering & Mining Journal*, August 5, 1922, 262-264.

Chapter Seven

1.   Arnold Zweig, *Sergeant Grisha*. (New York: The Viking Press, 1928).

Chapter Eight

1.   C.L Berrrian, "C.L. Berrien Gives Interesting Paper before Western Mining Convention on Development in Butte of the Hawkesworth Bit" *Montana Standard*, October 5, 1929.11.
2.   "The Gilded Age-52 Great Getaways" April 22, 2005.<http://www.ct.gov >. Connecticut's state quarter features an oak tree. In 1687 the Governors of Mass. and RI accompanied by sixty heavily armed troops had a long meeting in Hartford. A candle was knocked over and extinguished. Capt. Wadsworth grabbed the state's charter, dashed down Main Street and hid it in an oak tree hollow. The significance

was that only Conn. maintained self rule until the Rev. War. Hence "The Charter Oak Tree" symbolizes this event.

3. Asher, Robert, "Connecticut Inventors", Sept. 10,2005, <Connecticut Heritage Gateway >.

Chapter Nine

1. Lewis Wickes, "Jackie Coogar", photograph taken on Aug. 26,1924.

Chapter Ten

1. Michael Bell, 'The Face of Connecticut" (State Geological and Natural History Survey of Connecticut. Bulletin 110.ISBMO-942081-01-3).

Chapter Eleven

1. "Connecticut Roads",Sept. 2,2005, links to History and New England States.
2. "Canals",July,14, 2005,<http://www.ctheritage.org >.
3. Ann Finer and George Savage, ed., *The Selected Letters of Josiah Wedgwood*, (New York:Born & Hawes Publishing Co. 1965). 30-31.
4. "Yale University" Aug. 12, 2005,< *http://www.yale.edu* >.
5. "The History of Bigelow Carpets", March 30,2005, search: Bigelow Carpets.

Chapter Twelve

1. Bushnell Park, March 5, 2005,<http://www.Bushnellpark.org >. This site provides a visual tour and history of America's first public park.

Chapter Thirteen

1. Felix Wormer, 262-264.

Chapter Fourteen

1. Ellen Baumler, "Devil's Perch: Prostitution from Suite to Cellar in Butte, Montana." (Montana Historical Society, 10 October 2004),1-21. <http://www.montanahistoricalsociety.com/education/ccirguides/buttearticbaumler.asp >
2. George Everett, "How Keno was Born in Butte, Montana.", Dec.31, 2004. <http://www.butteamerica.com/keno.htm >.
3. Marcosson, 75.
4. Charles Mutschler, *Wired for Success*, (Washington State, Pullman,WA,2002), 94.
5. Marcosson, 226.

Chapter Fifteen

1. Robert G. Rodden, "Fighting Machinists", April 14, 2005, 3, <*http://www. iamawlodge1426.org/hisupdate33.htm* > Butte was also known as the "Gibraltar of Unionism."

Chapter Sixteen

1. Montana State Genealogical Society, *First Families & Early Settlers of Montana*, Vol. 1 and II, (Allegra Print and Imaging, Helena, MT 2005). 9,93.
2. Meyer Weinberg, *A Short History of American Capitalism*, "The Testing of American Capitalism," Chapter 9, 1920-1945, 326.
3. Marcossan, 347.

Chapter Eighteen

1. R.R Rice, Correspondence with Hawkesworth Drill Company from Porcupine Mine District in Canada, July 15, 1934. Hawkesworth family private collection.

Chapter Nineteen

1. "A Century of Progress: Chicago World's Fair."<chicagohs.org/history/century. html >.
2. Mary Murphy. *Mining Cultures* (Chicago: UP of Illinois,1997)205.
3. Nedra Bayne, "The Broadwater: Relic of Elegance," (Montana Historical Society: Helena, Montana, 1969).

Chapter Twenty

1. Fort Peck Dam. *Encyclopedia Britannica CD*.
2. Kinsey, Item 35.
3. Marcosson, 226.

Chapter Twenty-One

1. Robert Margo. "Employment and Unemployment in the 1920s",Sept. 19,2005. Search "Interwar Unemployment" for complete coverage of this topic.
2. Toole,93.
3. "Roy Alley Dies at Pipestone Springs", *Fallon County Times*, Sept. 4, 1940.
4. "Pioneer of Old West Summoned", *Montana Standard*, Dec. 28, 1942. 1.
5. Jeffrey St. Claire and Alexander Cockburn, Jan. 4,2005.

Chapter Twenty-Three

1. Hawkesworth, Maurice. Series of fatality accident reports occurring on the Butte Hill from June 17, 1946-Mar. 1948, private Hawkesworth family collection.

Chapter Twenty-Six

1. "Berkeley Pit", <pitwatch.org >, fall 2005.

Chapter Twenty-Seven

1. Timothy Egan, "Seeking Clean Fuel for a Nation, and a Rebirth for Small-Town Montana", *New York Times*, November 24, 2005, A15.
2. "Mining and Mineral Activity in Montana in 2004", *Mining Engineering Magazine*, March 2005. Search: OTMining.
3. First Underground Mining Class Graduates from Montana Tech",*Montana Standard*, April 2, 2004.
4. Jim Robbins, "Dam and Waste Will Go, Freeing Two Rivers", *New York Times*, Aug. 4, 2005, A12. "In a Town Called Opportunity, Distress Over a Dump", *New York Times*, Aug. 24, 2005, A8.
5. "Mike Mansfield", *Biographical Directory of the United States Congress*, Feb. 12,2004, <bioguida.congress.gov/scripts/biodisplaypl?index=M000113 >. Sherry Devlin, "Death of a Statesman: Mike Mansfield", Oct. 6, 2001, search Mike Mansfield.
6. Terry Lonner, producer. *The Beef Trail: A Pioneering Montana Ski Area*, (Bozeman, Mont:Mediaworks & KUSM-TV Montana PBS. 2003 or<www.mediawks4u.com > or <www.montananpbs.org >.
7. John Hart, *Environmental Theology*? (New York: Paulist Press,2004)13.

Bibliography

Emmons, David. M. *The Butte Irish*. U. of Illinois Press, 1990.

Finn, Janet L. *Tracing the Veins of Copper, Culture and Community from Butte to Chiquicamata*. U of California Press, Berkeley, 1998.

McGrath, Jean. ed. *Butte's Heritage Cookbook*. Butte-Silver Bow Bicentennial Commission 1976.

McGrath, ed. *Books of the Century*. "A Hundred Years of Authors, Ideas and Literature." New York Times: Random House, 1998.

"Millwright". *Webster's Third New International Dictionary*. 1993. p.1435.

Nenortas, Tomas J. *Victorian Hartford*. Arcadia: Chicago, 2005.

Rasmussen, R. Kent. *Quotable Mark Twain*.Contemporary Books: Chicago, 1998.

Stout, Tom.ed. *Montana: Its Story and Biography. A History of Aboriginal and Territorial Montana and Three Decades of Statehood*. "Arthur L. Hawkesworth." American Historical Society, Chicago and New York, 1921. Vol. III, p. 1173-1174.

Steindl-Rast,Br. David. *Gratefulness, the Heart of Prayer*. Paulist Press, New York, 1984.

Steinhilber, Berthold. *Ghost Towns of the American West*. Harry Abrams. New York,2003.

Taylor, Bill and Jan. *The Butte Short Line*. Pictorial Histories. Missoula, 1998.

Tickle, Phyllis. *Greed*. Oxford University Press,2004.

Weisberger, Bernard A. *"The Age of Steel and Steam."* Vol. 7, 1877-1890. *New York Times Incorporated*, 1964.

Newspaper Articles

"Al Hawkesworth Called by Death at the Age of 55." *Butte Daily Post. 14* June 1925.

"Anaconda Kiwanis Club Address by Inventor." *Butte Daily Post*. 22 Feb. 1923.

Clark, Irene. "Woman 89 Years Young Says Life Just Beginning." *San Diego Union*. 1931. p.10.

Drew and Oppel. "Friends in the White House Come to Coal's Aid." *New York Times*. 9 Aug. 2004. p. A1 and A11.

"Gallwey, Civic Leader in State, Called." *The Montana Standard*. 28 Dec. 1942. p.1+.

Morgan, Donna Lou. "Baked Pies are just 'a letter from' ome'." *Salt Lake Tribune*. 3 Mar.1983. E1+.

"Loved Inventor Called by Death as Fame is Won." *Anaconda Standard*. 17 June 1925. 1+.

Robbins, Jim. "Butte Struggles Against Death of Copper Mine." *San Jose Mercury News*. 13 Feb. 1983.

PAMPHLETS, ADDRESSES, MAGAZINE ARTICLES

Alley, John. R. "Shannon Roy Alley", Essay submitted to the Ann Cote Smith Essay Contest, Butte,MT,1996.

Hawkesworth, Maurice. "Progress in the Development of the Rock Drill Bit." American Mining Congress. 22 Sept. 1950.

Hawkesworth, Maurice. "Advantages of Single Use of Carbide Bits." National Western Mining Conference. Denver, Colorado. 7 Feb. 1957.

"Official Gazette of the United States Patent Office." Washington: Government printing office. July 11,1922.

Marcus, J.J. "Butte: The Richest Hill on Earth." *Engineering & Mining Journal*. Feb.1,2000.

Additional Web Sites

"About the Silver Bow Creek/Butte Area Site." U.S. Environmental Protection Agency. 22 July 2004.< http:www.epa.gov/region08/superfund/sites/mt/silver. >

Clark, William Andrews,1839-1925." *Biographical Directory of the United States Congress*. 2 Sept. 2004.< http://bioguide.congress.gov/scripts/biodisplay >

Guggenheim, Daniel." *Britannica Student Encyclopedia*. 17 July 2004. < *http://www.* Britannica.com/ebi/article?eu=350221. >

Mercier, Laurie *"City of Whispers." Anaconda: Labor, Community, and Culture in Montana's Smelter City.* "City of Whispers", 15Nov.2004<http:www. press,uillinois,edu/epub/books/mercier/ch1.l >.

Shorers, Brian. "Remaking the Wide Open Town: Butte at the end of the Twentieth Century." *Montana Historical Society*. 14 June 1905.

Wolberg, Beth. "Cornelius Francis Kelley". *The 100 Most Influential Montanans of the Century*. 26 Sept. 2004.< *http://www.missoulian.com* >.

Private Family Collections

"Assignment of Letters Patent: No. 1,296,078." Arthur L. Hawkesworth to Hawkesworth Drill. Manufacturing Company 17 Apr. 1920. J. D. Murphy, Notary Public

"Assignment of Letters Patents: No. 1296078, 1328325" and applications for Letters Patent numbers 283951,283953,283954,283955. Arthur L. Hawkesworth to Hawkesworth Drill Manufacturing Company. 17 Apr. 1920.

"Buck O'Donnell Original Cartoons."

Letters of Julia Clark Hawkesworth. 1920-1937.

"Collected Correspondence of Arthur Hawkesworth:1904-1924."

"Collected Correspondence of Maurice and Tecla Hawkesworth:1911-1987."

Metallic Packing for Piston-Rods Patent. 17 Jan. 1899. (Seventeen Years Protected.)

Hawkesworth Drill Company Stock Certificates.

Photographs and diagrams pictured in *Butte: An Unfinished Story*. Photographs were enhanced and made ready for publication by Brother Charles McBride, C.S.C. Computer advise and aid was provided by Brother Charles Devron, C.S.C. Without these two professionals this work would never had been completed. Thanks, too, to those who proof read the manuscript and made suggestions particularly Bill and Lynn Hawkesworth, Br. Bernard, Donahoe,CSC, Br. Don Fleishaker,CSC and Charles Tull, historian.

BVG